"After a period of intense fluidity and flux, *The Brexit Effect* provides a sophisticated account of exactly how the landscape of British politics has changed."

Matthew Flinders, *University of Sheffield* and
Vice President of the Political Studies Association, *UK*

"This is an excellent analysis of the ways in which Brexit has had an impact on the British political system, taking into account the peculiarities of British political culture. It is essential reading for scholars and students interested in British politics and the consequences of Brexit."

Sofia Vasilopoulou, *King's College London, UK*

THE BREXIT EFFECT

This book examines the seismic impact of Brexit on the British political system, assessing its likely long-term effect in terms of a significantly changed political and constitutional landscape.

Starting with the 2015 general election and covering key developments up to "Brexit Day", it shows how Brexit "transformed" British politics. The unprecedented turmoil – two snap elections, three Prime Ministers, the biggest ever defeat for the Government in Parliament, an impressive number of rebellions and reshuffles in Cabinet and repeated requests for a second independence referendum in Scotland – as a result of leaving the EU, calls into question what sort of political system the post-Brexit UK will become. Taking Lijphart's "Westminster model" as its reference, the book assesses the impact of Brexit along three dimensions: elections and parties; executive–legislative relationships; and the relationship between central and devolved administrations. Based on a wealth of empirical material, including original interviews with key policymakers and civil servants, it focuses on the "big picture" and analytically maps the direction of travel for the UK political system.

This book will be of key interest to scholars and students of Brexit, British politics, constitutional, political, and contemporary history, elections and political parties, executive politics, and territorial politics as well as more broadly related practitioners and journalists.

Gianfranco Baldini is Associate Professor of Political Science at the University of Bologna, Italy, and Research Associate at the Centre for Britain and Europe, University of Surrey, UK.

Edoardo Bressanelli is Associate Professor of Political Science at the Sant'Anna School of Advanced Studies in Pisa, Italy, and Senior Visiting Research Fellow at King's College London, UK.

Emanuele Massetti is Associate Professor of Political Science at the University of Trento, Italy, and Associated Fellow at the Centre on Constitutional Change, University of Edinburgh, UK.

Routledge Studies in British Politics

This series aims to promote research excellence in political science, political history and public-policy making, whilst addressing a wide array of political dynamics, contexts, histories and ideas. It will retain a particular focus on British government, British Politics and public policy, while locating those issues within a European and global context.

Series editors: *Patrick Diamond and Tim Bale of Queen Mary University, London, UK.*

For more information about this series, please visit: https://www.routledge.com/Routledge-Studies-in-British-Politics/book-series/RSBP

THE BREXIT EFFECT

What Leaving the EU Means for British Politics

Gianfranco Baldini, Edoardo Bressanelli, and Emanuele Massetti

Routledge
Taylor & Francis Group
LONDON AND NEW YORK

Designed cover image: © Getty Images

First published 2023
by Routledge
4 Park Square, Milton Park, Abingdon, Oxon OX14 4RN

and by Routledge
605 Third Avenue, New York, NY 10158

Routledge is an imprint of the Taylor & Francis Group, an informa business

British Library Cataloguing-in-Publication Data
A catalogue record for this book is available from the British Library

ISBN: 978-0-367-65055-1 (hbk)
ISBN: 978-0-367-65050-6 (pbk)
ISBN: 978-1-003-12768-0 (ebk)

DOI: 10.4324/9781003127680

Typeset in Bembo
by Deanta Global Publishing Services, Chennai, India

CONTENTS

FIGURES

TABLES

ACKNOWLEDGEMENTS

This book stems from a long-term collaboration between the Authors, two of whom – when the research for this book began in 2017 – lived and worked in England, in London (King's College London) and in Guildford (University of Surrey). All chapters have been discussed multiple times by the Authors, in their respective universities, and at several conferences. Preliminary results have been published in *The Political Quarterly* in 2018 ("Who is in Control? Brexit and the Westminster Model", vol. 89, no. 4, pp. 537–44) and in the *International Political Science Review* in 2021 ("Back to the Westminster model? The Brexit process and the UK political system"). Also, the book draws on – and significantly expands the argument presented in – our previous monograph, *Il Regno Unito alla Prova della Brexit*, published in Italian by Il Mulino, 2021. The book is the result of a truly cooperative effort. While we have contributed to all chapters, Gianfranco Baldini bears more direct responsibility for Chapter 3, Edoardo Bressanelli for Chapter 4, and Emanuele Massetti for Chapter 5.

We are very grateful to Andrea Pareschi, whose contribution in conducting and analysing the interviews has been very important. Our research has been discussed with several colleagues. Among them, we would like to acknowledge the generous feedback received from Daniele Albertazzi, Nicola Chelotti, Arianna Giovannini, Marco Giuliani, Andrew Glencross, Paolo Graziano, Luca Gori, Ben Jones, Louisa Parks, Arlo Poletti, Laura Polverari, Giuseppe Martinico, Alia Middleton, David Natali, Louise Thompson, and Salvatore Vassallo. The series editors, Patrick Diamond and Tim Bale, and the anonymous reviewers have provided valuable comments. Last but not least, the Routledge publisher, Andrew Taylor, and Sophie Iddamalgoda, the senior editorial assistant, have constantly supported our project.

We are also grateful to the audiences, the discussants, and the chairs of the panels in the conferences where we had the opportunity to present earlier versions of (parts of) this work, including the 2022 PSA Annual Conference in York, the 2019 EUSA Biennial Conference in Denver, Colorado, the Conferences of the Italian Political Science Association in Lecce in 2019 and online in 2021, and the 49th UACES Conference in Lisbon in 2019. Of course, only we remain responsible for all errors.

INTRODUCTION

On 23 June 2016, British voters narrowly voted (51.8 percent) in favour of leaving the European Union (EU), in the UK European Union membership referendum. Although successive polls had pointed to the possibility of a Leave victory, the outcome still came as a shock to many, and it went against the wishes of the great majority of the political establishment, starting with Prime Minister (PM), David Cameron. The 2016 referendum was only the third national referendum in the UK. However, the previous two – in 1975 on the continuation of membership in the European Economic Community (EEC), and in 2011 on electoral reform – both resulted in the confirmation of the status quo. Whereas the 2016 referendum had an immediate effect, with Cameron's resignation, further consequences developed over the following months and years. It soon became clear that 23 June 2016 was only "Act One" of the long Brexit theatre production. The prequel was, of course, the electoral pledge unwillingly made in the electoral manifesto of the Conservative Party ahead of the 2015 general elections – committing to "legislate in the first session of the next Parliament for an in-out referendum to be held on Britain's membership of the EU" (Conservative Party Manifesto 2015, 73) – which had far more implications, including for his own career, than the PM was able to foresee.

On 31 January 2020, Brexit was formally concluded. The UK became a former member of the EU – a "third country" to use Brussels' jargon – and Brexit could finally be implemented during the year of transition, with new rules designed for trade, migration, agriculture, and all policy areas where policy competences had been repatriated. The deal with the EU – the Trade and Cooperation Agreement (TCA), whose negotiations were concluded on Christmas Eve 2020, just a few days before the end of the transition – marked the new beginning of the relationship between the UK and the EU. Yet, the new relationship was characterised by difficulties. The special arrangements for Northern Ireland proved to be very

DOI: 10.4324/9781003127680-1

contentious and led to protracted negotiations with Brussels and Dublin, and strong political tensions between the Democratic Unionist Party (DUP) and the PM, Boris Johnson, and within the Conservative Party itself. There was also internal dissent within the governing party on the legislative implementation of Brexit – to a large extent overlapping with the pandemic crisis – as voting on the Internal Market Bill clearly illustrated.

While Brexit has not unleashed a *domino effect* (i.e., Frexit, Nexit, Italexit, etc.) in other countries, which many had feared (Hobolt & Tilley 2022; Walter 2021; Glencross 2016), it has caused major tensions within British politics. Between June 2016 and July 2019, Britain has had three different Conservative PMs. David Cameron and Theresa May fell because of Brexit; Boris Johnson emerged as the real architect of the country's exit from the EU, gaining a strong majority in the 2019 general election, which was held on the slogan "get Brexit done" (Ford *et al.* 2021).

Between the 2015 referendum pledge and "exit day" in January 2020, Brexit has twisted and shaken British politics like no other event since the end of WWII.[1] But if the 2016 referendum was the major *event* (although, as we will see, many others can be identified), a long *process* of withdrawal unfolded shortly after it. This book aims to investigate the dynamics and the political as well as institutional domestic implications of this process. To be sure, the latter played out at different levels. First, the UK Government had to negotiate the terms of exit with the EU (Martill 2020). Simultaneously, the Government had to pass legislation in Parliament, while also being significantly constrained in this by the rulings of the courts. Last but not least, and very significantly for a country that had seen the devolution of powers to the peripheries as one of its major constitutional innovations of the previous two decades (Bogdanor 1981), it had to cope with the fact that in both Northern Ireland (with 55.8 percent), and especially in Scotland (with 62.0 percent), "Remain" won the 2016 referendum.

All this proved to be far from easy to handle. Two snap general elections – in 2017 and 2019 – were held, with the main aim of sorting Brexit out, which had become Theresa May's nightmare (Allen 2018; Seldon 2020) in the second half of her three-year-long premiership (July 2016–June 2019). May was ultimately unable to get the necessary support in Parliament to deliver Brexit, even after having asked the EU for an extension of the two-year period of negotiation, as prescribed by Art. 50 of the Treaty on European Union (TEU). This meant that the country had to take part in the 2019 European Parliament (EP) elections. These elections were won by the newly founded Brexit Party, led by Nigel Farage, who, as leader of the United Kingdom Independence Party (UKIP), had been one of the protagonists of the Leave campaign in 2016 (Goodwin & Heath 2016). May's ensuing resignation led to the election of Johnson as the Conservative Party leader, and immediately after as PM. As a leading Brexiteer, Johnson ousted some of the "Remainers" from the parliamentary party and then managed – in the December 2019 general election – to gain a significant majority of 80 seats in the House of Commons.

On 31 January 2020, less than 50 days after these elections, as the world increasingly shifted its attention to Wuhan, China, some British newspapers appeared triumphant. "A New Dawn for Britain" (*Daily Mail*), "Our Time Has Come" (*The Sun*), "Yes, we did" (*The Daily Express*); while these tones were hardly shared by other papers, such as *The Guardian* ("Small Island"), and *The i* ("UK's Leap into the Unknown"). And yet, more than two years after the exit, many uncertainties still lie ahead, especially as far as the long-term economic consequences of the divorce are concerned. Meanwhile, the UK's exit, especially given its major economic, political, and cultural weight, raises important questions for the process of EU integration, which has been examined in the context of the so-called theory of European disintegration (Rosamond 2016; Schimmelfennig 2018; Huhe *et al.* 2020), and for its institutions which have, nonetheless, shown a strong adaptive capacity (Bressanelli & Chelotti 2021).

Brexit has attracted a lot of attention within the scholarly community (Diamond *et al.* 2018; Oliver 2019). In fact, according to Colin Hay, it is "rare for political analysts to be as heavily invested in processes that are still unfolding as they are with Brexit" (Hay, 2020, 191). Brexit is a sort of high-stake experiment for social scientists that has been running live. In political science, this attention has been channelled along different routes.

A first strand of the literature analysed the causes and the events that led to the Brexit referendum. Several studies highlight the important role played by the rise of UKIP (e.g., Glencross 2016) in Cameron's promise to hold a referendum in the 2015 general election. While not all share the idea of the "inevitability" of such a vote (Thompson 2017), the pressure for "exit" had been boiling inside the Conservative Party for many years (Bale 2016; Bogdanor 2019; Shipman 2016). This was also related to the fact that "the British public has consistently been the most Eurosceptic electorate in the EU ever since the UK joined in 1973" (Hobolt 2016, 1259–60). Some authors even go as far as to identify a "first Brexit" in the "six days" which led, in September 1992, to the exit of the pound sterling from the Exchange Rate Mechanism (Keegan *et al.* 2017). For that matter, historians go even deeper, with a prominent scholar claiming that Brexit was a "hundred years in the making" (Conway 2019).

Second, several studies have investigated the outcome of the Brexit referendum and the determinants of the Leave victory. Both individual and district-level data have shown support for the Leave campaign to be correlated with "low educational attainment, low income, age, recent increases in (but not aggregate levels of) in-migration, anti-migrant sentiment, political disaffection, prior UKIP and Conservative support, and national (as opposed to European or British) identification" (Hay 2020, 195). These elements point to the development of a cultural conflict in the UK, a transnational "European cleavage" (Hooghe & Marks 2018) whereby Brexit – in very similar ways to the support of populist parties around the European continent, and for Donald Trump in the United States – can ultimately be explained by the intensification of a sense of insecurity of "left behind" citizens (Clarke *et al.* 2017). While Brexit has often been portrayed as either the consequence of economic distress or – more often – of a cultural backlash, these two fields are in fact very difficult to disentangle (Carreras *et al.* 2019; Gidron & Hall 2020).

Third, some scholars have analysed the negotiations between the UK and the EU on the UK's withdrawal from the bloc. This literature has illustrated the key actors and objectives of the UK Government (e.g., McGowan 2018; Martill 2021a) as well as the reasons behind the EU's unity (e.g., Bressanelli & Chelotti 2021; Jensen & Kelstrup 2019; Schuette 2021).

These are just a few examples from a field that is constantly growing. So, why do we need a new book on the topic? In this volume we analyse the British "domestic" perspective to trace and map the political tensions that occurred between 2015 – when the referendum entered the legislative agenda – and 2020 (though our *terminus ad quo* and *ad quem* slightly differ depending on the dimension analysed, see below). We argue that Brexit – through the combination of the referendum *event* and the ensuing *process* – has already had some important effects on the political system, which we aim to capture empirically.

To be sure, the concept of "political system" encompasses dimensions and issues which we cannot reasonably cover in this book. In a nutshell, we are mostly interested in the "input" and "throughput" (rather than output) sides of the founding scheme of Almond and Powell (1966) on the analysis of political systems. To reiterate, our focus is placed on the domestic political implications of Brexit and, more specifically, on the *politics* and *polity* – rather than the *policy* – consequences of withdrawal. Gamble (2018) identified the following long-term implications of Brexit: on the UK as a multinational state, on the constitution and governance (in particular, the future of referendums); on the party system (how Brexit reshaped the social bases and identity of the two main parties); on political economy and economic consequences, and on geopolitics. Among these, we focus mainly on the first three, while not covering the last two.

Of course, several works (far too many to quote here, but we will refer to them in due course), have already shed light on some specific institutional and/ or electoral consequences of Brexit. However, so far, what is missing is a more encompassing analysis which, while not pretending to be exhaustive, or to have any kind of final word on the topic, aims at the broad picture, trying to offer a balanced perspective of the "direction of travel" of the UK political system post-Brexit.

Jennings and Lodge (2019) have shown that Brexit can be analysed along three main perspectives. First, at the level of electoral politics, as a manifestation of anti-politics. Second, at a policy level, as the silent crisis of the neoliberal policy paradigm of the global capitalist state. Third, at the state level, as "spectacle politics to overcome failure of party politics to resolve conflicts". At the crossroads of the second and third perspectives, Jessop has defined Brexit as a manifestation of the "organic crisis of the British state" (Jessop 2017). By focusing on the consequences of Brexit on the UK political system we follow a different path, which aims to combine quantitative and qualitative evidence in order to assess how citizens, political parties, and institutions have so far handled the strains provoked by Brexit.

To understand the domestic implications of Brexit we have built our theoretical framework on some of the most important long-term peculiarities of the British political system. Three of them are particularly important: the majoritarian nature of its political institutions (often summed up under the label of the "Westminster model"), the uncodified nature of its constitution with the centrality of parliamentary sovereignty, and, last but not least, the persistence of the British Political Tradition as the "cultural glue" (Flinders *et al.* 2018) underlying the behaviour of British political elites (Diamond & Richards 2012).

In a recent scholarly exchange published in the journal *Government and Opposition*, some prominent experts of British politics have argued about the utility of the "Westminster model" as a concept for studying British, and especially comparative, politics (Russell & Serban 2022; Flinders *et al.* 2022; Russell & Serban 2022). While Meg Russell and Ruxandra Serban believe that the concept has been "stretched beyond repair", especially in the field of comparative politics, Flinders *et al.* argue that the concept remains useful in comparative research.

In this book, we engage with this debate arguing that the Westminster model, as adapted from the comparative analysis of democracy proposed by Arend Lijphart, is still of great value to understand the political change in Britain today. In particular, we consider Lijphart's work to be very appropriate for our scope, essentially for three main reasons. First, it allows mapping the changes experienced *longitudinally* by the political system in the four years between 2016 and 2020, when compared to the previous phases of development of the political system. Second, and related, in doing this it also allows some *replicability*, since other scholars (Flinders 2005; 2010; Matthews & Flinders 2017) have used Lijphart's framework (though without the adaptations we propose here). As these works were all conducted before Brexit, our comparison with them helps to single out the Brexit effects more precisely. Third, and finally, our framework also helps to secure comparability across other experiences since it focuses on the case study while not losing track of the comparative framework underlying Lijphart's analysis, allowing one to see whether Britain has become more or less majoritarian because of Brexit.

With this in mind, we want to clear the field of a potential conceptual and terminological misunderstanding. The British political system is the subject of the empirical research of this book. In particular, the analysis focuses on three dimensions that have been particularly affected by the Brexit process: the party system, the relationship between government and parliament, and the relationship between the state and the devolved administrations of Northern Ireland, Scotland, and Wales. For Lijphart, the Westminster model – as opposed to the consensual model – represents a reference point, (or a "polar type"), within a conceptual map for the study of democracy. It is in this perspective that it can be used to make sense of the observed changes, identifying a direction of travel (towards or away from the reference point) and measuring the movements which have taken place during the period under investigation.

We claim that Lijphart's framework can indeed be used in order to trace how parties, voters, and institutions faced the many challenges created by the Brexit process. However, neither voters, nor political parties, nor institutions operate in a void. On the contrary, they all act in the context marked by norms and values inherited from the past. Compared to other European experiences, this inheritance is particularly important in the British case. To name just a few elements, the Conservative Party is arguably the oldest political party in the world. A similar point can be made about British institutions. Such institutional and cultural peculiarities are summed up in the concept of the "British Political Tradition" (BPT). Hence, we argue that Lijphart's framework should be complemented by other works more focused on the specific operations of the BPT. In doing so, we propose a new research framework, in a close dialogue with the most important works that have sought to understand political change in Britain.

Outline of the book

This book analyses the most important effects of Brexit on the political system in the early years following the 2016 EU membership referendum. It does so by cross-fertilising literatures on the comparative study of democracy, British politics domestic perspectives, and studies of (de-)Europeanisation. It seeks to identify the ways in which the Westminster model can be adapted as an analytical construct in order to make sense of the party system and institutional dynamics in the wake of the Brexit referendum. The latter was famously conceived as a means of "taking back control". Given that the repatriation of powers is far from an easy and fast process, our research aims at seeing how the main actors of the political system – citizens via the election, and the main institutions in London and the other regions of the UK multinational system – have dealt with the complex task of exiting the EU.

Accordingly, in Chapter 1, we draw on a broad canvas, tracing the origins of the general institutional architecture of the country. In this chapter, we start from the definition of what – in the language of political science – is our dependent variable: the nature and general functioning of the British political system. Indeed, from a comparative perspective, the British political system has been identified for decades as a prototypical majoritarian or Westminster democracy (Lijphart 1984; 1999; 2012). Moreover, while no constitution is free from "gaps and abeyances" (Foley 1989), this is particularly the case for the British constitution. The chapter engages with the debates regarding the changing nature of the political system. In doing so, it justifies the choice of the conceptual framework as derived and adapted from Lijphart's comparative study of democracy. It also justifies the empirical focus of the volume on three dimensions: electoral dynamics and the party system; the relationship between executive and legislative powers;

and the political-institutional relations between the central and devolved administrations of Northern Ireland, Scotland, and Wales.

Chapter 2 discusses our independent variable, presents the key argument developed by this book and introduces the research design. In our understanding, Brexit is not a singular, "discrete" event but rather a process – or a set of processes – unfolding over time. Treating Brexit in such a way means using extreme care when trying to "disentangle" the politico-institutional changes brought about by the Brexit process from other triggers of change. To do so, we triangulate different data sources, including more than 70 semi-structured interviews with practitioners, experts, and colleagues conducted from 2018 to 2019 between London, Belfast, Cardiff, and Edinburgh. We argue that the completion of the Brexit process – i.e., the actual termination of membership of the UK in the EU – has pointed to the persistence of the Westminster model, albeit with several caveats, uncertainties, and adaptations. To be sure, we do not naively expect the post-Brexit UK to go back to a classic version of the Westminster model, of the kind the country had experienced in the three decades after WWII. Yet, solid theoretical arguments lead us to expect, in a nutshell, a reduction in party system fragmentation and a centralisation of power in the hands of the executive, vis-à-vis both Parliament and the devolved administrations.

In analysing the nature of Brexit as an electoral shock (Chapter 3), we leave in the background the dynamics which brought about the success of the Leave campaign in the 2016 referendum. Indeed, in addition to a group of "hyper-globalists" (Baker 2002), the UK's exit from the EU is mainly related to the profile of voters defined as "globalization losers" (Clarke *et al.* 2017), who have contributed to the success of many populist parties in Europe (and of Donald Trump in the United States). One of the slogans that made the most of these voters recalled the desire to regain control of the sovereignty ceded to Europe: "Take back control" (or, to a lesser extent, "we want our country back"). These slogans were successful because they were conceived in a context marked by profound distrust and by nostalgic sentiments, which promised to restore sovereignty to the country and its citizens. In this chapter, we deal with the realignments of the electorate and of the party system, showing the emergence of a peculiar hybrid form, where the return to a two-party system format, which is typical of the period of the classic Westminster system, is combined with a fragile predominance of the Conservative Party.

Chapter 4 focuses on the relationship between the executive and the legislature, asking to what extent it has changed over, and because of, Brexit. The traditional Westminster model *à la* Lijphart – whose enduring validity in its "pure" form has been challenged by most recent empirical literature – features a power-hoarding executive which controls its own cohesive majority in parliament. In theory, Brexit was designed to bring back control and reinstate parliamentary sovereignty. In practice, however, the executive could strategically use the process to strengthen its own competences and powers. Through the in-depth analysis of case studies and the use of quantitative indicators, the chapter shows that the Brexit years have tested and put under strain several conventions and parliamentary rules, first and foremost relating to agenda control, and were characterised by a very intense and, at times, dramatic conflict between the executive and parliament. Parliament stretched its powers to challenge the traditional dominance of the executive, but its assertiveness – strongly supported by the Speaker – did not ultimately lead to significant reforms. In the end, the executive pursued "its" version of Brexit and Parliament was incapable of moving beyond opposition to "no deal". Overall, the chapter argues that the Westminster model maintains an enduring validity to understanding the functioning logic of the system post-Brexit.

Chapter 5 analyses the impact of Brexit on the relationship between the three Celtic peripheries – Northern Ireland, Scotland, and Wales – and the central institutions of the UK. Traditionally, the UK rested on different territorial settlements, all underpinned by a unitary constitution based on parliamentary sovereignty. The rise of centre–periphery politics from the late 1960s, and the adoption of subsequent devolution reforms from the late 1990s, have set the territorial constitution in flux. Against this backdrop, Brexit has reignited a series of pre-existing tensions by touching upon issues of devolved *self-rule* (i.e., the width and salience of competences assigned to devolved administrations) and *shared-rule* (i.e., the power of devolved administrations to concur to UK law-making). In particular, the chapter analyses the struggle for the allocation of repatriated powers (in the EU Withdrawal Bill) and two legal clashes before the Supreme Court: the so-called *Miller case* (2016–17) and the so-called *Scotland Continuity Bill case* (2018). After taking stock of the institutional impact of Brexit, this chapter analyses the political backlash of the Brexit process, in particular the growth of secessionist attitudes in the three Celtic peripheries.

Chapter 6 has a dual purpose. On the one hand, it summarises the main findings of the empirical chapters. On the other, it reconsiders them, taking into consideration the two-year period after Brexit Day, which overlapped almost completely with the Covid-19 crisis. In 2020, the UK was still subject to EU law – albeit in a transitory way – and it started to pass legislation to implement Brexit. Almost in parallel, the pandemic crisis led to a refocusing of public attention and Brexit became a somewhat lesser issue, although withdrawal was not only *de jure* but also *de facto* accomplished on 1 January 2021. All in all, the chapter argues that the pandemic crisis led to a further centralisation of executive power in a context, however, of continuous tensions with Parliament – with huge Conservative rebellions on the plans to contain the spreading of the virus – and with the devolved administrations.

Chapter 7 returns to the broad canvas by examining the main implications of Brexit for British democracy. Arguing that the Westminster model is still appropriate as an analytical framework to assess continuities and change in British politics, we tackle some of the most important questions for the future of the British political system. If British institutions were considered in crisis before the referendum (Richards *et al.* 2014), how have they performed in such troubling circumstances created by the Brexit process? Have British institutions really regained sovereignty by exiting the EU institutions? And what does this ultimately tell us in terms of the overall functioning of British democracy?

Note

1 The importance of Brexit is also reflected in the increasing attention reserved to it by textbooks on British Politics. To give just one example, one of the most popular mentions the word "Brexit" no less than 600 times in the 825 pages of its latest edition (Jones *et al.* 2022).

1

THE WESTMINSTER MODEL AND THE UK POLITICAL SYSTEM BEFORE BREXIT

UK political institutions are among the oldest in the world (Judge 2005). While significant reforms have recently taken place with regard to devolution and the territorial distribution of power in general, the UK still preserves many elements of the institutional architecture developed over the last two centuries. As a matter of fact, Britain carries particularly important historical baggage given that its main institutions have been shaped not by a specific constitutional moment, such as, for instance, the constitutions that emerged after the American or French revolutions at the end of the eighteenth century. On the contrary, British institutions emerged gradually and they were shaped by a spirit of "Club government" (Bagehot 2001 [1867]) and by what the historian Peter Hennessy called the "good chap" theory of government, based on mutual respect between the main players, as well as "a sense of restraint all round" (Hennessy 1995). This system was primarily based on the prioritisation of top-down mechanisms of accountability at the expense of more bottom-up participatory dynamics (Richards *et al.* 2019). Hence, the Westminster model (henceforth WM) cannot be understood in isolation from the cultural elitist climate which informed its emergence, as summed up in the principles of the British Political Tradition (henceforth BPT).

During the twentieth century, the country experienced changes that came to define the dynamics of its political system – in the years around WWI and in those following the end of WWII – as a prototypical case of majoritarian democracy (Lijphart 2012). Lijphart's model of democracy is built on ten institutional variables, which we analyse in this chapter. However, before pursuing this task, we examine (Section 1.1) how the WM has been used in comparative and British politics literature, and how the BPT is particularly important for the functioning of the UK political system. We then move (Section 1.2) on to the normative debate on the WM and to the way in which we adapt Lijphart's framework to our scope (Section 1.3). Section 1.4 discusses the nature of Brexit, which we regard

DOI: 10.4324/9781003127680-2

as the key trigger of change in the period analysed here. Finally, Sections 1.5 and 1.6 deal with two elements – respectively, membership in the EEC/EU (Europeanisation) and the "constitutionalisation" of referendums – which, in the last decades, have significantly impacted on the functioning of the UK political system and transformed the WM.

1.1 Westminster, British politics, and the BPT

For many years after WWII, British politics was very much a two-party game (see Chapter 3). This was primarily because all the different arenas – electoral, parliamentary, and governmental – were dominated by the Conservative and Labour parties, with the Liberals long distanced in third place.[1] Politics was centralised in London, in Westminster and Whitehall. The Parliament of Northern Ireland replicated the same majoritarian dynamics as Westminster but without alternation in power, constantly celebrating British unionism. The constitution was uncodified, and no judicial review was provided by any Constitutional or Supreme Court. Very few veto powers could interfere with the power-hoarding instincts of the government of the day. In every general election up to 1970, the combined vote of the two main parties totalled around 90 percent. Their combined representation was even higher in the seats of the House of Commons. In the governmental arena, single-party majority governments were the rule, again with no exception until 1974.

Although some changes soon started to emerge in the early 1970s – incidentally, just around the time when the country was joining the EEC (1973) – the above dynamics were still in place at the end of that decade. The nature of this two-party game was theorised by Arend Lijphart in the first edition of his comparative book *Democracies* (1984), which was soon to become a classic in the field, even more so after the two successive editions that were published respectively in 1999 and 2012. The concept of the "Westminster model" is used here in the meaning attributed to it by Lijphart (Crepaz *et al.* 2000; Bogaards 2017). However, although its name comes from the seat of one of the most historic representative assemblies (The Houses of Parliament in the Palace of Westminster), the eponymous model does not fully coincide (and it never did) with the British political system. Rather, as per Lijphart, the WM represents the extreme of a continuum whose opposite polarity is the consensual model (Lijphart 1999; 2012) – initially defined as the "consociational model" (Lijphart 1984).

In other words, for Lijphart, the empirical cases (including the British system) are distributed between the majority/Westminster pole and the consensual/consociational pole. Obviously, the UK and some former dominions and colonies of the British Empire are close to the majoritarian pole – which is why this is also called the "Westminster model" – than to the consensual model. Consequently, it is convenient to use the WM as a reference point with respect to a specific case (the British political system in this book), which can approximate or move away from it by strengthening (or acquiring) some characteristics of the consensual model.

However, the expression "Westminster model" (or "Westminster system") did not originate with Lijphart's work. It was used long before, with different meanings and connotations. These different meanings have circulated in various strands of political science literature – from case studies on the UK itself, to comparative studies in the Commonwealth context, or on a broader scale, but within a different conceptual framework.

Therefore, before introducing Lijphart's analytical framework, and the way we adapt it here, we offer the reader a brief survey of the literature on the WM, with specific attention to two aspects. From a conceptual point of view, it is important to keep in mind the ambiguities of the use of this expression, which is often considered a synonym of the UK's political system as a concrete case. From a normative point of view (cf. Section 1.2), it is also useful to stress that although the WM has often been considered as a model of democracy to be imitated (especially abroad: e.g., APSA 1950; Perez Diaz 1999), in the UK this has been increasingly criticised as dysfunctional (e.g., Smith 1999; Richards *et al.* 2014).[2]

1.1.1 What's in a name? The Westminster model and British politics

How did the WM emerge in the study of British politics? And how can we understand its different conceptualisations? Russell and Serban (2021, 746) map the first wave of the increasing use of the concept of the "Westminster model" in the 1960s, with the classic work of J.P. Mackintosh on "British government and politics" at the end of that decade (1970), which became the first political science textbook to use it as a "framing device" (ibid.). Although Mackintosh referred to it mainly regarding the period from 1880 to 1914, the concept was increasingly used by the literature for around 15 years after this book was published (ibid.). At the turn of the millennium, by reviewing several key textbooks on British politics, it has been argued that if Mackintosh "outlined *the collapse* of the Westminster model, the model nevertheless continue(s) to shape how British politics is perceived and taught" (Smith 1999, 108).

By analysing the rich literature on the "Westminster model", we can note that, first of all, many authors refer to "system" rather than "model". This occurs especially among those who comparatively study the importance of the British institutional heritage in the former colonies, which are now members of the Commonwealth (primarily Australia, Canada, and New Zealand). For example, in a special issue of the journal *Governance* dedicated to the "Westminster system", the editors identified four different meanings of the term within these countries (Grube & Howard 2016, 469):

(1) a type of political system characterised by the presence of several objective traits;

(2) a web of meanings shared by key governmental actors;
(3) a set of persistent and stable traditions that structure political and administrative behaviour;
(4) a series of reciprocal exchange relationships between governmental elites.

It is the first of these four meaning – referring to institutional issues – that is of particular interest for this book. The other ones concern cultural elements, which specifically emphasise the common background of the political and administrative elites in the country. However, while focusing on the institutional elements of the WM, we agree that culture matters, since institutions do not work in a void. Their functioning is informed – sometimes significantly – by the environment in which they are located, and by the interpretations that the most important actors give, not only to the rules and norms, but also to the practices and behaviours that have contributed to shape them.

This is all the more crucial for a country like Britain, where the existence of an uncodified constitution is combined with customs, codes of conduct, and norms which are often poorly specified. The classics of the British constitution – starting from Walter Bagehot (2001 [1867]) – highlighted the importance of these elements in the definition of a sort of "Club government", a form of "standing wonder", which were, during the Victorian age of limited electoral suffrage, based on a high degree of trust in the governing elites (Loughlin 2013).

The crucial importance of cultural elements is at the core of the Interpretivist school of the WM, most notably Mark Bevir and Rod Rhodes (2001), when they claim that "the instinctive understandings of what Westminster means are ingrained not just in the minds of political leaders but in the practices of individual public servants based on shared traditions and stories that shape views about how things should be done" (cited in Grube & Howard 2016, 470). While taking on board the core suggestion on the importance of analysing the cultural elements in the behaviour of the actors, we still believe that, together with qualitative data as the main means of research used by the interpretivist approach, it remains important to use also quantitative indicators.

The ambiguities about the meaning of the "Westminster model" have also affected the specialist literature on the UK, fuelling a series of debates on the analytical usefulness of the model itself which, taken together, end up increasing the conceptual confusion of the expression. Moreover, these debates reflect the conceptual shifts that have already emerged in the comparative literature on the Commonwealth countries.

As a matter of fact, these criticisms developed around two themes, which are the "paradigm shift" from "Government" to "Governance", and the importance of cultural aspects in the functioning of the political system. While not entirely dissimilar, these two perspectives differ since the first one is more centred on the need to look beyond the core institutions of London. As for the first theme, the debate was triggered by Roderick Rhodes with the launch of the "Governance" paradigm in one of the most cited political science works of the last 25 years

(Rhodes 1997).[3] This study of Rhodes has been defined as "the most prominent and influential account of governance theory in British political science"
(Marinetto 2003, 562). A key element is the concept of a *policy network*, which
indicates the presence of multiple centres of power, thus opposing the imposing
and "power-hoarding" vision of the majority model and, instead, favouring a
model of power-sharing by consensus and by "bargaining", especially by pressure groups. In 1988, Rhodes began his volume *Beyond Westminster and Whitehall*
arguing that "the study of British politics is too often the study of Westminster
and Whitehall" (1988, 1).

The influence of the Governance paradigm is very clear in the approach taken
by the academic journal *British Politics*. In 2006, in the journal's opening article,
the two editors, Peter Kerr and Steven Kettell complained about the excessive
static status of the study and teaching of the discipline, which was still too centred
on a "classic" conception of the WM, More specifically, they emphasised how
the discipline had suffered from the deficiencies of the so-called "Westminster
model" and its central concern with examining the narrow mechanics of British
central government (2006, 6). Also, they argued that, despite new approaches
and research paradigms, "many authors continue to defend too narrow a conception of what is political" (ibid. 2006, 6–7). Kerr and Kettell's conclusion
targeted the static and excessive flattening of the central government in studies
that "focused on relations between prime ministers and their cabinets, the role of
civil service and the work of parliament". While one of the best-known electoral
geographers reminded these authors of the many important advances in electoral
research (Johnston 2006), the underlying agreement between these authors was
on the fact that the study of British politics had hitherto been marked by a strong
institutionalist bias.

In 2013, writing in the same journal, Jordan and Cairney took up the theme
with similar tones: "most analysts argue that the 'Westminster model' is out of
date and has been replaced by new approaches based on governance" (2013, 233),
which would be much more useful for the study of public policies. However, a
few years later – again starting from a policy perspective, and again in the same
journal – Richardson highlighted "several trends that suggest that the British
policy style is moving towards the tax pole of the spectrum (...), more in line
with the traditional Westminster model of government" (2018). This point is
very interesting because it comes from one of the authors who first questioned the
important majoritarian dynamics in the functioning of British politics (Jordan &
Richardson, 1979). Furthermore, it is placed in a context in which many important policy experts are noting the advent – in contemporary democracies – of a
more assertive style of government (Capano *et al.* 2015).

The criticism of the "Westminster model" launched by the proponents of the
paradigm shift (from "Government" to "Governance") has had such an impact
on British political science that it has provoked reactions in the opposite direction. According to John (2018), the spread of the "Governance" approach led to
the neglect of central government institutions:

in their enthusiasm for governance, many students of British politics have eschewed studying the rules of central-state institutions and the incentives they place on political actors. Classic topics from the study of political institutions, such as prime ministerial powers, ministerial appointments, and cabinet governments, are seen as synonymous with the much-criticised "Westminster model" and are thought to embody its questionable normative assumptions.

(p. 3)

There is a danger that by moving to a more governance-focused and decentered accounts of British politics, less attention is placed on the core institutions, but where political actors are still using them to get things done and where key choices made by politicians are only comprehensible within this set of constraints and opportunities. Not only are the choices of these core state actors important in this framework, the institutions affect the behavior of other actors, such as legislators, interest groups and, in turn, voters.

(p. 9)

Taking a look at the second theme, the criticisms that we consider more appropriate for our work regarding the concept of the "Westminster model" have been raised by two main groups of scholars: constitutional law experts and those who emphasise the importance of the BPT for the functioning of British institutions. Both tend to emphasise the importance of the interaction between constitutional norms and some cultural aspects. The first group is mainly associated with the work of the Constitution Unit (CU) based at University College London. According to Glover and Hazell (2008), Lijphart's model is not adequate to capture the transformations of the country due to its scarce focus on the contextual (especially cultural) elements in which the constitutional change, especially in the last 25 years, has taken hold in the country. Furthermore, this group criticises Lijphart's analytical framework by contesting the usefulness of some variables, such as interest groups and the autonomy of the central bank (ibid., 24) and stigmatising a certain superficiality in the treatment of other variables more specifically dedicated to constitutional elements.

The second group, on the other hand, emphasises the importance of the cultural codes of institutional functioning, within the aforementioned BPT. The basic idea is that the nature of the British constitution – not codified in a single constitutional text – derives from the secular evolution of its institutions and from a profound osmosis with the traditionalist values of society. The flexible nature of norms having constitutional rank is accompanied by a high rate of politicisation of the rules. In particular, governments with a majority in parliament have great discretion in pursuing their agenda. Although the BPT is formally more in tune with the values of the Conservative Party, Labour has also ended up adapting to it (Diamond & Richards 2012; Dorey 2008). But how does the BPT interact with the evolution of British institutions and with the interpretation of its constitutional rules?

1.1.2 The BPT, historical inheritance, and institutional persistence

In the country traditionally considered the cradle of representative government (Manin 1997), and where the early birth of public administration is considered to have favoured a virtuous relationship between the development of the state and the democratisation process (Fukuyama 2014), the historical development of the institutions is strictly associated with the emergence of the BPT. The latter is based on the importance of stable, strong, and majoritarian leadership and on the key principle of the "sovereignty of parliament", whereby a government commanding a majority is practically unconstrained in its power. This is at the core of the UK political system, as it has traditionally been based on

> a constitution in which power was highly concentrated, where the prerogatives of the Crown had become the powers of the executive, and where formal constraints on that power were notable due to their absence. In international terms, Britain was out on a limb. There was no book of constitutional rules; no supreme court to guard the constitution against the politicians; no charter of citizens' rights that had to be complied with; no other tiers of government that enjoyed constitutional status and protection; no second chamber with power to rival the first; and no electoral system that enforced proportionality between votes cast and seats won. This was a "winner-takes-all" system with a vengeance, not just in terms of how the first-past-the-post electoral system worked, but in terms of the governing resources available to a winning party. Getting your hands on the great prize of government, with all its unconstrained power, conditioned everything. The style and culture of political life, with its ferocious adversarialism and yah-boo polarities, both reflected and reinforced the essential nature of this system.
>
> *(Wright 2020, 25–6)*

To understand the "Brexit effect" on the political system, we need to focus on the close relationship between constitution and tradition in the evolution and current configuration of the British political system. In the absence of a single constitutional text, examining the context in which institutional rules have taken shape can be a complex exercise. However, it remains a necessary task for us in order to identify the *status quo ante*, i.e., the main characteristics of the political system before the 2016 referendum.

This means tracing the main constitutional principles, as elaborated above, by the works of Albert Venn Dicey (1885) and Walter Bagehot (2001) [1867]. With some approximation, it can be said that, while the first author focused on legal aspects, the second was more interested in the political aspects. In Dicey's analysis, three fundamental principles are emphasised: the centrality of the Parliament of Westminster (understood as "parliamentary sovereignty"), the rule of law (centrality of rights; supremacy of law and, in this context, judgements of the courts in the common law), and last but not least, the relevance of conventions (Norton 2020). Bagehot, on the other hand, highlighted the dual nature of the English constitution (*sic*). Criticising the theory of the division of powers canonised a century earlier by Montesquieu, Bagehot identified its "efficient secret" in the fusion between executive and legislative powers, with clear pre-eminence of the government over parliament.

Bagehot and Dicey published their works as Britain was still going through a phase of gradual extension of the electoral franchise, typically considered among the key elements of the democratisation process (by key classics such as Robert Dahl and Stein Rokkan). In democratic regimes, the writing of a constitution often takes place in conditions of great uncertainty and evolution. In many cases, democratic constitutions were written after traumatic events, such as wars or revolutions, which triggered historical caesuras from a political-institutional point of view. Although with important variations, through a "constitutional moment" many Western democracies have developed a genetic phase that defines the institutional imprint – and the functioning dynamics – of the various organs of the state, giving an important imprint to the model of democracy as well. The British case is different. Unlike two other cases, such as the United States with the Constitution of 1787 or, a few years later, France,[4] with the first constitutions after 1789, in the UK the constitution does not derive directly from a revolutionary break. Of course, the civil wars of the seventeenth century (1642–51) led to the first codified text, the Commonwealth "Instrument of Government", which however, in terms of elaboration, cannot be compared to a real constitution (cf. Loughlin 2013, 15).

Moreover, in the drafting process of constitutions, one often finds a relationship of mutual contamination between the elites who lead the process and the social and cultural context in which the text is embedded. Values influence the writing of the text, which in turn contribute to conditioning a country's process of modernisation and cultural – as well as institutional – change (Acemoglu & Robinson 2012; North *et al.* 2009). British institutions have evolved, above all, from the influence of Edmund Burke's conception of representation and the hostility to political rationalism expressed by the philosopher Michael Oakeshott. Burke's fiduciary conception of the electoral mandate "also implied limited access to decision-making by the people, which would not have been affected by the progressive enlargement of electoral suffrage" (Hall 2018, 2). British constitutionalism is, instead, based on gradualism, tradition, and anti-rationalism as theorised by Oakeshott (Loughlin 2013; Norton 2020). The consequences of these particularities can be grasped through three aspects: the political nature of the constitution, the centrality of the concept of parliamentary sovereignty, and the importance of the BPT.

As a matter of fact, these three elements are strongly intertwined. Although Bagehot was not explicit on this, the implicit corollary of his analysis was clear.

The British constitution has a highly politicised nature. The ruling party maintains a great deal of discretion in the interpretation of the rules, also because "the absence of a constitution codified in a single document has meant that the dividing line between what a constitution represents and what does not (be) very nuanced" (Bagehot 2001 [1867, 94]).

The political nature of the British constitution can be grasped by briefly surveying the emergence of its key institutions. In a comparative perspective, the UK represents a model of gradual and unbroken democratisation (Dahl 1971; cf. also Fukuyama 2011) and is an important example of early developments in an open social order (North *et al.* 2009). For Dahl, the British path is distinguished from that of other European continental democracies due to the precocity of liberalisation (civil rights, for which symbolic dates such as that of the Magna Carta of 1215 and the Bill of Rights of 1689 could be cited) with respect to inclusiveness (i.e., the granting of political rights, primarily the extension of the franchise). The British process of democratisation is the most solid path for the subsequent stabilisation of a polyarchy (the name with which Dahl defined democracies). According to North and colleagues (2009), thanks to the early development of property rights, England matured the conditions to limit the prerogatives of the monarch, thus being able to manage the transition from "natural society" to "open access orders" in an orderly way.

The idea that secure ownership of land provided the basis for stable political and constitutional development over the centuries between the Norman Conquest in 1066 and the Glorious Revolution of 1688 is a staple element of traditional Whig history. Whig history interprets English history as the natural and inevitable development of a constitutional structure that is capable of providing limited government and, ultimately, open access (North *et al.* 2009, 78).

Therefore, it was also thanks to these dynamics that while several other European countries were in a period of constitutionalism, the UK did not experience a clear and univocal "constitutional moment". There was no founding phase of new institutions which, at the same time, anchored the progressive stabilisation of citizenship rights and civil, political, and social freedoms. Contemporary British (formal and informal) institutions emerged during the turn of the nineteenth and the first half of the twentieth centuries (Norton 2020). More specifically, during the Victorian age (1837–1901) some of the essential elements of the British political-institutional system were consolidated, such as the single-member plurality (SMP) electoral system, the principles of "party government", with the alternation – and the adversarial dynamics – between the two main parties (Conservatives and Liberals at the time).

As emphasised by the historical-institutionalist approach (i.e., Fioretos *et al.* 2016; Pierson 2000), institutions go through long periods of stability, which are only rarely interrupted by sudden and strong moments of discontinuity, the so-called "critical junctures", which can lead to an important reshuffling of the balances of power that were consolidated previously (over the centuries in the British case). The British institutional set-up took shape from a strongly political act such as electoral reform, which initiated the enlargement of suffrage, but which did not end with the latter. British politics in the Victorian age was structured following the reform of 1832 (of the so-called "rotten boroughs"). This is the event that most closely approximated a critical juncture (Ertman 2010). There are three important reasons for this. First, it put an end to the corrupt practices of suburban voting control, also triggering a feeling of national identity and participation. It also imported a new source of political order, namely, a two-party system built around the religious cleavage. Finally, it acted as a model for future expansion of the franchise in 1867, 1884, and 1918. If, after WWI, the religious cleavage would be replaced by the class cleavage (with Labour replacing the Liberals as the second most-voted party), then for the genesis of British institutions, Ertman (2010) stresses the importance of the political/electoral dimension, as well as that of the gradual nature of the subsequent enlargements of the franchise. Surely, the constitutional dimension has also played a key role in the transition of the UK political system to democracy. In this respect, the watershed can be identified in the Parliament Act 1911 (later completed by the Parliament Act 1949), which considerably limited the legislative powers of the House of Lords, leaving the elected chamber as the cornerstone of the political system. From then on, any party commanding a majority in the House of Commons could express a government capable of imposing its legislative agenda, which was in principle approved by voters in the previous general election.

The political nature of the constitution has a fundamental implication: Parliament can repeal any law and – while bound in its action by a wide range of sources, statutory laws, and conventions – prime ministers who control their party face few obstacles in the pursuit of their objectives. Parliamentary sovereignty, and the prominence of the executive which has a majority in parliament (i.e., in the House of Commons), and the political nature of the constitution are, therefore, two sides of the same coin. With the expression "political constitution" we mean precisely this aspect, the subject of the analysis of another great jurist, Ivor Jennings, who, among other things, spoke of a constitution with a "small c" (Jennings 1933), providing the starting point for the definition of a "political constitution" that was later developed by John A.G. Griffith, who stated, "the constitution is what happens" (cf. Gordon 2019; Gamble 2016).

In this respect, other scholars have come to argue that "the dynamics of the BPT mean that parliamentary sovereignty corresponds to executive sovereignty" (Richards & Smith 2017, 2). Besides, it has been said that these shared attitudes ended up in "collusive club spirit that holds Conservatives and Labour together in a cartel that minimized the costs of settlement of political elites" (Dunleavy 1999, 204).[5] Classic authors such as Birch (1964), Beer (1965) and Greenleaf (1983) highlighted the conservative nature of the concept of tradition. Continuity and stability are considered as integral parts of the system, which legitimises historical conventions and the concentration of power in the hands of those who govern (Diamond 2014), based on a liberal conception of representation and a conservative conception of responsibility.[6] Writing in the same year, two very different authors, Anthony Birch (1964) and Leo Amery (1964), argued that only the first two elements of Lincoln's trilogy of government "of the people, for the people and by the people" could apply to British democracy.

This means that tradition matters much more than any rupture, which is what political regimes normally experience when they democratise through the constitution-making process. More specifically, the essential principles of the BPT are defined through

> a limited, liberal notion of representative democracy, encapsulating the view that it is the executive that governs in the interests of the nation, and thus, power should rest with the government; and also a conservative notion of responsibility prioritising top-down accountability at the expense of alternative, more bottom-up, participatory approaches.
>
> *(Richards et al. 2019)*

How does Brexit affect this state of affairs? According to Bogdanor (2019), Brexit could represent the very first and fundamental "constitutional moment" for the country. The "Brexit moment" actually takes place in the wake of the important institutional changes that occurred during the New Labour era (1997–2010). Due to these changes – and, in particular, the devolution and the Human Rights Act of 1998 – Bogdanor referred to the advent of a "new constitution" (2009). What we have outlined so far were the dynamics of the "old" British constitution, of the political order that, according to King (2015), began entering into crisis in 1974, the year after joining the EEC, and immediately preceding the first referendum in the history of the country. While we leave it to the constitutionalists to determine whether and to what extent these and many other innovations have actually led to a new constitution, we are more interested in analysing how these elements are put under great pressure by the Brexit process. This can be done by more precisely singling out the contours of the WM concept for our approach.

In general, we agree with Russell and Serban (2021) when they argue that the use of the concept is extremely varied and often indefinite. In fact, some use it to describe the institutional system of the UK; others to characterise countries influenced by the British model, especially within the Commonwealth. Furthermore, scholars interested in different aspects of the political system identify it with (or emphasise) different characteristics. Therefore, Westminster, for parliamentary scholars, indicates the British bicameral parliamentary system, and the building in which Parliament meets; while for scholars of public administration, Westminster refers to the historic independence of the civil service, the bureaucratic apparatus serving the government. Even worse, many use it without specifying its meaning.

However, it seems to us that the criticism of Russell and Serban (2021) cannot be applied to Lijphart's research and to those who connote the concept of the "Westminster model" in the wake of the American political scientist. Our anchoring to Lijphart's scheme is in fact clear in its objectives, tracing the defining elements to institutional (not administrative or cultural) arrangements, and helps to set a benchmark for research, such as ours, which only concerns the United Kingdom in a specific and restricted time frame.

Moreover, as we have anticipated, the concept of the "Westminster model" is not used by Lijphart to characterise a specific country or group of countries, but rather as an ideal-typical category and as the pole of a continuum at the opposite end of which the "consensual model" is placed. The empirical cases may approach the features of the abstract category but there is no attempt, in Lijphart's empirical analysis, to make the UK the fulfilment of the ideal-typical model. By way of example, although the WM (*à la* Lijphart) presupposes unicameralism, the UK Parliament is bicameral (albeit asymmetric), being composed of the House of Commons and the House of Lords.

Therefore, it appears appropriate to speak of the UK political system when referring to a specific empirical reality, while the expression "Westminster model" refers to Lijphart's polar category. It also seems to us that, despite the awareness that the UK has probably never been, and now is certainly no longer, a "perfect" example of a majoritarian system, the terms "Westminster model" and "Westminster democracy" can continue to be used in order to capture the essential dynamics of its political system.

1.2 The normative debate on the Westminster model

The "Westminster model" has often been associated with institutional effectiveness and efficiency. In its application to British democracy, features such as government stability and its control of the agenda, an emphasis on accountability; the SMP electoral system and a two-party system have made the political system a paradigmatic example of a majoritarian democracy. From the UK, the SMP was then exported to the (former) British colonies, thus facilitating the replication of many dynamics – from North America to India and Oceania – of the "Westminster model". It suffices to mention here that, until its electoral reform in 1993, New Zealand was considered to be a country which conformed to the model even better than Britain (Lijphart 1999).

Back in 1950, in the annual report to the conference of the American Political Science Association (APSA), the British party system was significantly praised as an example to follow of a responsible party system. Stability, responsibility, and accountability were the merits of a political system built on the combination of secular political institutions, shaped by an early liberalisation and which, together with the progressive consolidation of political parties during the nineteenth century, favoured the emergence of strong and accountable leadership. The "efficient secret" of this system – in the words of Walter Bagehot (2001) [1867] – lay in the "almost complete fusion of executive and legislative powers in the Cabinet" – that is, in the combination of one-party government and cohesion at the parliamentary level.

Similarly, several classics of political science had also expressed admiration for British institutions and their stability and efficiency. Already at the end of the nineteenth century Woodrow Wilson, the future American president, looked with admiration at the British parliamentary system and at the merger of executive and legislative branches (1885). In the pioneering comparative research on political culture, conducted by Almond and Verba (1963), the British system was praised as the closest thing to the ideal conditions for a healthy democracy, that is, civic culture. Similarly, Robert Dahl (1971) emphasised the country's early and solid path to democratisation. Moreover, Giovanni Sartori (1976) identified in the British case the archetype of the two-party system, which favoured timeliness in government action and the mechanism of alternation, also thanks to the presence of the SMP electoral system.

Of course, the WM was also widely criticised (as was the British political system). In the United States, as early as the mid-1960s the United Kingdom had become "an example of a dysfunctional and pathological system" (Moran 2017, 140), as was clear from the works of the leading American expert on British politics, Samuel Beer. In the 1970s, before Margaret Thatcher came into the government, a wave of journalism was consolidated on the decline of the United Kingdom, which was for some, "the sick man of Europe" due to the economic decline of the country, the conflicts in industrial relations, the important social transformations and, last but not least, the Northern Ireland question.

Also, on the political-institutional side, the 1970s were particularly problematic. In 1974 Harold Wilson led – for the first time in the post-war period – a minority government, while in 1977 James Callaghan lost his majority and struggled to remain in power. The concentration of the vote in the two large Conservative and Labour parties began to crumble, leaving room for a more fluid system, in which "third forces" emerged, such as the Liberal Party, nationalist parties in Scotland and Wales, and revolts against the party leadership (like that of Enoch Powell among the Conservatives). As Kenneth O. Morgan put it: "British politics appeared pluralistic, almost unrecognizable" (Morgan 2017, 6–7).

According to Lijphart, consensual systems are "kinder and gentler", and are associated with greater economic wellbeing and satisfaction with politics. The conclusions reached by Lijphart completely overturned the predominant view after WWII, indicating a superiority of consensual democracies, both in terms of economic performance and citizens' satisfaction with the political system (Lijphart 2012). While the substance of these conclusions has been shared by other authoritative scholars (Bingham Powell 2000), it has also been openly contested by others (Bernauer et al. 2016). However, here, we are not interested in the extensive academic debate that Lijphart's analysis has sparked (Boogards 2017; Andeweg & Luwerse 2018; Bormann 2010), but in how to profitably adapt his analytical framework to our scope.

1.3 Lijphart's analytical framework: discussion and adaptation

A discussion of Lijphart's framework for the analysis of democracies cannot ignore the great theoretical debates in which his scholarship emerged. In the first decades of the post-war period, comparative politics was dominated by the behavioural approach, which was based on the analysis of individual values, orientations, and cognitive elements that form the "political culture" (Almond & Verba 1963); as well as by the historical-sociological approach based on the analysis of important social divisions (cleavages) of historical origin (Lipset & Rokkan 1967). This was the cultural and epistemological context in which the praises of the British political system are situated, which helped to reinforce the conviction in the superiority of the WM.

Both theoretical approaches – behavioural and historical-sociological – tended to overshadow the role of state institutions, which were, however, brought back into vogue in the form of the "new institutionalism" (March & Olsen 1984) at the beginning of the 1980s, immediately regaining a central position in comparative politics (Evans 1985). It was in this phase of transition that Lijphart's voluminous and authoritative contribution to the comparative study of democracies took shape. Lijphart's starting point, emerging from his work on the Dutch case (Lijphart 1968) and from the comparative work on cases marked by the co-presence of important cleavages and consociational politics (Lijphart 1977), was clearly influenced by the behavioural and historical-sociological approach. In the first version of the volume on the types of democracy, the variables referring to the number of relevant cleavages and the political culture of direct democracy were still present (Lijphart 1984). However, the institutionalist turn was consolidated in the second and third versions, in which societal cleavages and political culture disappeared from the formal analytical framework (Lijphart 1999; 2012).

In his works, the American scholar analyses and classifies democratic systems on the basis of the level of concentration of power, imagining a continuum that unfolds between two ideal poles: on one hand, that of majority democracy and, on the other hand, that of consensual democracy. Given the relatively limited number of cases, especially in the first volume written in 1984, the majority model is largely populated by the UK and by countries which, as former British colonies, have inherited important political-institutional traits from the UK, starting from the majority electoral system and a two-party system. For this reason, in the conceptual apparatus (which is broadly taken up here), the expression "Westminster model" coincides with the "majoritarian model".[7]

Although Lijphart starts from (and then traces his analysis back to) a conceptual distinction of a linear (one-dimensional) type – a majority model vs a consensual model – he develops an analytical framework based on the intersection of two dimensions. The first, called "governments–parties", refers to the horizontal distribution of power among central institutions. The second, called "federal–unitary", refers to the vertical distribution of power between the central administration and any regional or local administrations. The more power is concentrated within a one-party government (first dimension) and in the central administration (second dimension), the more one approaches the majority (or Westminster) model. On the other hand, the more power is distributed among the various parties present in parliament (first dimension), and between different levels of government (second dimension), the more one approaches the consensual model.

In the most recent version, Lijphart identifies a total of ten variables, five of which belong to the first dimension and five to the second. As reported in Table 1.1, the former are party system (V1), type of government (V2), government–parliament relationship (V3), electoral system (V4), and type of intermediation–organised interests (V5). The latter are vertical division of powers (V6), types of parliaments (V7), types of constitutions (V8), control of the constitutionality of laws (V9), and relationship of dependence/independence from the government of the central bank (V10). Each variable is calculated on the basis of an indicator or by making a synthesis of several indicators. These indicators are presented and discussed in detail in subsequent empirical chapters. For now, it is worth dwelling on the connections between the variables within each

TABLE 1.1 Lijphart's model: dimensions and variables

Majoritarian (Westminster) democracy	Consensus democracy
Executives–parties dimension	
V1) Two-party system	Multi-party system
V2) Single-party majority government – party in office dominates	Broad coalition government – parties share cabinet/ministerial posts
V3) Executive predominance over parliament (due to party discipline)	Balance between executive and legislative power
V4) Majoritarian electoral system	Proportional electoral system
V5) Pluralist approach in interest representation	Corporatist (or neo-corporatist) approach
Unitary–federal dimension	
V6) Unitary and centralised government – absence of territorial self-government	Federal and/or decentralised system of government
V7) Unicameral parliament (or weak bicameralism)	Strong bicameralism (similar powers but different modes of representation)
V8) Flexible constitution: parliamentary sovereignty – no formal distinction between ordinary and constitutional laws	Rigid constitution: special majorities for constitutional laws
V9) No judicial review – no Constitutional Court	Judicial review and arbitration of constitutional controversies by a Constitutional Court
V10) Central bank under executive (direct or indirect) control	Independent central bank

dimension and between the two dimensions, also considering that this book concerns a single case study (the UK) with a focus on a relatively short period, while the analytical framework was mainly designed for comparative analysis between countries.

As for the first dimension, much of the debate has focused on whether including the variable of the intermediation of interests (V5) along with the other four. As argued by authoritative scholars (Keman & Pennings 1995; Taagepera 2003, 7), no theory or logical model explains this connection. Indeed, Lijphart himself admits that, despite a good empirical correlation with some other variables (1999, 244), V5 is not structurally related to the others (1999, 306).

On the contrary, the remaining four variables are firmly connected to each other. In particular, V4–V1 and V2–V3 logically appear as two interconnected combined variables. A majority electoral system (V4) tends to favour the formation or maintenance of a two-party system (V1). In turn, this combination tends to produce single-colour majority governments (V2), which result in government dominance over parliament (V3). On the other hand, a proportional electoral system (V4) favours the formation or maintenance of a multi-party system (V1). This combination tends to translate in the formation of coalition or minority governments (V2), which produce a more balanced relationship between government and parliament (V3).

The remaining four variables appear logically connected. In fact, some are perhaps too much, in the sense that they are partially overlapping on a conceptual level. Regarding this problem, it is useful to start by ascertaining the two-dimensional nature of the variable "(vertical) division of power" (V6). This variable concerns both the so-called *self-rule*, i.e., the level of autonomy of the regions and local authorities with respect to the central administration (centralised state vs decentralised state), and the so-called *shared-rule*, i.e., the power of the regions to intervene in the central decision-making process regarding constitutional and ordinary laws (unitary state vs federal state). Indeed, the V6 measurement scale starts from a minimum value "1" ("unitary and centralised" system) and reaches a maximum value "5" ("federal and decentralised" system), passing through the various combinations of self-rule and shared-rule: "2" ("unitary and decentralised"), "3" ("semi-federal") and "4" ("federal and centralised"). In other words, V6 overlaps the entire "federal–unitary" dimension, not only in terminology but also substantially, taking shape as a dimension in its own right. Furthermore, V6 conceptually overlaps the variable on types of parliaments (V7) with regard to federal systems, which (by definition) necessarily need a bicameral parliament (in which one of the two chambers represents the federated entities). Indeed, although there is no relationship of necessity in the opposite sense (a bicameral parliament is not necessarily part of a federal system), the empirical correlation between V6 and V7 is the strongest within the second dimension (Lijphart 1999, 244).

In addition, as noted in other works, including comparative ones (Druckman *et al.* 2005), the variable relating to the type of parliament (V7) is also logically connected (and above all) to other variables of the first dimension, specifically to the combined V2–V3 (type of government and government–parliament relationship). Indeed, bicameral parliaments, regardless of the federal or unitary nature of the "upper house", tend to require larger majorities and/or longer periods of time for the deployment of government action, thus producing, at least tendentially, coalition governments (V2) and, in any case, a greater balance of power between government and parliament (V3). This general argument is particularly valid in the case under examination, as the UK's bicameralism is not connected to Lijphart's second dimension, but it can have some effect on the first, if only with regard to V3 (government–parliament relationship) (see Chapter 4).

Finally, the variables relating to the type of constitution (V8) and the control of the constitutionality of the laws (V9) are strongly connected with each other and with the other variables of the second dimension, as well as with the first dimension. The presence of a rigid constitution and a Constitutional Court guarantees – just as their absence does not guarantee – the legitimate exercise of power of the various levels of government and of the various organs of the central state. In turn, this contributes to the production of laws that are in line with the constitution. These two variables (V8 and V9) are, therefore, configured as transversal to the two dimensions, more than pertaining exclusively to the second.

Considering the above, the empirical analysis presented in this book adapts the analytical framework just examined, regarding the number of dimensions, while making use of the same variables. Three dimensions have been identified as particularly salient with respect to the tensions created by the Brexit process: the "electoral–party" (V4 and V1); government–parliament relations (V2, V3, and V7); and "centre–periphery relations" (V6). The "remote" variables – interest brokerage (V5) and central bank (V10) – are not considered here (in the wake of what Hazell 2008 has done); while the variables V8 and V9 are included as context factors that can have an impact on all three of the dimensions identified.

1.4 The Brexit process as a case of constitutional and political change

After having defined the object of our study – i.e., longitudinal changes in three key dimensions of UK political system: party–system, executive–legislative relations, and centre–periphery relations – and the abstract point of reference that allows us to detect the direction and intensity of change – i.e., Lijphart's WM and the relative indicators – now we need to discuss the nature of what we present as the main motor of change during the analysed period: Brexit.

Brexit has been broadly understood as a complex process with multiple different causes, as well as with many and very diverse effects or implications (Evans *et al.* 2018; Adam 2020). As a consequence, it has generated a wealthy scholarship approaching the subject from different perspectives and disciplines, such as sociology (Davies 2022), economics (Whyman & Petrescu 2020), political economy (Lavery *et al.* 2019), constitutional law (Gordon 2020), and political science (Evans & Menon 2017).

In this book we are interested in the impact of Brexit on the UK's political system. As such, the causes of Brexit, albeit of clear interest to us, remain outside of the focus of the analysis. Similarly, the effects/implications of Brexit on specific policy areas are beyond the remit of this book, unless they clearly affect the main political institutions – e.g., by deeply reshaping lines of competition amongst parties or engendering institutional contestation between the executive and the legislative or between the centre and the peripheries. In short, we are interested in the impact of Brexit on UK polity and politics, not on UK policies.

In line with our main interest, we conceive of the Brexit process as a case of constitutional reform, implying some institutional change and entailing political adaptation or reaction. In so doing, we place ourselves within the mainstream literature that has investigated Brexit from the point of view of the UK (Keating 2018; Taylor 2019; Bogdanor 2019; McConalogue 2020; Sumption 2020; Wincott *et al.* 2021; White 2022).[8] Clearly, the key constitutional reform of the Brexit process consists of a reappropriation of the exercise of sovereignty and a repatriation of legal authority. As such, it could be seen as a simple restoration of the pre-1973 UK constitution. However, the institutional transformations induced over 40 years of EEC/EU membership, the adoption of domestic constitutional reforms, as well as societal and political change, make the Brexit process a more complex *affair*. Indeed, as a consequence of intervened changes, the exercise of sovereignty and the repatriation of powers can (and did) become a source of contestation. In turn, the Brexit decision and the process for carrying it out could induce further institutional and political change.

Like many processes of constitutional reform, it can be rather complicated to disentangle the process itself from the outcome, as constitutional reforms are conducted by political forces acting within those political institutions that are then affected by the reform. In other words, the political process can be as important as the institutional reform, and the two are deeply interlinked. This is even more the case for political systems, such as the UK, that have a flexible/political constitution (Tomkins 2010). Indeed, from the outset of the Brexit process, constitutional lawyers warned that leaving the EU would constitute a challenge both *of* and *for* the UK's constitution (Gordon 2016).

The comparative/theoretical literature on institutional reforms in established democracies has highlighted the strategic and self-interested nature of institutional reforms from the perspective of political elites, who tend to act only when they see a clear advantage or when they come under pressure from public opinion (Bedock 2017). In this respect, a systematic exposition of the actors and motivations for reforms was provided by Alan Renwick (2010), albeit in regard to a specific type of institutional change, that is, electoral reforms. Many of his considerations, however, apply to institutional reforms in general and can be of much use to further categorise the Brexit case. Renwick identifies three broad types of reforms (Renwick 2010, 11–16). First, most reforms are wanted and carried out

by political elites either by majority (*elite majority imposition*) or through a negotiated agreement between the political majority and minority (*elite settlement*).
Secondly, there can be reforms that are carried out independently or against the
will of political elites. This type of reform occurs when there is an intervention by constitutional/supreme courts (*judicial decision*), or when political elites
undergo an imposition either from external actors (*external imposition*) or from the
masses (*mass imposition*). Thirdly, there can be reforms in which political elites are
prompted to act according to the will of external actors or of the masses, but they
maintain control of the process and (at least partially) the content of the reform:
elite external interaction and *elite mass interaction* respectively.

Fitting Brexit into one of the above-mentioned categories is not straightforward
and requires a degree of subjective evaluation. Yet, surely, the Brexit process was
put in motion neither by the will of political elites, nor by judges, nor by external
actors. This uncontroversial view takes out *elite majority imposition, elite settlement,
judicial decision,* and *external imposition.* Conceiving of Brexit as a case of *mass imposition* reform, might capture important aspects of the decision and, to some extent,
of the process. Indeed, one of the main reasons why Brexit has been perceived as a
"shock" is that neither the majority of the British government nor the opposition
wanted it. UK voters' decision to leave the EU in the Brexit referendum was a failure of and a revolt against the political elites (Copus 2018; Rodriguez-Pose 2018;
Rudolph 2020; Lees 2021). In addition, while Theresa May's governments seemed
to take the cue from voters (Bresenbauch Meislova 2019), the political class as a
whole remained unable or unwilling to deliver a result (Thompson 2020; Martill
2021a),[9] until voters gave another push on the occasion of the European Parliament
election of May 2019 (Martill 2020; Vasilopoulou 2020).

Yet, interpreting Brexit as a *mass imposition* reform would blanket the fact that
political elites, and in particular the successive governments, maintained control
of the domestic process and relative control of the content of the reform. If anything, the constraints on the final outcome of the reform – including domestic
constitutional issues (e.g., the status of Northern Ireland) – came primarily from
the need to negotiate a deal with external actors, namely the EU. Brexit can,
therefore, be conceptualised as a process of constitutional reform that falls in
between *elite mass interaction,* as far as the political decision and the direction of
change are concerned, and *elite external interaction,* as far as important provisions
of the final outcome are concerned. In other words, the British political elites
were, to some extent, squeezed between the will of British voters to leave the EU
and the conditions posed by the external (EU) actor. However, they maintained
some room for manoeuvring vis-à-vis both counterparts.

1.5 The difficult Europeanisation of the UK political system

Brexit terminates the 47-year long and often difficult membership of the UK
in the EU. The UK can be seen a peculiar and somehow extreme case of
early and problematic politicisation of the European issue. Well before Brexit,
British peculiarities have been famously summed up in the image of the

country as the "awkward partner" (George 1994), a "stranger" (Wall 2008) or a "semi-detached member" (Bulmer 1992) of the EU. Such an attitude gave Euroscepticism a British coin, as we first find the word mentioned in the British press in the mid-1980s, at a time in which the UK was, ironically, a key contributor to the approval of the Single European Act (1986). Margaret Thatcher's famous Bruges speech (1988) incorporated some of the historical, geographic, economic, and political factors which have both defined the nature of British "awkwardness" in the EEC/EU and the roots of Euroscepticism as a political phenomenon more generally. As Grande and Schwarzbözl (2017, 2) summed it up, the UK's (early) politicisation of Europe was characterised by the absence of an elite consensus on Europe, weak support for integration in public opinion; polarisation between the two mainstream parties; the formation of new challenger parties based on European issues; deep divisions within both mainstream parties.

The early roots of politicisation of Europe in Britain can be found in the uncertainties experienced by the governments of the late 1950s in facing the decline of the British empire (Gamble 2003; Gifford 2014). Internal party divisions on Europe characterised the party system ever since the first (unsuccessful) applications to join the EEC in 1961 – under Conservative PM Harold Macmillan – and 1967 – under Labour PM Harold Wilson (Smith 2012; Baker *et al.* 2008). President De Gaulle's departure from office with the lifting of the French veto finally allowed Britain to start negotiations to join the EEC and the House of Commons to vote on the conditions of membership on 28 October 1971, in what has been described as very divisive vote, with significant splits in both major parties (Norton 2011, 248).

However, after the UK joined the EEC in January 1973, it quickly became clear that Edward Heath's government (1970–4) was to become a parenthesis of authentic Europeanism in a long story of Eurosceptic, or at best "mildly-Europeanist" prime ministers. Both main parties were divided on whether to join. In an early phase the Conservatives were more in favour than the Labour Party and, as proof of that, the outspoken Conservative MP Enoch Powell invited voters to support the more Eurosceptic Labour Party in the 1974 February general election. Indeed, Labour had promised voters to renegotiate the terms of membership with the EEC and hold a referendum, which is what it did after winning a narrow majority in the October election (cf. Section 1.5).

Britain was the only member state in which membership was to be *confirmed* by a referendum (rather than *allowed* by a preventive consultation, as happened elsewhere). The decision to hold the first-ever UK-wide referendum was mainly dictated by Harold Wilson's (forlorn) hope to placate dissent inside his recently formed minority government (Smith 1999; Butler & Kitzinger 1976), in a deeply troubled economic situation. The 1975 referendum represented the first clear instance in which the institutional dynamics of the UK political system – and particularly the "near fusion" of executive and legislature – became enmeshed with sovereignty issues. In any case, the option to continue with membership won a comfortable majority, albeit with a rather limited participation (64.5

percent) for that time, putting to a rest – temporarily, at least – conflict on the European issue.

In the 1980s, the governments led by Thatcher resolutely pressed for the completion of the Common Market through the Single European Act (1987). At the same time, however, she stressed the need for reshaping the British financial contribution to the Community (with the so-called "rebate"). Thatcher resolutely opposed any instance of political integration and pushed the Conservative Party, increasingly divided internally, into Eurosceptic positions. On the other hand, the Labour Party had split in the early 1980s, when a group of dissidents, who were critical of the party position under Michael Foot's premiership – it had both moved to the left and embraced strong Eurosceptic positions, proposing in its manifesto for the 1983 general election to leave the EEC without a referendum – established the Social Democratic Party.

The end of Thatcher's leadership (November 1990) came in the shadow of the preparations for the Maastricht Treaty (1992). Internal dissent in the Conservative Party became unbearable, and Thatcher's successor, John Major, had to deal with a very fractured party. When the Maastricht Treaty was finally ratified – also by removing the "social chapter" from the text of the Treaty and guaranteeing an opt out for the UK on the single currency – the salience of the EU issue had exploded, marking the end – in the UK earlier than in other member countries of continental Europe – of the so-called "permissive consensus" on integration (Hooghe & Marks 2009). In 1997, when Blair became PM, the salience of Europe among public opinion reached its peak and a brand-new party like the Referendum Party received 3 percent of the vote in the 1997 general election – a result which for a Eurosceptic party would today look rather meagre, but which at the time was far from irrelevant. Incidentally, on this result the United Kingdom Independence Party (UKIP) went on to build its rise by gaining one position – from fourth to first place – at every European Parliament (EP) election from 1999 to 2014, quadrupling its score from 6.6 percent to 26.6 percent, and obtaining a remarkable 12.6 percent in the 2015 general election. If, in the 1990s, the EU still had a limited impact on European party systems (Mair 2000), the success of the Referendum Party and UKIP anticipates a development that, in the 2000s, will affect many other countries in continental Europe.

Although Blair's decisions on Europe could be seen as "a missed opportunity" (Menon & Scazzieri 2020), Blairite strategies were mainly aimed at containing the salience of Europe, by indefinitely delaying the possible adoption of the single currency and by promising a referendum on the Treaty on the Constitution of Europe. As aptly emphasised, Blair's strategies can be unpacked in four main aims, respectively "(1) to defuse the European policy cleavage between the two main British parties, (2) to depoliticise European policy decisions, (3) to delegate veto power to the general public, and (4) to defer the making of conclusive decisions on contentious European issues" (Oppermann 2008, 178). Blair was helped by French and Dutch voters, who ditched the "Constitution" in their referendums in May–June 2005, thus sparing the PM to fulfil the pledge made in the election manifesto for the 2005 general election. As a result of this, in 2007 the salience of Europe among British voters was back to the irrelevance experienced during the 1980s, and it would remain at this level until the early 2010s (Grande & Schwarzbözl 2017, 31).

When the Conservatives were back in government and David Cameron became PM (2010), he was soon to be haunted by the ghost of the increasing inevitability of the referendum on EU membership, as the combined pressures of UKIP as a single-issue party claiming exit (Ford & Goodwin 2014), the increasingly internal Euroscepticism of the parliamentary party (Lynch 2015) and of public opinion more in general (Curtice 2016) became difficult to push back. Cameron's decision to endorse the formation of a new Conservative group in the EP, following the exit of the Conservative Party from the European People's Party after the 2009 EP elections (Lynch & Whitaker 2008) was a sort of anticipation of what was going to happen. When Cameron became the leader of the Conservative Party, he asked his party to "stop banging on about Europe". As it is well known, history proved to be quite different, and Cameron eventually ended his political career banged by Europe (Table 1.2).

TABLE 1.2 EU membership, institutional change, and politicisation of the EU issue

Period	Nature of change	Impact on institutions	Politicisation
1973–79 "Silent revolution"	EEC membership: absorption of the *acquis communautaire* and primacy of EU law	Weakening of Parliament Issues of intra-party cohesion	Relatively low salience despite the referendum on membership
1979–97 "Centralisation and *opt-outs*"	Creation of the single market and establishment of the EU with Maastricht	Strengthening of Euroscepticism Centralisation	End of permissive consensus High salience for the ratification of the Maastricht Treaty
1997–2010 "Reluctant reforms"	Devolution Further deepening and widening (enlargement towards Eastern Europe)	"Bi-constitutionalism" (Flinders 2010)	Depoliticisation of the EU issue
2010–16 "Illusion of control"	New rules post-Lisbon Economic and financial crisis Migration crisis	Referendum Importance of third parties (Lib-Dem, UKIP)	Failed attempt at depoliticisation Stronger salience for the EU, particularly if linked to immigration

As we know well, Cameron's political career was terminated by the results of a referendum: an institution that has gradually become part of UK politics after having been considered, for a very long time, alien to British democracy. Since the referendum is not only at the origin of the Brexit shock but it has also accompanied previous reforms – and might generate other reforms in the future – it is important to briefly trace the history of this institution in British democracy, in a view to highlight the role that it has acquired.

1.6 Referendums in the UK

As discussed above, key principles of the UK constitution – such as parliamentary sovereignty – and of the BPT – such as "government knows best" – have traditionally converged on attributing absolute prominence to representative and even elitist practices of democracy vis-à-vis participative ones. This explains why referendums not only remained absent in British politics until the 1970s, but they were also considered to be alien to British democracy. Yet, in the last 25 years, referendums have become familiar elements of the UK political repertoire and, most importantly, they have featured prominently in the Brexit process. Not only the Brexit saga has originated from the June 2016 referendum, but the ensuing political debate and political struggle has involved referendums in various ways (Gordon 2020). First, a general reflection has emerged on the use of referendums in democracies and the quality of decision-making (Offe 2017; Rose 2020), particularly in relation to the fairness of information communicated during referendum campaigns (Banks 2016; Marshall & Drieshova 2018; Renwick *et al.* 2018). Secondly, the debate has invested the transformative effect of referendums in the relationship between the principles of parliamentary sovereignty and popular sovereignty in the UK (White 2022). Thirdly, in Scotland and Northern Ireland, where voters backed the Remain option, the interpretation of the referendum results as a univocal mandate for UK's withdrawal from the EU was fiercely contested (Keating 2018; Murphy 2018). Fourthly, in turn, the Brexit-related grievances coming from these two Celtic peripheries translated into demands for a second independence referendum in Scotland and for an Irish unification referendum in Northern Ireland (Daniels & Kuo 2021). Finally, especially in the first two years after the Brexit referendum, a lively debate has emerged on: a) whether the result of the referendum should be interpreted as a mandate for a *soft Brexit* or a *hard Brexit* (Allen 2018); and b) whether there should be a second referendum, either to confirm/dismiss the choice adopted in the first one or to approve/reject a final Brexit deal (Bellamy 2019).

Before analysing the impact of the Brexit process on the UK political system, it is therefore important to take stock of all pre-Brexit changes in the constitution and in the BPT, especially those that cut across our three dimensions: party–system, executive–legislative relations, and centre–periphery relations. In this respect, a preliminary overview on the role acquired by referendums in British politics is in order.

It is perhaps paradoxical that the first requests for holding referendums came from Conservative scholars, starting from Albert Dicey (the theorist of parliamentary sovereignty), and politicians, including Winston Churchill. Those first calls highlight two recurring features of the use of referendums in the UK: an instrumental approach and a constitutional content. In open contradiction with the principle of parliamentary sovereignty, Dicey aimed to use referendums to stop the constitutional reforms proposed by the Liberal governments in the 1890s (Home Rule for Ireland) and by the Lib–Lab majority in the early 1910s (the subordination of the Lords to the Commons – as per the Parliament Act 1911). The instrumental positioning on the referendum was crystal clear, as this was advocated by the party that was weaker in the House of Commons (Conservatives) and was rejected by the parties that commanded a majority (Liberals and Labour). Similarly, in the spring of 1945, Churchill wanted to prolong his premiership until the end of the war in the Far East and, for this reason, he proposed a referendum for a further extension of the parliamentary term (Norton 2020, 69). In that occasion, Labour's leader Clement Attlee rejected the proposal adducing a principled argument: "I could not consent to the introduction of our national life of a device so alien to all our traditions as the referendum" (House of Lords 2018, 4–5). However, the conflict of interest between the two leaders in the upcoming general election was all too evident.

In the post-war context, the lack of referendums in British politics was not perceived as a democratic lacuna, as the most salient issues were politicised by mass parties, well connected with (and largely trusted by) their respective social constituencies. The 1970s brought two novelties. First, a new idea of democracy gradually emerged in the UK: less attached to the elitism of the BPT and to the intermediary role of parties, and more open to principles of responsive government and grassroots participation (King 2009, 250–1). Secondly, the UK came to be in front of a key political/constitutional issue that parties tended not to politicise because they were internally divided on it: membership of the European Economic Community. It was primarily the second novelty that pushed referendums inside UK politics. The Conservative government that supervised UK's entry in 1973 resisted the call for a UK-wide *ex ante* referendum – in contrast to what happened in Denmark, Ireland, and Norway – but it still held an *ex post* consultation on the constitutional status of Northern Ireland. The so-called 1973 Border Poll was the first (non-local) referendum in the history of the UK and contributed to change the view of the Labour leadership on the possibility of calling a UK-wide referendum (Butler & Kitzinger 1976, 18–19). In this context, the first UK-wide referendum was held in 1975 on EC membership, after Labour had committed to it in the 1974 general elections (Saunders 2016, 318). It would remain the only UK-wide referendum for 36 years

However, these first referendums, induced both leftist and conservative intellectuals to reconsider the compatibility of this instrument with the British political system (Baham & Burton 1975; Goodhart 1976). Indeed, referendums remained present in UK politics throughout the 1970s, as Labour governments proposed devolution for Scotland and Wales. Also in this case, referendums were deployed on constitutional matters and with a clear instrumental approach, i.e., with the aim of shifting responsibility of the final decision from a very divided Labour Party to Scottish and Welsh voters. As is widely known, the 1978–79 devolution reform did not pass because Welsh voters turned it down by a huge margin (Balsom & McAllister 1979), while Scottish voters did not support it convincingly enough (Bochel & Denver 1981).

With the electoral victory of Margaret Thatcher in 1979 and the beginning of a long Conservative predominance, referendums disappear from British politics for about two decades. Not even the ratification of the Maastricht Treaty, which contributed to a change of premiership in the UK, was subject to a referendum. It took the arrival of Tony Blair as PM and the reformist agenda of New Labour to inaugurate a new era of British politics in which the referendum devise featured prominently. Five regional referendums were held between 1997 and 2004 in a view to implement devolution reforms: with the ones held in the late 1990s – London, Northern Ireland, Scotland, and Wales – being a success, and the one held in 2004 (north-east of England) resulting in a fiasco (cf. Chapter 5). The former represented an important novelty in the political motivation for using referendums in the UK. By late 1990s, the Labour Party had become rather resolute and united across all constituent nations of the UK on the project of devolution.

Therefore, the referendums were not held to shift responsibility to voters but to seal the constitutional reforms with a sort of "double legitimacy" process: Westminster approval of the relative act(s) from above and popular approval(s) from below. The political/constitutional implication of this move is not trivial, as it might introduce a potential element of rigidity in the UK (otherwise) flexible constitution. In principle, the UK Parliament must retain substantive powers to scrap any previous law, including constitutional laws – as it did, for instance, with the abolition of the Northern Ireland parliament in 1973 (cf. Chapter 5). As a consequence, according to some, the requirement of holding a referendum for adopting a new reform (or deleting a previous one) is incompatible with the UK constitution (Goldsworthy 2010). However, at a political level, it might come to be perceived as illegitimate to scrap a previous "double legitimacy" reform by a simple act of Parliament. In other words, the referendum would become a virtual (i.e., politically) mandatory requirement for repealing reforms adopted (also) by referendum. A recent tendency to adopt pre-emptive statutory requirements for referendums by law appears to reinforce this trend (Gordon 2020), particularly (but not exclusively) for those approved through a "double legitimacy" process.[10] Yet, the academic debate remains open on the legal value of these requirements and on the supposed protection offered by the "double legitimacy" process.

The last four referendums occurred under the premierships of David Cameron (2010–16): the 2011 (Wales-only) referendum on the attribution of legislative powers to the Welsh Assembly; the 2011 (UK-wide) referendum on the reform of the electoral system for general elections (from first-past-the-post to Alternative Vote); the 2014 (Scotland-only) referendum on Scottish independence; and the

2016 Brexit referendum. Leaving aside the 2011 Welsh referendum, which was "inherited" by a law of the New Labour era (Government of Wales Act 2006), the other three stand out for two characteristics. First, differently from Blair's referendums, the prime minister was against the proposed change. The motivation was not to seal a pursued reform with a "double legitimacy" process but, on the contrary, to crash mounting challenges against the constitutional *status quo*. In other words, the idea was to face up calls for unwanted reforms, win the referendums, and to get these issues out of the agenda for good. Secondly, the three referendums held under Cameron's premiership stand out for the extremely high stakes, namely, the voting system, the territorial integrity of the state, and EU membership. Some scholars stigmatised Cameron's choice to gamble with referendums up to the bitter end (Glencross 2016), but these kinds of considerations fall outside the remit of the present book. Surely, Cameron's strategy worked fine with the 2011 referendum on the voting system, and it brought home the result (though with some suspense and unintended consequences) on occasion of the 2014 Scottish independence referendum; but it failed with the Brexit referendum, albeit by a narrow margin.

Surely, the bitter defeat suffered by the political establishment (and by 48 percent of voters) in the Brexit referendum triggered a long polemic on the quality of referendum campaigns (Renwick *et al.* 2018). However, referendums seem to have established themselves in the nomenklatura of British politics. After all, the adversarial nature of referendum questions and the majoritarian nature of referendum-based decision-making (at least for how referendums are organised in the UK), fits very well with some traditional features of British politics. In time, a sort of customary practice has been slowly emerging, revealing some patterns in the use and scope of referendums in the UK. First, as envisaged in the theoretical literature, the introduction of this instrument of direct democracy in a majoritarian political system has resulted in referendums remaining *ad hoc* initiatives, at full discretion of the governmental majority of the day (Vatter 2009, 130). Albeit suggesting some regulatory frameworks, authoritative reports on the subject have confirmed that this (i.e., *ad hoc* initiatives by the parliamentary majority) is indeed considered the way in which referendums should be used in the UK (House of Lords Constitution Committee 2010; Independent Commission on Referendums – UCL Constitution Unit 2018). This prerogative of parliamentary majorities puts governments *de facto* in control of the decision whether to hold a referendum or not. However, as David Cameron's era has demonstrated beyond any doubt, it does not exclude that governments might be pushed by other actors to hold referendums that they would not want. Second, so far, referendums in the UK have been solidly linked to constitutional issues (Kavanagh 2012; Curtice 2013).

Of course, not every salient constitutional reform has been triggered or approved by referendums. The ratification of Maastricht (1993) or Lisbon treaties, or the establishment of a Supreme Court (2009) are clear examples of salient constitutional reforms conducted without referendums. However, anytime a referendum was held, either regional or UK-wide, it posed a constitutional question – a practice fully endorsed by the above-mentioned authoritative reports (House of Lords Constitution Committee 2010; Independent Commission on Referendums – UCL Constitution Unit 2018). As a consequence, referendums in the UK tend be relatively rare but extremely salient events. This is perhaps a (perceived) paradox of the UK political system. On the one hand, the principles of parliamentary sovereignty and "government knows best" would suggest a certain closure of the system to popular input. Yet, on the other hand, the holding of referendums on potential reforms that the government opposes signals a strong degree of systemic openness to popular input. Indeed, some scholars have hypothesised a shift based on democratic constitutionalist thinking (White 2022). In addition, some referendums – e.g., the one on Scottish independence – have offered citizens the opportunity to have a say on matters that, in most other European democracies, are (constitutionally) set beyond the realm of decidability. The instrument of referendums has, therefore, significantly affected the way in which British democracy works, perhaps even to the point of upsetting traditional equilibria. The usage of referendums is progressively consolidating but the precise legal status, position, and impact of this device in the UK constitution remain questioned.

1.7 Conclusions

In this first chapter we have presented the object of our study, the UK political system, the main challenge that it went through in recent years – i.e., Brexit – and the conceptual tools that allow us to track longitudinal change, i.e., Lijphart's taxonomy for types of democracies. In particular, we have identified Lijphart's "Westminster model" as a useful point of reference for ascertaining the extent to which the UK political system has moved towards it or away from it as a result of Brexit. We have selected three dimensions of analysis out of Lijphart's model: the elections–parties; the executive–legislative relations; and the centre–periphery relations. In the abstract model, these dimensions are characterised respectively by single-member plurality (SMP) and the two–party system; single-party majority and government and executive dominance over the legislature; and a unitary and centralised state. We have explained that the UK political system has never fully coincided with the "Westminster model", in spite of the fact that the latter takes its name from the central political institution of the former. In addition, we have mentioned how, starting from the early 1970s, changes in electoral behaviour (i.e., decline in two-party vote) and, perhaps more importantly, in the constitution (Europeanisation, devolution, and the Supreme Court) have gradually moved the UK further away from the "Westminster model". Moreover, drawing on the British politics' scholarship, we have argued that a comprehensive understanding of the UK political system requires due consideration of a series of established political behaviour and attitudes that go under the label of the British Political Tradition (BTP). Finally, we have recalled that also the BTP has undergone some important changes in the last decades; not least the inclusion of an instrument of direct democracy, the referendum, in a political system centred on the principle of parliamentary sovereignty and traditionally characterised by the culture of "government knows best".

Indeed, it was a referendum that provided the Brexit shock. Drawing on Renwick's typology of electoral reforms and applying that typology to constitutional reforms more in general, we have presented the Brexit process as a case of constitutional reform, characterised by a mix of *elite mass interaction*, as far as the political decision (leaving the EU) and the relative domestic arrangements are concerned, and *elite external interaction*, concerning the withdrawal and post-withdrawal UK-EU agreements. The rest of the book provides an in-depth empirical analysis of the strains that emerged during the Brexit process and the political-constitutional outcomes. Before doing that, however, the next chapter presents our working hypotheses and explains the research design and methodology.

Notes

1 This pattern was also reflected in the way British politics was taught in the 1960s. To give an example, in 1966, in an anthology dedicated to British politics for American students (with "People, Parties and Parliament" as a subtitle), the editor, Anthony King, explained that "almost all of the selections deal with Britain's two major parties" (viii).

2 While Britain was admired, especially in the United States, for the dynamics of party system responsibility in the two decades after WWII (Ranney 1962), several dysfunctionalities have emerged, in particular, during the 1970s including within its party system (Epstein 1980). As an eminent scholar put it, "in the 1970s the British model ceased to be the object of envy and emulation and came to be seen as the European basket case, the home of an adversarial kind of politics that prevented effective policy-making and brought the country to its knees" (Wright 2020, 4).

3 This work has more than 10,000 Google Scholar citations as of September 2022.

4 For a comparison with French political traditions see Hazareesingh (1994). In one of the most important studies on the formation of British national identity, Colley (1992) highlights how the latter came to be based on the twin elements of insularity and Protestantism as opposed to France, continental and Catholic. Speaking of a political tradition obviously does not mean ignoring the existence of different currents of thought which, during the twentieth century also confronted each other in a bitter way (Hall 2011). However, only the most radical currents (which have always been largely minoritarian: Marquand 2008) have questioned the assumptions of the BPT as a political tradition and as the "cultural glue" of the UK political system.

5 It should be noted that a similar reference to cartelisation by the two parties that have governed the country alternately since 1945 was absent in what is now considered the most important theoretical model of analysis of political parties, that of the cartel party (Katz & Mair 1995), which instead referred to a greater propensity for cartelisation in consociational democracies.

6 In the important volume of Flinders (2010), dedicated to constitutional change after the New Labour years (1997–2010, already seen in Chapter 1), the author identified five principles or values that form the background to "meta-constitutional orientations": 1) the belief in the value of an unwritten or "small c" constitution; 2) the emphasis on pragmatic adaptation and flexibility; 3) the "good guys" theory of

government (literally "good chaps", meaning an elitist conception of power, with "familiar faces" from the same social background); 4) a political constitution; 5) majoritarianism (2010, 21); all elements very close to those mentioned here. King (2015) instead lists the following five points regarding the importance of historical legacy in the British government: 1) strong centralisation; 2) the concentration of power (power-hoarding); 3) the weight of the establishment; 4) the adversarial nature of politics; 5) the centrality of accountability as a mechanism for verifying power.

7 For the sake of clarity, we use the term "model" to refer to an abstract concept. The expression "Westminster model" is used as synonymous with "majoritarian model", and it has to be considered as a polar type, opposed to the "consensus model", along an ideal continuum. We refer to UK empirical case with the general expressions "UK political system" or "British political system". Finally, we use the expression "Westminster system" when we refer to the UK case in a specific period of time (1945–70), in which the empirical case was particularly close to (albeit not fully coinciding with) the abstract model.

8 The conceptualisation of Brexit as a case of constitutional change has also been adopted by many scholars who take the perspective of the EU, or both perspectives – UK and EU – at the same time (e.g., Cooper 2017; Patberg 2019; Glencross 2021).

9 Although an important faction of the Conservative Party (including future PM Johnson) was of course in favour and actively campaigned for Brexit.

10 In particular, the Northern Ireland Act 1998 prescribes the requirement of a referendum for a change of constitutional status of the region; the Scotland Act 2016 and the Wales Act 2017 require a referendum (in Scotland or in Wales) for the abolition of the devolved administrations; finally, the (now defunct) European Union Act 2011 had introduced the requirement of a referendum for any further significant transfer of powers from the UK to the EU (Gordon 2020, 231).

2

UNDERSTANDING THE BREXIT EFFECT

2.1 Introduction

This book's main goal is to understand the impact of Brexit on the UK political system. In a nutshell, we argue that the completion of the Brexit process, i.e., the actual termination of membership of the EU, is likely to lead to a resurgence of the Westminster model, albeit with several caveats, uncertainties, and adaptations. To be sure, we do not naïvely expect the post-Brexit UK to go back to a classic version of the Westminster model of the type it had experienced in the three decades after WWII. Yet, there are solid theoretical arguments leading us to expect a reduction in party system fragmentation and a centralisation of executive power, concerning both Parliament and the devolved administrations. Although the executive finds itself currently operating in a very different institutional context – e.g., because of the existence of a Supreme Court and the powers of the devolved administrations – we argue that the process of Brexit provides a window of opportunity for the executive to "get back (some) control". Needless to say, this is not an uncontested or inevitable outcome, as the strains of Brexit often point in different and contradictory directions. Yet, some distinguishing features of the majoritarian model are likely to emerge stronger, across our analytical dimensions, after and because of the Brexit process.

This chapter is structured as follows. Section 2.2 discusses the independent variable – Brexit – and the way it is understood and conceptualised in the book. Section 2.3 moves the focus to the dependent variable – the UK political system – focusing specifically on its Europeanisation. In Section 2.4, we theorise on the impact of Brexit on the UK political system, submitting hypotheses for each of the three dimensions (adapted from Lijphart) introduced in Chapter 1. Finally, Section 2.5 describes the research design and the data collected to assess our claims.

DOI: 10.4324/9781003127680-3

2.2 The Brexit process: periodisation and analytical issues

In order to assess the impact of Brexit on the UK political system, it is crucial to clarify what is meant by "Brexit" here (cf. Chapter 1, Section 1.4). Indeed, "When is Brexit?" is a key question addressed in one of the first comprehensive studies of Brexit (Oliver 2018). We acknowledge that there is – or, rather, there are – several "Brexit Day(s)", such as 31 January 2020, the formal termination of the UK's membership of the EU; or 31 December 2020, when the transition period ended and, as a consequence, the EU rulebook effectively stopped applying. There are also several announced – and then postponed – Brexit Days, the first one being 29 March 2019, exactly two years after the triggering of the procedure spelt out in Art. 50 of the Treaty of Lisbon. Brexit is often used to indicate the day of the UK referendum on EU membership (23 June 2016), although the referendum only provided, in formal terms, a non-binding political recommendation. In our understanding, Brexit is not a singular, "discrete" event. It rather indicates a process (or a set of processes) unfolding over time. For analytical purposes, we track them from the moment PM Cameron, leading a single-party Conservative government after the 2015 general election, implemented the pledge to hold a referendum on membership, to the actual Brexit Day, following which the Brexit agenda shifted to its implementation, or the "future relationship" between the UK and the EU (see the detailed timeline in Appendix B).

In principle, the idea of "Brexit as a process" could be challenged and rejected, for instance, by conceiving Brexit to be a distinct event that occurred at midnight on 31 January 2020 (Brexit Day). In this case, anything that occurred before or after Brexit Day could be seen as respectively short/medium/long term causes or effects of Brexit. However, we believe that such a thin conceptualisation of Brexit (as the instant in which the UK formally left the EU) misses two related and important points. First, it would underplay the extent to which the theme of leaving the EU has held a hyper-dominant position in the UK public sphere, inside, and outside political institutions. Writing in the middle of what we consider as the "Brexit period", Tim Oliver stated that "to a large extent Brexit has become British politics" (2019, 3). Indeed, the Brexit period can be clearly set apart from previous and quite possibly future periods due to the extent to which political debate and political energies in the UK were absorbed by the Brexit issue. Secondly, "Brexit as an event" does not encompass the sense of purpose and/or direction that has emerged from the Brexit referendum, although it has been openly challenged by some or endorsed with different sets of preferences and different levels of commitments by others. It is precisely the presence of an expressed purpose that reveals and demonstrates the high level of interconnectedness between the referendum and most of the salient political events in the UK in the following years. In turn, this evident interconnection between the analysed events is at the core of the concept of "process".

Treating Brexit in this way means that we should be particularly careful when trying to "disentangle" the politico-institutional changes brought about by the

Brexit process. Quite obviously, not all changes, reforms, or tensions observed during the Brexit years are causally linked or in some way connected to the complex process of withdrawal from the EU. The relatively long duration of the process – four and a half years from Cameron's electoral pledge, three and a half years from the referendum, and almost three from the notification of withdrawal – further complicates the picture as confounding effects, both endogenous and exogenous in nature, continuously enter the story (cf. Figure 2.1). As has been noted elsewhere, studying the impact of a similarly long process – that is, the EU enlargement towards Central and Eastern Europe (Best & Settembri 2008) – causal connections should be established with great care. Indeed, linking all institutional changes following enlargement to the expansion of the EU would lead to a *post hoc ergo propter hoc* fallacy. Some institutional changes were long due and simply "happen" to follow enlargement, while others are prompted by different causes.

To be sure, interconnectedness does not mean determination. We are not arguing that the Brexit process could only follow one (predetermined) path and get to one (predetermined) outcome. In fact, though presenting empirical evidence on how the process has actually unfolded, we do consider alternative courses and alternative (partial or final) outcomes. We do that both *ex ante*, when we present our theoretical/analytical framework and our working hypotheses (see below), and *ex post*, when we discuss the findings and their broader implications (see Chapter 7). So, by the expression "Brexit process" we mean a series of clearly interconnected events that were triggered by placing the issue of the referendum on membership on the legislative agenda. In this period, the issue of EU membership became the top priority and dictated the direction of change. Since February 2020, instead, not only was Brexit formally concluded but, since March, the UK (as most other countries in Europe and in the world) had to tackle the Covid-19 pandemic emergency. Therefore, the year 2020 cannot be considered as a Brexit year only but, rather, as a Brexit and Covid year (Harvey 2021; Morphet 2021; Ward & Ward 2021). For this reason, we devote a specific chapter (Chapter 6) to it, while the core of the empirical analysis is presented in Chapters 3–5.

Brexit had an impact on a political system which was already under strain in several respects before the prospect of leaving the EU entered the policy-making

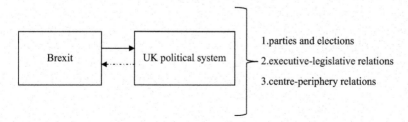

FIGURE 2.1 Brexit and the UK political system

agenda. The "classic" Westminster system had already been partly transformed (Hazell 2008). Indeed, the years of a coalition government and, earlier, the devolution reforms, had shaken its foundations (Flinders 2010; Matthews & Flinders 2017; Matthews 2017). Leading experts of British politics discuss growing anti-party sentiments, the increasing distrust towards political and representative institutions, rising inequalities, policy failures, and separatist tendencies in the context of the "crisis" or "bad health" of British democracy (e.g., Judge 2014; Richards & Smith 2015; Rose 2021). This book does take into serious consideration the broader context in which our institutional analysis of the Brexit process is located. However, in order to track down the specific impact of Brexit, we embrace a narrower theoretical and empirical focus and discuss the broader implications of our work in a dedicated chapter (Chapter 7).

Finally, we do not treat Brexit *a priori* as a "critical event", a transformative moment, or a critical juncture leading necessarily to radical change for the UK political system. We treat it more agnostically as a "shock", bearing important implications for British institutions and politics. Indeed, as Wincott put it, "for good or ill, Brexit unsettles the practices and structures of the UK state; it makes reorganization of the state unavoidable" (2020, 1579). This is not to downplay the significance of Brexit, but rather to analyse it *sine ira et studio* and let more normative speculations follow (rather than precede or even guide) the empirical analysis.

2.3 Europeanisation and the weakening of the Westminster system

Brexit represents an attempt – so far unique – to "reverse the gear" of integration (Gravey & Jordan 2016) and de-Europeanise (or rather de-EUropeanise) a domestic political system. Since the UK entered the EEC in 1973, a process of Europeanisation occurred, through which the UK absorbed the *acquis communautaire* while, on the other hand, developing itself the EU regulatory system. Even though the UK has greatly contributed to "differentiate" integration (Gänzle *et al.* 2019), through a number of opt-outs from key policies (e.g., the Schengen agreement; monetary union; the social chapter of the Maastricht treaty), in the 47 years in which the UK was a member of the EEC/EU, the UK political system became – willingly or unwillingly – Europeanised (for the historical account, see Chapter 1, Section 1.4).

In their systematic analysis of the Europeanisation of the UK political system, Ian Bache and Andrew Jordan (2006) have used the concept of Europeanisation both to capture the capacity of the UK to influence EU decision-making ("bottom-up"), and the impact of the EU on the UK political system, that is, its institutions, actors, and policy outputs ("top-down"). It is this second aspect – relatively under-researched until the early 2000s at least (Bache & Jordan 2006, 4) – which is of particular relevance here, treating member states as the "dependent variable" and the EU as the "independent variable".

Unsurprisingly, the UK has traditionally been considered a difficult case in terms of Europeanisation. By joining the EEC at a later stage (1973), it had to absorb the existing *acquis,* which it did not have the chance to contribute to shaping from the start. Later, even its more pro-EU governments (i.e., the New Labour government in the late 1990s and early 2000s) did not fully subscribe to political integration. The perspective of a European federation has been rejected by the vast majority of public opinion and political elites, which is in stark contrast with some "older" member states, such as Germany or Italy. More generally, the UK provides a very good illustration of the "goodness of fit" hypothesis (Börzel & Risse 2000). According to it, the lower the fit of a member country in the EU political system – in terms of its functioning logic and political culture – the more extensive the required adaptation will be. As for the UK, since membership began, difficulties have been immediately clear. According to Vernon Bogdanor, the UK was indeed required "to make far greater adjustments than any of the other member states" (2019, 39).

This claim could, however, be spelt out more precisely. In this regard, Vivienne Schmidt (2006) provides a useful analytical distinction between policies, governing practices, and ideas. Looking at public policies, the UK has shown a good absorption capacity with little need to substantially change its own policies or institutional arrangements. Indeed, the UK has been actively shaping the EU agenda on the common market and has led the way in deregulation and privatisation. In this aspect, member countries such as Germany or France have faced more difficulties adapting their domestic markets to integration.

The picture is different for governing practices, which display greater problems of adaptation. The institutional "fit" of the UK in the EU is indeed complicated. Although the EU is a compound polity – that is, a system based on a "multiple diffusion of powers which guarantees that any interest can have a voice in the decision-making process, and no majority will be able to control all the institutional levels of the polity" (Fabbrini 2010) – in majoritarian political systems, governing activity concentrates "in a single authority through unitary states, statist policy-making and majoritarian politics" (Schmidt 2006, 19). The founding treaties of the EEC/EU established a hierarchical legal system in which the norms stated in the treaties are protected by a Supreme Court – the EU Court of Justice, based in Luxembourg – and created a multilevel governance system, with powers distributed both horizontally among the EEC/EU institutions and vertically between the EU and its member states. Generally, the functioning logic of the EU is based on consensus, with broad coalitions among member states (in the Council) and super-grand coalitions among parties (in the European Parliament), grounded on compromises often forged after long negotiations. Evidently, this stands in stark contrast with majoritarian systems, where the winner of general elections "takes all", there is a centralised and centralising executive and a weak system of checks and balances. Susanna K. Schmidt (2020) has recently underscored the "significant" institutional mismatch between the EU and the UK polity.

In this aspect, the UK was under stronger pressure to adapt. The "federalising" pressure brought in by EU membership, with sub-national units directly implementing EU regulations and administering EU projects and funds (Bache 2008), contributed to the devolution of powers to sub-state authorities. The "deparliamentarisation" (cf. Raunio 2009) of decision-making, with the very limited involvement of national parliaments in EU affairs (EEC/EU regulations have direct legal effects, without the need to transpose them into national law), further weakened parliament. Finally, "judicialisation" occurred because national judges were asked to ensure the compliance of domestic law with EU law, thus strengthening the role and independence of the judiciary.

As Schmidt (2006) emphasises, however, the misfit between the EU and the UK is stronger in the very idea of how democracy should work. The key source of tension with the EU is the backbone of the UK's political system: the principle of "parliamentary sovereignty" (Norton 2011, 79). According to this principle, Parliament can approve whatever legislation it wants to without any external constraint, as there is no hierarchically superior authority with the power to declare an Act of Parliament null and void. As acutely observed by Alexis de Tocqueville, the UK Parliament is "both a legislative assembly and a constituent one" (cited in Bogdanor 2019, 189). Acts of Parliament are primary law, which can be amended only by subsequent Acts of Parliament.

The principle of the sovereignty of Parliament has been severely challenged by EEC/EU membership. When the UK became a member of the EEC, the Court of Justice had already recognised the direct effect of EC legislation (*van Gend en Loos case*) and the primacy of EC over national law (*Costa vs ENEL case*). With such rulings, the principle that there is no authority over and above parliament was fundamentally challenged. EEC/EU membership was then seen as a threat not only to executive autonomy (as in France), but also to parliamentary sovereignty (Schmidt 2006).

Of course, the delegation of law-making powers to Brussels was made possible by a specific Act of Parliament (*the European Communities Act 1972*) and, as Brexit itself demonstrates, another Act of Parliament sufficed to "repatriate" them (*the European Union (Withdrawal) Act 2018*). Formally, therefore, the principle of parliamentary sovereignty was unscathed by membership in the Community/ Union. In substantive terms, however, the story is very different, since membership makes Acts of Parliament subject to EU law and jurisprudence.

According to Bogdanor (2019), EEC membership has clashed in two main ways with the UK legal-political tradition. First, a written constitution has come into being almost by accident, without a full engagement of citizens and a proper debate in the public sphere about the implications of this fundamental change. The UK constitution has been subject to a process of formalisation because of the EEC/EU Treaties, beginning with the Treaty of Rome (signed by the six founding members in 1957), and ending with the Treaty of Lisbon. Second, the courts have been empowered making a "constitutionality" check of national laws through referral to the Court of Justice of the EU. The creation of the Supreme

Court in 2009 has *de facto* introduced a tribunal of the last instance for the constitutionality of norms, although its remit is limited to human rights and conform-
ity with EU law. Therefore, the UK has found itself in a different legal regime
with a written "constitution" and a "constitutional" court, moving significantly
away from its long-standing legal and political tradition.

A different stream of the Europeanisation literature has instead focused on
political parties and party systems (cf. Ladrech 2002). Until the early 2000s,
the EU was hardly a salient issue for political parties, and party competition
on integration matters was limited (Mair 2000). In this context, British parties
are quite exceptional. A single-issue party in the EU, the Referendum Party,
was established as early as 1994 calling for a referendum on EU membership.
UKIP has been a frontrunner of Eurosceptic/populist movements, challenging mainstream parties in Europe. Its growing electoral success (particularly
in by-elections) played no small part in Cameron's decision to hold a referendum on EU membership. The internal party splits on Europe characterised the
major British parties ever since the first (unsuccessful) applications to join the
EEC in the early 1960s (Smith 2012; Baker *et al.* 2008). Through the 1970s,
Eurosceptic tendencies were mainly expressed by the left wing of the Labour
Party while, from the mid-1980s, political integration fuelled anti-EU sentiments within the Tory ranks. Furthermore, EU membership introduced a
new arena of party competition where different rules apply. From 1999, UK
members of the European Parliament (EP) were chosen according to proportional electoral rules (Scully & Farrell 2007). This allowed parties that have
been penalised by the Single-Member Plurality (SMP) system used in general
elections to obtain representation in the EP and make themselves more visible
(Goodwin & Milazzo 2015; Baldini & Chelotti 2022, 4). Nigel Farage, the
leader of UKIP, and later of the Brexit Party, excelled in using the EP to boost
his popularity (cf. Brack 2015).

Overall, it can be argued that British membership in the EEC/EU led to a
weakening of the majoritarian system (see Chapter 1) by challenging the principle of parliamentary sovereignty, introducing a sort of rigid constitution, pro-
moting federalising tendencies, and lowering the entry barriers for third parties.
Furthermore, with the extension of Qualified Majority Voting (QMV) in the
Council of Ministers, and with the strengthening of the EP in law-making,
the UK government lost its capacity to fully control EU policies (which it
could previously veto, if considered unacceptable or damaging for the country).
Incidentally, when the UK government was on the losing side in the Council
of the EU, the accountability of ministers was also negatively affected, since no
one could be held accountable for a policy agreed by a majority of EU members.

2.4 Back to Westminster? The impact of exiting the EU

Disentangling the complex knot of relationships with the EU is a difficult and
untested exercise that will need some time in order to be brought to completion.

Impact assessments on the economic consequences of Brexit have been a contentious issue during the process, to the point that the then Brexit minister, David Davis, faced a charge of "contempt of parliament" in 2017, due to his refusal to release them in full. Understanding the political and institutional consequences of the Brexit process could be an equally difficult task. As the EU is removed from decision-making, Brexit inevitably entails internal change, as both policies and governing practices need to be adapted or reinvented. While we share, in principle, the proposition that "in itself Brexit does not determine the extent or form of this restructuring" (Wincott 2020, 1582), we believe that hypotheses on the most likely directions of change can be formulated.

2.4.1 Dimension 1: elections and the party system

To start with the first dimension, our expectations are the result of the interplay between the implications of the 2016 referendum (as an event) and of the ensuing Brexit process to implement the exit from the EU. The immediate expectations for the first elections after the referendum were related to a reduction in party system fragmentation, mainly through the reabsorption of UKIP, a single-issue party that was formed to bring the country out of the EU and which had won 27 percent of the votes in the 2014 EP elections, thus increasing its electoral threat to the Conservatives (but also to Labour: Ford & Goodwin 2014). This party had also experienced great success in the 2015 general elections when its breakthrough in Westminster was only avoided by the mechanics of the SMP electoral system. At the same time, Theresa May's inability to get the Withdrawal Agreement through Parliament led the country to take part in the EP election in May 2019 (see Chapter 1), leading to the birth and the massive electoral success of a sort of UKIP 2.0, namely the Brexit Party. The resurrection of Farage's crusade to bring the UK out of the EU put the entire party system under considerable strain, to say the least. On the third anniversary of the membership referendum, Britain witnessed yet another resignation by an incumbent Conservative PM (May announced her retirement from the post just after her party was crushed in the EP elections). Therefore, what had become clear by this time was that there was no majority in Parliament to carry the country out of the EU in a context marked by extreme fluidity in the opinion polls.

Moreover, all opinion polls conducted during 2018 and 2019 showed that public opinion was still divided down the middle, with a slight move towards Remain. More significant, perhaps, was also the fact that more and more voters were priming Brexit identities over party identities, thus reinforcing the expectation – already driven by a stall in parliament – that the next general elections would be dominated by Brexit itself as the key moment to finally "break the deadlock" (Allen & Bartle 2021).

As the Brexit referendum was broadly interpreted as a key manifestation of a new "cultural" cleavage centred on globalisation (also referred to as the transnational or demarcation/integration cleavage), whereby old social alignments were replaced by new divisions broadly based on socio-demographic elements such as age and education, as well as on geography (Ford & Jennings 2020; Sobolewska & Ford 2020), the dynamics of party support were also expected to be affected by the realignment process. This is especially the case since the Conservative Party, after Cameron's and May's resignations, morphed more and more significantly towards the "Exit Party" which, in the view of many voters, meant regaining control of the borders. In this respect, an analysis of the social background of the voters of the two main parties becomes important, especially in light of an electorate which has become increasingly volatile. This volatility also involves – significantly enough – the issues on which voters base their electoral choices. Hence, our expectation with regard to the second electoral event after the referendum – namely the 2019 general election – can be linked to the increasing importance of the parties' capacity to be seen as the true interpreters of the "Leave" and "Remain" camps. Moreover, the relevance of the multi-level nature of the party system should be considered. The country's exit from the EU implies that it will no longer take part in EP elections, thus reducing opportunities for the possible success of yet another party inspired by Brexit.[1]

In general, albeit with further caveats that we specify in the next chapter, we posit that:

H1 Brexit leads to a reduction in party system fragmentation

2.4.2 Dimension 2: executive–legislative relations

Brexit can be seen as a shock altering the politico-institutional equilibrium. Building on a rational-choice, institutionalist perspective (Héritier 2007), it could be argued that Brexit upset the status quo and opened up new opportunities for power-maximising actors. The act of "giving back control" in a context of institutional uncertainty could result in the empowerment of different institutional actors, giving rise to a conflict-prone political situation. It is, therefore, likely that actors will engage in strategic bargaining to maximise their power and to obtain an institutional outcome (i.e., a type of Brexit agreement; more control over repatriated powers) that is closer to their own preferences. Asymmetries in resource ownership – such as time, information, bureaucratic resources, etc. – and the fall-back position of the actors explain the outcome of the bargaining process (Knight 1992).

There are strong elements suggesting that de-Europeanisation could lead to an empowerment of the executive over Parliament and the devolved administrations. With the disappearance of the EU "external constraint" (Dyson & Featherstone 1996), a window of opportunity has opened up for the more powerful actors to renegotiate an institutional settlement, placing them in a stronger position compared to the status quo. The first element to consider is that executives normally have the upper hand in international negotiations. They lead them directly, negotiating with the other parties in secluded settings, facing limited parliamentary scrutiny. Historically in the UK, international negotiations have been the exclusive domain of the executive, under "royal prerogative". The Brexit negotiations were conducted directly by the UK government, distinctively No. 10 and the *ad hoc* Brexit minister, and treated as if they were international negotiations. Although the Supreme Court restated the constitutional need to obtain a parliamentary mandate (through an Act of Parliament) to trigger Art. 50 TEU and start the withdrawal process, the intervention produced little change for the actual conduct of the negotiations (with parliament giving a "blank cheque" to the executive).

A second element to consider is that the Brexit process unfolded under tight deadlines. From the triggering of Art. 50, only two years were available to conclude the negotiations. In several circumstances, the government urged its own recalcitrant MPs to vote according to its wishes, because, otherwise, a "no deal" (the least favourite option for most MPs) was likely to occur. The "spectre" of no deal, bringing with it a frightening scenario of a policy vacuum with high economic costs, was used to convince MPs to accept whatever offer was put on the table. The need for a decision, pending the deadline that the government itself agreed upon with the EU, was meant to focus the MPs' minds and allow for Brexit (that is, Brexit as negotiated by the executive) to take place.

Beyond the formal deadlines of the withdrawal procedure, there was a real urgency for finalising Brexit in order to provide legal certainty for businesses and citizens. Executives can benefit from emergencies – also skilfully constructed as "emergencies". They can use crises to empower themselves and, in specific circumstances, "grab" repatriated powers from the EU. Indeed, "deadlines are useful for a certain kind of emergency politics" (White 2019). The executive seeks to put itself in a position where it can capitalise on the state of emergency, which it has itself contributed to create. As Ginsburg and Versteeg put it, it is almost common knowledge that "emergencies require massive delegation of power to the executive, which is the only branch of government with the information, decisiveness, and speed to respond to crises" (2020, 4). Given the massive effort required to exit the EU regulatory framework, only the executive could swiftly and decisively act to "get Brexit done". In such circumstances, checks and balances are weakened or need to disappear altogether, in order to leave space for the executive's action.

Indeed, in Carl Schmitt's classic definition (2005), "sovereign is he [sic] who decides on the state of exception" and the seemingly paradoxical concept of "constitutional dictator" implied a temporary concentration of all powers in their hands to preserve constitutional order. Delegation of powers to the executive becomes a functional necessity, as legislatures are ill-suited to deal with emergencies, given their more limited information about events, party political divisions, and weaker administrative resources (Posner & Vermeule 2011). Legally speaking, executives could rely on constitutional provisions on the state of emergency, or they could be provided by the legislature with broad statutory authorisation for action. In this context, courts play an enhanced role to guarantee that the state of emergency does not breach other constitutional provisions and is not overstretched, but their action can also face specific constraints, or be curtailed by the executive (e.g., through the threat of restricting their legal remit or powers). New institutional rules created to tackle the emergency may survive it, thus resulting in permanent empowerment of the executive over other governing institutions. Overall, it can thus be expected that:

H2: Brexit leads to an empowerment of the executive over the legislature

2.4.3 Dimension 3: centre–periphery relations

As for the territorial dimension (i.e., the vertical distribution of powers), even before the Brexit referendum occurred, it was widely expected that the UK withdrawal from the EU would have important repercussions and unleash the dynamics of "politico-territorial restructuring" (Minto *et al.* 2016), also because of different preferences on EU membership across the UK nations (Henderson *et al.* 2016). After all, territorial dynamics were already changing before the Brexit referendum, as a string of events, such as the referendum on Scottish independence and the ongoing expansion of the powers of the Welsh assembly and of the Scottish parliament all indicate.

A seemingly straightforward outcome would be the *de facto* expansion of devolved competences, since Europeanised policy areas that formally fell under the remit of the devolved administrations would be repatriated and assigned to them. However, the effective expansion of regional competences cannot be taken for granted for two main reasons. First, withdrawal from the EU is, first and foremost, a matter of international politics. As argued above, it is managed by the central government and the PM, with a keen interest for ensuring minimal interference from other levels of government. Having the first-mover advantage, by setting the content of the negotiations (together with the EU), it is unlikely that the government will champion the interests of the devolved administrations. Second, the Brexit process has unfolded in a period of electoral dominance of the Conservative Party and, hence, Conservative governments. Notwithstanding the fact that the Tory party has adapted to devolution and has, itself, contributed to it (Convery 2014), the Conservatives remain the most vigorous defender of the unitary character of the British state, which is understood as an extension of the predominant English component (Gamble 2016). If any government exploits the window of opportunity of Brexit to enhance its own powers, this would be even more the case for a Conservative government.

Should this occur, the most likely political implication is that popular demands for secession will, as a reaction, become more vocal. Indeed, this is what theories of comparative territorial politics, such as the theory of "lost autonomy" (Sirkoy & Cuffe 2015), lead one to expect. In the medium term, therefore, post-Brexit centralisation of power may spectacularly backfire. On the contrary, in the long run, the theoretical scholarship sees membership of the EU as a facilitator of independence (Laible 2008; Cetrà & Lineira 2018). Therefore, the removal of the UK from the EU should make (at least Scottish or Welsh) secession more traumatic and, therefore, less appealing. Yet, as far as institutional change within the current UK polity is concerned, in the short/medium term, it can be expected that:

H3: Brexit leads to an empowerment of central government over the devolved administrations

2.4.4 Institutional change and stickiness

A note of caution regarding the expectations sketched above comes from a historical institutionalist perspective on the process of Brexit. Such an interpretation attaches particular importance to the "stickiness" of institutions and underscores the difficulties in leaving an ongoing trajectory of institutional development, or "path dependence" (cf. Pierson & Skocpol 2002; Thelen 1999). The "transformed" Westminster system (Hazell 2008) may not be so amenable to the executive, whose empowerment strategies may fail or clash against already consolidated institutional rules, thus diminishing its clout (i.e., coalition or minority government) or allowing other domestic actors to counterbalance its power (i.e., the Supreme Court, the devolved administrations). In addition, Brexit is likely not to be a "clean" process, as it mixes up with existing endogenous developments, interacting with the broader context and other exogenous crises, thus creating muddled and hybrid phases (Wincott 2017; cf. Baldini & Chelotti 2022, 5).

As for executive–legislative relations, Brexit occurs after a couple of decades of piecemeal but gradual empowerment of the legislature. The reform of select committees, the absence of a Conservative majority in the House of Lords, and the growing assertiveness of backbenchers are all factors which have concurred to partly rebalance the relationship between government and Parliament (Russell & Cowley 2016). As Brexit has been designed, in the words of the former Brexit minister, David Davis, to allow "Parliament to take back control of UK laws and policies" (2017), it could mark a significant enhancement of its policy influence.

Moving to the territorial dimension, since the creation of the devolved administrations in 1997–9, several of the competences attributed on paper to the nations were exercised either exclusively by the EU or in cooperation between the EU and the UK. As a consequence, the repatriation of policy competences from Brussels could bring with it, in the medium or long term at least, a significant expansion of the policy-making power of the nations and, therefore, a further shift of the UK political system towards more decentralisation, if not federalism.

Assuming that the repatriated powers will effectively be taken up by the nations (which is, in any case, far from guaranteed), different implications for centre–periphery relations exist. Building on the research on territorial politics (Levi & Hechter 1985; Rudolph & Thompson 1989), the expansion of local self-government, particularly if accompanied by reforms toward further devolution, could be expected to satisfy the demands of some autonomist voters, weakening electoral support for autonomist parties. In the long run, the political system would then be characterised by more devolution and the weakening of centrifugal tendencies. Alternatively, other scholars argue that the reinforcement of regional autonomy is most likely to strengthen secessionist tendencies (Brancati 2008; Massetti & Schakel 2016; 2017), because the repatriation of policy competences to the nations would neither eliminate nor reduce the existing tensions between the central government and peripheral nationalism but, rather significantly reinforce it.

2.5 Research design and data

We embrace a "process perspective on institutional change", shared by different institutionalist perspectives (cf. Héritier 2007; Pierson & Skocpol 2002), which leads us to focus on the factors driving institutional change – and, of course, Brexit in particular – with the underlying causal processes and outcomes. Ultimately, drawing on Lijphart's polar types – i.e., the Westminster model, on the one hand, the consensus model on the other (see Chapter 1) – our aim is to capture the direction of travel of the UK political system. In the post-Brexit period, has it moved closer (back) to the Westminster model, or has it taken further steps away from it?

In order to understand how the UK political system has changed during, and because of, Brexit, we have undertaken an in-depth empirical analysis based on process tracing. We aim to examine "intermediate steps in a process to make inferences about hypotheses on how that process took place and whether and how it generated the outcome of interest" (Bennett & Checkel 2015, 6). More specifically, we seek to uncover how a sequence of events, triggered by the Brexit process, led to specific outcomes in the three dimensions previously discussed (see, again, Chapter 1). Through a careful triangulation of different sources, we have sought to disentangle what has occurred *because* of Brexit from what has happened *during* the Brexit process.

We have relied extensively on primary sources (e.g., official documents of institutional actors at different levels of government; official declarations and interviews by key players), and the thriving literature on the UK and Brexit (both the academic literature and that produced by think tanks). At the same time, we also conducted 72 interviews with "privileged observers" of the Brexit process (see Appendix A for the complete list). We triangulated different sources to minimise any "selection bias" and carefully considered any alternative explanations.

Our interviewees are 28 renowned academic experts of UK politics and its constitution (mainly political scientists and lawyers); 40 party politicians drawn from across the political spectrum, (mainly within the Conservative ranks, the Labour Party, and the SNP, but also from all other "minor" parties), as well as elected representatives at all levels of government, the Westminster Parliament, the Scottish, Welsh, and Northern Ireland assemblies. We also interviewed four parliamentary clerks who played important roles when the Brexit legislation reached Parliament.

Interviews were conducted in three rounds. The first round took place from 9 to 20 December 2018, in London; the second round was held from 10 to 22 February 2019, partly in London and partly in Edinburgh; the third and final round was conducted from 18 September to 6 October 2019, with interviews in London, Cardiff, Edinburgh, and Belfast.[2] As our fieldwork was completed before the outbreak of the Covid-19 pandemic, the vast majority were face-to-face interviews. Only three of them were organised online, via Skype. The three rounds of interviews focused on somewhat different targets (i.e., for logistic reasons, the assemblies in Wales and Northern Ireland were targeted only in the third round). Yet, in some cases, we decided to go back and interview again one of our interviewees (or a close colleague) because the unfolding of the Brexit process required a reconsideration of some earlier findings or an update of the original questionnaire in light of new political developments.

We conducted semi-structured interviews. Some questions were prepared *ex ante* and were asked to all interviewees, while others were adapted to the specific interviewee or updated to take into consideration changes in the Brexit process (e.g., a major governmental defeat on a division in the Commons; new elections or cabinet reshuffling). More generally, we pursued a strategy to not "constrain" the person we spoke with by superimposing our own interpretations or hypotheses. As we interviewed *elites*, we considered it more appropriate to provide a loose grid only and allow the experts to express themselves as freely as possible (cf. Dexter 2006). Interviews were recorded – after obtaining the explicit consent of the interviewee – and anonymised. Interviews were held in the location chosen by the interviewees – often their office, sometimes a public space – and they often lasted around one hour.

Notes

1 Although this possibility cannot be totally ruled out, given the highly symbolic salience of the anti-EU battle (Jennings *et al.* 2021).
2 As we further specify in Chapter 6, the timing of the interviews and the different nature of the three dimensions mean that interviews are used less in the first than in the other two dimensions.

3

WESTMINSTER PRESERVED

Elections, party system, and the absorption of the Brexit shock

3.1 Introduction

From 1945 to 1970 two political parties – Conservative and Labour – dominated British politics with no major differences between the electoral, parliamentary, and governmental arenas. Most citizens identified with one of them, often voting for the same party through many elections. The representatives of these two parties occupied more than 90 percent of the seats in the House of Commons. Finally, after each general election, the leader of the party that won the most seats quickly moved to Downing Street to form a single-party government. During this period, the British party system was considered a textbook case for a two-party system. Building on the criteria first proposed by Duverger (1951), Giovanni Sartori's landmark study (1976) claimed that, beyond the rather obvious criterion of an electoral scene dominated by two main competitors, a two-party system can be identified on the basis of three further conditions: a centripetal pattern of competition, a willingness of one or the other of the two main parties to govern alone, and, last but not least, a frequent alternation between the two of them (Webb & Bale 2021).

During the period in which Sartori was writing, the British party system started to experience some changes. However, since 1945 the same two parties have alternated in single-party governments, with the only significant exception of the 2010–15 coalition between the Conservatives and the Liberal Democrats. In recent years, Sartori's work has been supplemented by several important studies, which have introduced other important indicators to assess change and stability in party systems. As a matter of fact, the structure and functioning of any party system are both the result of an interplay between institutional, political, and socio/psychological factors. Institutionally, electoral systems are particularly important, especially if they provide – for newcomers and challenger parties

DOI: 10.4324/9781003127680-4

– high barriers for entering the parliamentary (and ultimately the executive) arena. In this respect, the UK is both the mother country of a very selective system, such as the plurality electoral system (applied in single-member constituencies, henceforth SMP), and the only European country to still apply such a system to general elections (but not to most other levels of government, see below).

Politically, party strategies and leadership agency are also very important. While selective electoral rules can constrain party strategies, the decision regarding whether to field candidates is ultimately a political decision. Sociological and psychological factors must also be considered. At least until 1970, British general elections were marked by high stability, as testified respectively by the seminal works of Lipset and Rokkan on party systems, cleavages, and voter alignments (Lipset & Rokkan 1967; see also Webb & Fisher 1999), and of Butler and Stokes on the partisan identification model of electoral choice that is based on a combination of social and psychological factors (Butler & Stokes 1974). In one of the first systematic comparative studies of European party systems, Rose and Urwin argued that Britain then had the "most 'static' party system in Western Europe" (1970, 306). The prevailing view was that political parties competed on a single dimension, namely, the class cleavage.

In the early 1980s, these (and other) British peculiarities were captured by Lijphart's definition of the "Westminster" (or "majoritarian") model of democracy, built on a strong single-party executive as one of his core elements (Lijphart 1984). According to Lijphart, "[it is] the disciplined two-party system rather than the parliamentary system that gives rise to executive dominance" (2012, 12). The fabrication of single-party governments by the SMP system was, during the period from 1945 to 1970, a textbook case of the majoritarian effects of the electoral system, by which the latter turned a relative majority of votes into an absolute majority of seats.[1]

In analysing the electoral and party system dimension, it is crucial to also focus on electoral behaviour. In this respect, the 2016 EU membership referendum is commonly considered among the most – if not *the* most – significant *event* of the Brexit process. The latter was then marked by several institutional skirmishes. In this chapter, we aim to analyse how Brexit affected the party/electoral dimension in the years immediately following the referendum. This task is made possible by the fact that in order to facilitate (or unlock) the parliamentary process of exit from the EU, two snap elections were held, in 2017 and 2019.

Moreover, given that the two-year term for exit negotiations – established by Art. 50 of the Lisbon Treaty, approved in March 2017 – could not be respected, in May 2019 the UK also had to take part in the European Parliament (EP) elections. These elections resulted in the victory of no less than a "Brexit party" (Vasilopoulou 2020; Martill 2020), formed just five months before the vote by the former leader of the UK Independence Party (UKIP), Nigel Farage, a key figure behind the Leave victory in 2016. These events evoke several questions. Does the country still have a two-party system, or does it rather have a predominant party system (Quinn 2013)? How can we assess the importance of Brexit *as a process*, which, in particular, unfolded after the 2016 referendum and continued, at least until the 2019 general election? How can we make sense of Brexit's effects on the party system, considering the electoral bases on which the latter had been built?

While a rich stream of the literature has examined Brexit as an example of a populist vote that was brought about by the rise of a cultural cleavage based on the contraposition between liberal and authoritarian values (e.g., Inglehart & Norris 2017), this chapter builds on the literature on electoral systems, party systems, and voting behaviour in order to pursue three main aims. In assessing changes and continuities we consider insights coming from the following three fields of research. First, there are cross-fertilising analyses which too often tend to not speak to each other, thus, jeopardising the accumulation of knowledge and a full understanding of the topic. Second, and related to the first, this leads to a framework for the analysis of the first Brexit effects on the British party system, which is then applied to recent electoral events. Third, and finally, building on the recent work of De Vries and Hobolt (2020) on the rise of challenger parties, we briefly speculate on some future scenarios of the current configuration (from the end of 2021) of the party system.

The remainder of the chapter is organised in six sections. The next section provides an overview of the main changes in party systems and voter alignments before Brexit. The following section analyses the importance of the electoral system as a key institutional bulwark of the Westminster model. Then the analytical framework explains the choice of the indicators and the way in which the party system and electoral behaviour can fruitfully be combined. The empirical section analyses and comments on the data before moving on to some considerations regarding the weak bases of the party system and possible future scenarios. The final section discusses and concludes the chapter.

3.2 Before Brexit: the British party system and voter alignment – from stability to turmoil

Between 1945 and 1970, the Conservatives and Labour were the only two parties to field candidates in practically all constituencies, with the notable exception of Northern Ireland[2] (which, however, only sent 18 MPs to Westminster; see Chapter 5). In the 1950s – a period of crisis for the Liberal Party – between 70 and 80 percent of the English constituencies presented candidates from only two main parties (Gaines 2009, 122). The Liberals were able to field more candidates in the 1960s, when the Scottish National Party (SNP) also intensified its presence in Scotland, thus gaining more votes (as did Plaid Cymru – PC – in Wales, from 1970). Hence, the "menu" of political choices became more differentiated from the 1960s.[3] Experts agree that the social basis of party support started to erode in the early 1970s. Since then, electoral instability has grown as new dimensions of electoral competition have emerged at the different stages of the country's political development. Webb and Bale list sectoral and geographical cleavages as well as sex, age, education, and – most recently – the environment and European integration (2021, 68ff.). We return to some of these in due course.

From the mid-1970s, the country experienced more fragmentation with the rise of third parties and of several challenges related to the systemic functionality of political parties (Webb 2002). The first post-war minority government was formed in 1974 (Sandbrook 2012). This turbulent "double electoral year" – with two snap elections in February and October, also saw the rise of Scottish nationalism. By the end of the millennium, the two-party system still showed important signs of resilience (Webb 2000) even amidst growing levels of electoral instability and the opening-up of the electoral market. During this period, the most significant challenge was presented by the Maastricht Treaty in 1992. Elsewhere in the EU, the latter is considered as the turning point in public opinion towards Europe, from "permissive consensus" to "constraining dissensus" (Hooghe & Marks 2009). On the contrary, the British electorate had long been the most sceptical towards Europe among the founding member states and those that joined during the first enlargement in 1973 (Hobolt & Tilley 2021). And yet, Maastricht was also crucial for the UK, as a double challenge for the established parties, bringing about stark internal divisions regarding European integration, particularly for the Conservatives (Bale 2016; in a less dramatic way this was the case for Labour during the 1975 European Economic Community (EEC) membership referendum: Saunders 2016), and especially the frontal challenge of UKIP.

In general, new parties rise thanks to the combination of two elements: the loosening of the ties between voters and traditional parties, and the emergence of new issues of competition. From the early 1970s, the two main parties lost votes in two main directions: to the centre, where the Liberals, (Liberal Democrats from 1988, after merging with the Social Democratic Party [SDP], which itself was a centre-left splinter group of the Labour Party formed in 1981), stood at around 20 percent, and to other minor parties, such as the SNP and PC in the Celtic regions, as well as the Greens (from 1990) throughout the country. And, as we shall see in further detail below, to UKIP from 1993.

These developments only partly affected the patterns of political competition. As anticipated, during the period from 1945 to 1970, the two major parties – Conservative and Labour – frequently alternated in power (governing respectively for 13 and 12 years each). Voters had strong partisan attachments (often transmitted through family socialisation: Butler & Stokes 1974) and tended to remain faithful to the same party for several years, sometimes even decades (Denver & Garnett 2014). Electoral volatility, as measured by the classic Pedersen index,[4] was comparatively very low (Chiaramonte & Emanuele 2017).

At the turn of the millennium, an important study underlined that the "era of classic two-party majoritarianism" was, indeed, limited to the 1945–70 period (Webb 2000, 4ff). During that period – again borrowing from Sartori's terminology – both the two-party format (i.e., the number of relevant parties) and the mechanics (i.e., the mechanical properties of the party system) were strictly linked to both institutional and social peculiarities, namely, the electoral system on the one hand, and on the other, the prevalence of a left–right cleavage as the main dimension of electoral alignment. This pattern was captured by the widely quoted work of Pulzer, who stated, "Class [is] the basis of British Politics. All else is embellishment and detail" (1967, 98). However famous and well-cited, this statement should be qualified, as such, "around one in three British manual workers voted Liberal or Conservative in the 1950s and 1960s" (Stephens 1979, 404, cited by Hooghe & Marks 2018). This highlights the importance of not falling into the trap of "golden age-ism" (see Awan-Scully 2018).

In this respect, the significance of UKIP's challenge can again be grasped by referring to another crucial element of Sartori's work, namely, the distinction between parties with a *coalition* or a *blackmail potential*. In the case of the former, they can influence electoral competition by being deemed legitimate as potential coalition partners. This occurred with the Liberals (Liberal Democrats from 1988), which, after many years in opposition, and after making some agreements with Labour,[5] finally went to govern with the Conservatives in 2010. In the case of the latter, they can challenge and threaten another party or parties with electoral losses if they do not follow the challenger's ideological direction (Evans 2002). UKIP's rise in 2014–15 was a decisive case of blackmail potential since the party's electoral threat was a key factor for David Cameron's electoral promise to hold an EU membership referendum, first in his Bloomberg Speech in 2013, then in the 2015 electoral manifesto (Bale 2018).

However, it is in the last 15 years that the country has gone through unprecedented turmoil. The experts of the "British Election Study" (BES) have referred to several events – such as the rise of immigration (and the parallel success of the UKIP after 2004), the 2007–8 financial crisis, the birth of the first post-war coalition government in 2010 and the Scottish Referendum on Scottish independence in 2014 – as veritable "electoral shocks" in a context marked by high electoral volatility (Fieldhouse *et al.* 2020). Brexit, triggered by the 2016 referendum on EU membership, is the fifth – and perhaps most dramatic – electoral shock to date.

Different as they are, these shocks all stem from a decrease in voter loyalty and have resulted in higher volatility. While this is true for most voters, "party switchers" are particularly important in this dynamic: "Newly recruited party supporters are even less loyal than the average voters in our generally volatile electorate" (Fieldhouse *et al.* 2020, 186). Over the past decade, the UK has gone from one electoral surprise to another.

The literature confirms that Brexit was a "perfect storm" that was a long time in the making (Cutts *et al.* 2020; Ford *et al.* 2021; Green *et al.* 2021). In analysing the dimension of the electoral/party system, it is crucial to combine a focus on supply and demand in that citizens articulate their interests – and ultimately develop their voting loyalties – by following actions and policy proposals made by political parties. It is unfortunate that the literature on voters and on parties often tends to be isolated from each other.[6] More than 30 years ago, when analysing the state of Political Science as a discipline, Gabriel Almond talked about a "discipline divided", and more specifically, about political scientists working at "separate tables" (Almond 1990). Similarly, in a recent entry dedicated to "Party Systems and Voting Alignments", Asa von Schoultz highlights that

> Despite the fact that the supply and demand side of politics work in tandem, the evolution of voting behaviour and party system research have tended to be relatively separate fields of research. De- and realignment are commonly discussed and studied from the perspective of voters using a generic categorization of parties or party families, and the evolution of parties and party system that represents the organizational component of the cleavage concept is, in turn, commonly studied in isolation from that of voters and their behaviour.
>
> *(2017, 42)*

Looking at Brexit as both an *event* and a *process* allows a reconciliation of these otherwise separate lines of research. However, before doing this, we have to focus on the rules of the game. In his work, Lijphart focused on institutional variables. While the first 1984 edition of his comparative work on democracies also contained a variable on societal cleavages, this variable was then dropped in the successive editions. However, as anticipated in Chapter 2, in order to detect the effects of Brexit on the electoral and party system dimension, societal elements become very important. To understand why this is the case, we first have to focus on the importance of electoral legislation.

3.3 The institutional pillar of the two-party system: SMP and electoral legislation at other territorial levels of government

A majoritarian electoral system was instituted in the UK several centuries ago. Despite increasing pressure to abandon it in favour of more proportional legislation – which meant that more than 15 years ago SMP was considered "under siege" (Mitchell 2005) – it still resists today. SMP notoriously "protects" the two main parties from the challenges of the emerging parties, also favouring – as claimed by supporters (e.g., Norton 1997) – government stability and the identification of political responsibilities.[7] However, while some decades ago SMP was applied to elect assemblies – and send representatives to Brussels – at various territorial levels (from local elections, to the European Parliament), over the last 25 years both new assemblies and new electoral rules for the already existing ones were introduced (see Table 3.1).

Adopted in England in the thirteenth century (Norris 1995), and then extended to several countries of the Commonwealth, SMP became prevalent over other majoritarian systems in Great Britain only at the end of the nineteenth

TABLE 3.1 Electoral systems and reforms at different territorial levels

Territorial level	Operating system up to 1997	Pressures for change	Reform	Expected results	Consequences for party system
General elections	Plurality	Minor parties demand more proportionality (especially Lib-Dems since the early 1990s; then also Greens and others)	Failed referendum on alternative vote in 2011		Electoral reform effectively out of the agenda, given main parties' hostility (especially the Conservatives)[a]
European elections	Plurality	Adaptation to European standards (proportional systems)	1999: adoption of PR	More fragmentation	UKIP's progressive rise from fourth place (1999) to most-voted party (2014)
Nations (Scotland, Wales, Northern Ireland)[b]	STV in Northern Ireland	NI assembly re-convened; assemblies created in Scotland and Wales	1999 Assemblies elected in Wales (2/3 plurality, 1/3 proportional) Scotland (57 percent plurality, 43 percent PR);	New consociational rules for NI Labour aims to contain nationalist challenge	Since 2011 SNP becomes Scotland's predominant party

a After the 2015 general election, some of the leaders of the minor parties most penalised by the operations of SMP delivered to David Cameron in Downing Street a petition for a more proportional electoral system signed by almost half a million voters (https://www.theguardian.com/politics/2015/may/18/green-party-ukip-electoral-reform-first-past-post-elections).

b In 2004, voters in the north-east of England strongly rejected the creation of an elected assembly for the region in a dedicated referendum (77.9 percent against). The main reason that emerged for such a vote was the hostility to a further layer of government. Interestingly enough, one of the most prominent campaigners was Dominic Cummings, then Campaign Director of "Vote Leave" since 2015, before becoming Boris Johnson's Chief Advisor in 2019.

century. About a century ago, SMP also favoured a major realignment in the party system. Actually, while several other factors contributed to the replacement of the Liberals by Labour as the second largest party (including the prevalence of class cleavage over the religious factor, suffrage extension in 1918, the divisions of the Liberals, Irish autonomy: see Webb & Fisher 1999, 11), SMP also played a role – together with the crisis of the Liberals (Tudor Jones 2019) – in the emergence of a new pattern of Conservative–Labour two-party competition, institutionalising it especially after WWII.

SMP became the standard procedure in 1948 (Mitchell 2005, 158). Around this time, Maurice Duverger (1951), a true pioneer in the study of political parties and electoral systems, looked at Britain as a case where SMP favoured the emergence of a two-party system in a relationship so strong that it came close to a true "sociological law" (Duverger's so-called First Law; the second one being on the two-ballot system and proportional representation (PR) favouring multipartyism). Specifically, according to Duverger, a two-party system was favoured by the convergence of psychological and mechanical effects. While the former meant that most voters would vote "strategically" for candidates having a chance to win the seat, the latter played out in the conversion between votes and seats, also favouring the big parties.

Successive studies have criticised and qualified Duverger's views. With a different research design, Lijphart did not analyse the cause-and-effect relationships identified by Duverger. For our purposes, it is interesting to report the two main criticisms levelled at the French author, the first of which was in the context of application of his "law", and the second on the direction of causality[8] and the interactions between the variables. According to the first, Duverger had been too "assertive" in his law-like generalisation, not paying enough attention to the context of application as an essential condition for the causal relationship. Indeed, plurality often leads to bipartisanship *at the constituency level*. Only in the presence of homogeneous territorial competitions can such effects spread throughout a country (Cox 1997; Baldini & Pappalardo 2009). Second, according to Sartori, "the effects of the electoral system cannot be assessed without considering the manipulative properties of the party system" (1994). In particular, SMP is a "strong" electoral system with disproportional effects that are linked to two conditions. Beyond the previously mentioned homogeneous territorial distribution of support for the major parties (and the absence of parties with strong territorial bases), Sartori referred to the level of "structuring" of the party system. Let's briefly examine these two elements in turn.

First, geography is paramount to the operation of the UK electoral system (Johnston *et al.* 2021). To gain a seat, parties face a dilemma. They need to be active on the ground, but they have to prioritise territories where they appear to have some chance of winning, therefore, there is the risk of overlooking areas where they are either "sure of winning" or totally out of the game. To win, they must avoid being distant from local concerns (Middleton 2021), aiming to obtain a self-sufficient majority in the House of Commons. This means that in the UK the contest between parties (and candidates) has a peculiar territorial flavour that is significantly different from electoral competition that takes place in other countries under alternative electoral legislation.[9] Traditionally, political parties were able to build their strategies by learning from experience in previous elections in which results suggested how much to invest in any given constituency. But this worked in times of closed electoral markets, when citizens changed their vote very rarely in successive elections.

As far as the structuring of the party system is concerned, Sartori defined "structured" as those party systems where voters consistently supported the same party thanks to "stable ideological alignments", rather than a fragile and volatile support based on personalities. However, as we shall see below, this concept of party system structuring was not thoroughly elaborated by Sartori. Recent literature refers to the concept of party system institutionalisation instead. Hence, this is the concept that we shall use in our comparative assessment.

Given that the rise of minor parties increased the pressure for electoral reform, why does SMP voting survive for general elections? None of the conditions identified by leading experts as necessary for its reform occur in the country. Among these is the inability of the electoral system to bring about expected consequences (first of all, the manufacturing of a majority by the most-voted party in the most recent election), in combination with one of the following: an increase in support that a reforming party would expect for the popularity of the reform ("act-contingent"), or for the benefit that comes from the new rules ("outcome-contingent") (Shugart 2008; Renwick 2010). For reasons that we cannot detail here[10] due to lack of space, from the early 1990s SMP displayed a strong bias in favour of Labour, which then turned into a smaller bias for the Conservatives from 2015.

While the Conservatives explicitly advocate SMP for its effectiveness and contribution to government stability (Norton 1997), Labour was more open to change in several of its electoral manifestoes (Curtice 2013). But when the party had a clear opportunity to ditch SMP, with the strong majority of the Blair Governments – especially the first one (1997–2001), it decided not to follow up on the report of the Jenkins commission, which suggested the adoption of a complicated mixed system (Dunleavy & Margetts 1999). Thus, the mutual convenience of the two major parties has preserved SMP.[11] Even when the Liberal Democrats managed to hold a referendum in 2011, this was on the Alternative Vote, which is still a majoritarian formula. The proposal was then heavily rejected by the voters (see Chapter 1). However, significant changes took place at other territorial levels. Having been adopted in the first direct elections to the EP in 1979, SMP was then abandoned in favour of proportional representation (PR) in 1999, the same year in which the Parliaments of Wales and Scotland were elected for the first time, with mixed-member-proportional systems (cf. Table 3.1).

To fully understand the electoral dimension, one must never lose sight of the coexistence – in the intertwining of the electoral and party systems – of institutional and social elements. Following Sartori (1969), one can avoid the opposite extremisms of a sociological reading (which sees party systems as mere projections of cleavages) or an institutional reading (in which only the technical elements of the electoral law are emphasised). In the UK, both the institutional and social foundations of bipartisanship eroded from the 1970s onwards. However, this occurred in a very asymmetrical way. While SMP resisted the pressures for reform, social changes challenged the representation and responsiveness of the two main parties. The emergence of non-majoritarian systems (proportional or mixed) at other levels of government allows smaller parties to overcome the psychological and mechanical barriers identified by Duverger.

After 1999, the simultaneous birth of regional parliaments and PR for the EP elections strengthened the smaller parties. The SNP progressively grew in Scotland, to become the largest party in the 2011 Scottish elections (see Chapter 5). At the same time, UKIP used EP elections as a springboard. In 1999 UKIP was still marginal (the fourth party, with 6.5 percent, equal to only three seats). In each of the three successive European votes (2004, 2009, 2014) it climbed one position, becoming the most-voted party in 2014, with 26.6 percent of the votes. The effect of these innovations was evident in the early 2000s: in 2007 there were clear signs of "multi-Party Politics in a Multi-Level Polity" (Lynch 2007). Although both types of elections (European and regional) are "second-order" elections (Reif & Schmitt 1980), "they have created additional opportunities for smaller parties to establish electoral bases" (Fieldhouse *et al.* 2020, 65).

In conclusion, while at first sight the survival of SMP might give the impression that the electoral system can somehow be taken for granted in our electoral-party dimension, this is not the case. While we argue that SMP for general elections remains a strong bulwark in defence of the majoritarian patterns of the Westminster model, we must underline two important points. First, in times of open electoral markets, the psychological effects of SMP are also loosened and smaller parties can build strong credentials to challenge the status quo. Second, this challenge can, in turn, be helped by the increasing relevance of a multi-level structure of political competition. These processes do not happen overnight. Devolution was introduced in 1997–8. As we see in more detail in Chapter 5, the institutions of devolution ultimately favoured the nationalist parties. Similarly, despite a continuing low turnout, European elections gave a formidable platform for the rise of UKIP, especially thanks to the numerous seats granted to the party by a PR system.

Having explained the interplay of the various factors that are behind the electoral and party system dimension, then pointing out the importance of the electoral systems as the key institutional pillars of the Westminster model, we can now turn to the analytical framework.

3.4 The Brexit effect on electoral alignments and the party system

In 2009, a prominent scholar in the field argued that "it is probably fair to say that, within the contemporary literature, the notion of party systems is relatively under-theorized" (Mair 2009, 286). Shortly after, the field of cleavage research has been described as marked by "weak theorizing" (Franklin 2010). Since then, both the literature on party systems and that on voting behaviour have seen several innovations. In 2009, Mair was writing on the UK case, in a country where, over the last 25 years, the party system has been confronted with important challenges both with regard to the multi-level nature of the party system (Bardi & Mair 2008; Lynch 2007) and the rise of new parties (Ford & Goodwin 2014; Emanuele & Chiaramonte 2018). Also, the 2016 referendum can be seen as a litmus test for the rise of new cleavages, such as those related to the "left-behind voters", the so-called losers of globalisation (Kriesi *et al.* 2006).

In one of the last pre-Brexit analyses of the British party system, Quinn (2013) argued that, as of 2010 – after two consecutive long mandates by the Conservatives with Margaret Thatcher and John Major (1979–97) as well as Labour, with Tony Blair and Gordon Brown (1997–2010) – the classic two-party dynamic had been replaced by a pattern of "alternating predominance". More specifically, building on Sartori (1976), he argued that alternating predominance was

> a hybrid of one-party predominance and classic two-partism, in which both major parties enjoyed lengthy spells of single-party rule. Its defining feature was prolonged periods of weak competition until the major opposition party was able to modernise itself sufficiently to be trusted by voters.
>
> *(Quinn 2013, 379)*

Quinn's analysis contains a thorough assessment of the developments up to 2010. However, for the scope of this chapter, it has two main limitations. First, it is mainly focused on traditional party system indicators, giving less attention to voter alignments. Second, it stops when the electoral shocks mentioned above just started to unfold. These shocks show that the traditional bases on which the party system was built are weakening in many important ways. Voters are less trustful of political parties in general, they experiment with votes for other parties, and increasingly structure their electoral choice on new issues (such as immigration).

While these elements have been masterfully treated by recent works (Fieldhouse *et al.* 2020; Sobolewska & Ford 2020; Ford *et al.* 2021), there are fewer studies specifically on Brexit and party politics.[12] Moreover, the few existing ones either focus on single parties rather than on the interactions between them (e.g., Hayton 2022), or on some early implications of Brexit for party system realignment (e.g., Gamble 2019; Sanders 2017). In this respect, the main innovation of this chapter stems from its combination of data that allow a better comprehension of the overall transformations that are involving the party system, also considering the social bases on which the latter is built.

As explained in Chapter 1, in Lijphart's model, the electoral system and the party system are two key variables of what he called the "parties–executive" dimension. To assess them, he relied on some of the most commonly used indicators of disproportionality (i.e., the Gallagher index) and fragmentation (Laakso and Taagepera's indexes, see below). Lijphart's work has been considered as a reference for assessing the changes of the Westminster model in the UK (Flinders 2010; Matthews & Flinders 2017). As anticipated in Chapter 1, here we adapt and supplement Lijphart's framework with other indicators. Three main streams of research can be helpful in order to build an appropriate framework for understanding the significance of Brexit. We start from electoral alignments and voters' identities, then move to two other streams which are more focused on party system dynamics. This combination might seem unbalanced. However, aspects of electoral behaviour are also present in the last two.[13]

3.4.1 Cleavage politics: are there new alignments and Brexit identities in the place of party identities?

Against a backdrop marked by a rise in populism across Europe, Brexit is often considered to be the expression of a political conflict based on cultural values, which is orthogonal to the traditional right–left axis which had been dominating European politics throughout the twentieth century. Hooghe *et al.* (2002) coined the term "GAL/TAN" to indicate the contraposition between green, alternative leftist positions (particularly spread among the more educated, cosmopolitan, and young electorate) and traditional, authoritarian, nationalist values, which are more diffused among less-educated, elderly electorates (GAL voters would also be more spread in the qualified occupations, while TAN voters are more numerous among lower classes, the self-employed, unemployed, and the retired). Similarly, Kriesi and co-authors (2006; 2012) refer to these trends in mapping the rise of a cultural cleavage between winners and losers of globalisation. Hooghe and Marks (2018), have coined the term "Transnational cleavage". Most recently, when analysing cleavage politics in the context of the many "EU crises", Marks *et al.* (2021) use the term "neo-cleavage". Their analysis is worth quoting at length:

> The chief propositions of neo-cleavage theory are that the dynamism in party systems arises from exogenous social change; that the party-political response comes chiefly in the form of new political parties that rise on a new cleavage; and that processes of alignment and dealignment coexist as new divides become solidified among voters while old divides lose causal power. Neocleavage theory does not anticipate a wholesale restructuring of the electorate. A significant degree of volatility is likely to persist alongside structuration. This is because transnationalism concerns certain social categories more than others, and it is those individuals most directly affected who are most likely to form intense, durable political allegiances.

In 2016, the vote to "Leave" the EU was associated with regions with a greater proportion of less-educated voters, with a greater number of older voters, or regions that have experienced a recent rapid increase in the proportion of EU migrants, and those located outside Scotland or London (Goodwin & Heath 2016). However, in times of weakening electoral alignments and fluctuating political identities (Bludhorn & Butzlaff 2019), it is important to also focus on the context in which the elections of the "Brexit years" took place. Specifically, how important was Brexit as an electoral issue? What consequences had the result on the following phases of the Brexit process? What can be said about its effect on the party system? Following Bartolini and Mair (1990), the politicisation of a conflict can be analysed through three components: structural (presence of social groups with specific interests in a conflict, which can be a source of votes for a party), psychological (the perception of important divisions on ideologies, values, identity, and interests), and organisational (the mobilisation of these issues by a party actor, usually personalised by a leader). There are evidently important elements of overlap between these aspects (Mair 2006b). Deegan-Krause and Enyedi (2010) also point to the role of agency. Leadership effects are particularly important in the case of Brexit. What is also important to highlight is that divisions can take a long time to solidify into a cleavage. In this respect, one of the key areas in which the impact of Brexit can be assessed is the way in which voters are priming Brexit identities over party identities.

3.4.2 The classification of party systems

Sartori (1976) built his typology of party systems on two main dimensions: fragmentation – i.e., the number of relevant parties – and polarisation, which defines the ideological distance between them. However, as Nwokora and Pelizzo highlight (2014), Sartori did not give much consideration to alternation as a specific dimension of classification. In the British case, the relevance of alternation becomes all the more evident as the party system enters – with the 2010 general election – a new phase marked by uncertainty and instability. To be sure, since then the Conservatives have indeed managed to replicate the 1979 to 1992 record of four electoral victories in a row. This happened, however, with a substantial difference. That is, in both 2010 and 2017 the party did not obtain an overall majority in parliament, and in order to form a government it was forced – respectively – to form a coalition with the Liberal Democratic Party (Prime Minister: Cameron, 2010–15), and a minority government in a "confidence-and-supply" agreement with the Democratic Unionist Party (DUP), led by Theresa May: 2017–19). Hence, only in 2015 (Prime Minister: Cameron, who resigned after the 2016 referendum) and in 2019, (with Boris Johnson), did the Conservatives manage to win an overall majority of seats. The reasons why this happened are related to a number of factors that are linked to the combined effects of the electoral system, strategies of the political parties, as well as voters' shifting loyalties.

As Sartori himself acknowledged, both two-party and predominant party systems tend to be fragile configurations. The distinction between the two categories can also be complicated. Therefore, we need to complement existing indicators on fragmentation with others. Writing in the age of mass parties and stable voting alignments, in a period in which new parties (or electoral earth-quakes) were extremely rare, Sartori (1976) did not pay much attention to the stability and predictability of the patterns of competition. This meant that the question of party system institutionalisation was not thoroughly considered. According to Casal Bértoa (2017, 407), the institutionalisation of the party system is "the process by which the patterns of interaction among political parties become routine, predictable and stable over time". Also, Chiaramonte and Emanuele (2017) have elaborated on the meaning of electoral volatility for party system institutionalisation, focusing on "regeneration", i.e., the component of change, (and possible de-institutionalisation), due to the emergence of new parties in the electoral arena. Hence, together with more traditional indicators, we also make use of other indexes elaborated by this recent literature.

3.4.3 One or many party systems? The importance of horizontal, vertical, and functional divisions

As argued by Bardi and Mair (2008) a polity can have different party systems when it displays one or more of three types of divisions: horizontal, vertical, and functional. In the UK, existing horizontal divisions have experienced important variations in the last 25 years, at both sub- and supra-state levels. These have been so important that "the classic two-party system of early post-war Britain has given way to a more complex picture in which distinctive party systems operate at national, regional, local and European level" (Lynch 2007, 323). We have seen that, since 1999, new institutions/electoral laws were introduced at both sub- and supra-national levels. Then, politically these territories increased their relevance with the increasing successes of the SNP in Scottish elections (in 2006 and 2011) and of UKIP in the EP elections (in 2009 and 2014).

Secondly, vertical divisions are mainly associated with the "pillarised polities". As a Union State of four polities (Keating 2021), the UK has different degrees of "regionalised party systems". While in Scotland and Wales "British" parties also compete against the SNP and PC respectively, only Northern Ireland has a totally "regionalised" party system in which British parties do not contest elections. In Northern Ireland, most of the parties either belong to the nationalist/secessionist (mainly Catholic) camp, which aim for the reunification of Ireland, and the unionist camp (mainly Protestant), which has, so far, gained more votes. With regard to Brexit, most of the big parties in these three polities were against it, with the exception of the DUP in Northern Ireland (see Chapter 5).

Finally, functional divisions can be understood in terms of the distinction between electoral, parliamentary, and governmental arenas. While in countries using a proportional electoral system with permissive electoral formulae the differences between the first two arenas can be very limited, in majoritarian democracies small parties can either not make it to parliament or be confined to the opposition for long periods. For example, UKIP only obtained one seat in 2015 with almost 12.6 percent of the vote (with a level of disproportionality unseen in any other European country), and the Liberal Democrats only managed to access governmental positions with the 2010 coalition government.

However, following Chiaramonte and Emanuele (2017), this chapter mainly refers to the electoral arena for the same reasons they identified:

> First, the electoral arena is the only one where the interactions between parties and voters can be taken into account; second, from an empirical point of view, the electoral ground comes first with respect to other arenas (parliamentary, governmental or policy-making ones): if electoral competition becomes unpredictable, it is very likely that this unpredictability will be reproduced in the other arenas, while the other way round would be much more difficult to conceive.
>
> *(Chiaramonte & Emanuele 2017, 377)*

Moreover, as the previous section on electoral legislation has shown, party systems and electoral competitions are now intertwined on a multi-level territorial basis. Hence, the analysis to which we now turn can also be considered as a fundamental step in order to understand the societal bases on which the institutional tensions have played out in the wake of the 2016 referendum, which will be the focus of the next two chapters.

3.5 Data and analysis: Brexit as an electoral shock

The empirical analysis on the effects of Brexit starts from three combined considerations. The first one is on timing and context, the second is on methods and causal mechanisms, and the third is on speculations on future scenarios. First, the most important literature on electoral behaviour in the UK views Brexit as a consequence of long-term changes. In particular, according to Sobolewska and Ford, "Brexit is the expression of conflicts that have been building in the electorate for decades, not their cause" (2020, 2). As anticipated in the latest volume of the British Election Study (BES, Fieldhouse *et al.* 2020), Brexit is considered to be the fifth "election shock" in less than 15 years. As such, it cannot be considered an isolated event, as something that just happened out of the blue.

Since the beginning of the new millennium, both the institutional and social foundations on which the British two-party system traditionally rested have significantly weakened. If new electoral systems have been introduced at the sub- and supra-state levels, cultural divisions, and in particular immigration (Kaufmann 2018), have challenged the ability of the two main parties to respond to societal challenges. In this respect, it has been persuasively argued that Brexit is not the result of a shift towards more anti-immigration positions. Rather, the British electorate has recently become slightly more socially liberal (Surridge 2021; Wheatley 2019). In this respect, it is particularly important to look at the role of agents (Deegan-Krause & Enyedi 2010), as political entrepreneurs that are able to politicise or reframe new issues, significantly changing the structure of political competition.

Second, the methods we use combine insights from qualitative and quantitative research in an attempt to consider not just both the supply and demand sides, but also to identify the causal dynamics of the effects of Brexit. While precise causal mechanisms remain difficult to isolate, the attention to the context in which each election was fought significantly strengthens our analytical leverage. Third, by considering a multiplicity of factors, we can form some speculations on future scenarios for the party system, which will be developed in the next section. Let us now look at the main results of the empirical analysis.

3.5.1 Electoral alignments and cleavages

Over the last 20 years, Britain has experienced a rise in new anti-EU (and anti-immigration) parties with a significant blackmail potential – first UKIP, then in 2019, the Brexit Party. In different ways, these parties have affected the patterns of political competition, both by gaining votes (UKIP in the 2015 general election; the Brexit party winning the 2019 EP elections, with over 30 percent of the votes) and by contributing to a realignment of the electorate for the main parties.

To be sure, the rise of cultural values as determinants of electoral choice is not new. Back in 1999, analysing the landslide of New Labour in 1997, Evans noted that despite Europe's low salience as an electoral issue, the decline in class voting was interpretable "at least in part, [as] a consequence of party realignment on Europe" (p. 219). Even during Westminster's golden age, class was not the only factor determining electoral behaviour. Leadership evaluation, the role of the media, new issues,[14] and the political parties' competence to face them: all these factors have long been relevant, and there is no overall agreement about their precise, increased relevance (Webb-Bale 2021, Ch. 5–6).

In analysing alignment and cleavages it is important to combine the dimensions of analysis proposed by Bartolini and Mair (see above), with a focus on agency, which is particularly important given the many instances of elite actions (and leadership turnover) which affected the course of the Brexit process (see Table 3.2).[15]

To begin with, the 2015 general election broke several records, which were related to the rise of third parties and to electoral volatility in general (see also Table 3.4). While running somehow short of the expectations raised by its double victory scored in the two by-elections held in 2014, (when Douglas Carswell and Mark Reckless became the party's first two MPs, after having defected from the Conservatives), the party not only obtained almost 4 million votes, but greatly distanced the Lib-Dems as the third most-voted party. Moreover, it came in second in as many as 120 constituencies, thus, credibly aiming to win many seats in future general elections, especially if no referendum on the EU were to be called. In these elections, the UKIP voter was found to be very close to the typical image of a globalisation loser, that "recruited the bulk of its support from financially vulnerable,

TABLE 3.2 Contests in context: the relevance and implications of Brexit in recent elections

		2015 General	2017 General	2019 European	2019 General
Brexit as a process	**Brexit as an electoral issue**	Important for rise of UKIP (12.6 percent)	Very relevant (but other factors matter, e.g., austerity)	Crucial → triumph of Brexit Party	Conservative triumph on "Get Brexit done" slogan
	Consequences on next steps of exit process	Conservative victory triggers (2016) referendum; split of Conservatives	No conservative majority in Westminster to trigger legislation	May's resignations and leadership change; new withdrawal agreement	Fast approval of exit legislation. Key signpost in Brexit political process
	Brexit effect on party system	UKIP's success increases the Conservative internal tensions on EU	Resurgence of two-party vote (82.4 percent, not seen since 1970). After 2016 referendum UKIP suffers from "winner's curse" (Whiteley et al. 2018, 95)	Farage's second victory electoral earthquake and great uncertainty[a] (four different parties leading in April–July 2019 voting intentions)	Return of a Conservative predominance?
Cleavage dynamics	**Structural elements**	UKIP strengthens dynamics of "revolt on the right" (Ford & Goodwin 2014), but also on the left (Roberts 2014)	Increase in age and education as predictors of vote for two main parties: Conservatives move closer to TAN pole, and older (though no real "youthquake"; Prosser et al. 2020)	Brexit Party strongly popular among retired voters (but also in the 55–64 cohort)	Strong decrease of class as vote predictor; age and education confirmed as important, if slightly less than in 2017

(Continued)

TABLE 3.2 Continued

	2015 General	2017 General	2019 European	2019 General
Realignment and identity dynamics	Anti-EU voters of the right move to UKIP and, as done in north of England former Labour voters	Conservatives attract more Leave voters (63 percent) than Labour do with Remainers (54 percent). Brexit identities stronger than party identity	Brexit Party's triumph (especially in areas where Leave vote won in 2016); similar demographic to UKIP, yet more protest-motivated (Evans *et al.* 2021, 9)	Widening gap between Conservative appeal among Leavers and Labour's among Remainers. Still strong Brexit identities
Selected agency elements (elite actions; inspired by Deegan-Krause & Enyedi 2010, 705)	Cameron respects pledge for EU referendum; referendum rules (with significant decisions on franchise) (Goodwin & Heath 2016)	May's call of snap election backfires (Allen & Bartle 2018)	Creation of Brexit Party (and of Change UK);[c] strong divisive appeal by Brexit Party (Vasiliopoulou 2020)	Johnson's capacity to absorb Brexit party challenge (Evans *et al.* 2021)

a In the words of one of the doyens of British psephology, during these months "The foundations of the country's traditional two-party system looked as weak as they had ever been" (Curtice 2022, x).

b As confirmed also by Interviewee 9, a prominent scholar in electoral research.

c "Change UK" was a splinter centrist group in which seven former Labour MPs were joined by three other Conservatives and one Lib-Dem MP to contest the 2019 EP election. With only 3.3 percent and no MEP elected, the party then dissolved after an equally unsuccessful general election in December that year (Thompson 2020).

TABLE 3.3 Party system types across time (with some comparative cases)

Type	Period(s) in Britain (with governing party) (foreign cases in Italics)	Fragmentation	Polarisation[a]	Alternation
Predominant	1979–97 (Con) 1997–2010 (Lab) 2010–? Con	1+n	Trivial	Possible but infrequent
Two-party	1945–70	2+n	Low	Regular and wholesale
Moderate pluralism	Tendency after 1970; (Germany, among others)	3–5+n	Medium	Regular (wholesale or partial)
Polarised pluralism	(Italy, at least until 1992)	6–8+n	High	Regular/frequent but partial

Source: Author's compilation, after a scheme proposed by Nwokora and Pelizzo (2014, 104).

a While in the context of current debates on a radicalisation of identitarian elements, the triviality of polarisation in a context of party predominance might seem a debatable element, "Sartori defined polarisation as the ideological distance between relevant parties, so there can be no such distance when there is only one relevant party" (Nwokora & Pelizzo 2014, 103). This is also the reason why we devote limited attention to polarisation in this chapter (but some considerations on this element are included in Chapter 6).

TABLE 3.4 Selected indicators on party system and elections (1945–2019)

	Classic Westminster model 1945–70	Rise of minor parties 1974–2005	Multiple electoral shocks[a] (2010–15)	The Brexit years 2017–19
V1 Fragmentation Effective number of parliamentary parties (... of electoral parties)	2.0 (2.4)	2.2 (3.2)	2.5 (3.8)	2.3 (3.1)
Two-party vote	91.2	73.8	66.1	79.0
Volatility	4.8	8.3	12.6	12.9
Regeneration	0.7	6.1	11.4	9.2
Strong party ID	45	16	15	17 (2017)
V 4 Disproportionality (Gallagher index)	7.1	16.1	15.0	7.1
Marginal seats	26.1	17.3	14.0	15.4
Turnout	77.5	71.6	65.6	68.0

Sources: Author's calculation; Fieldhouse et al. 2020, 53.

a See Fieldhouse et al. (2020) and the list below.

disaffected, working-class and, to a lesser extent, self-employed voters who tended to be older, white and with few, if any, qualifications" (Goodwin 2015, 14).

In the two and a half years between the 2017 and 2019 general elections, the context, dynamics, and consequences of the vote all changed quite radically. If both were convened to complete the exit process (see the next chapter), first of all, the exceptionality of three general elections in less than five years should be noted, an event that had not happened for almost 50 years. At the same time, it is important to highlight that elections – as opposed to the Brexit process – are discrete events, placed at a specific moment in time and, therefore, affected by the specific contingencies of the time in which they take place.

Brexit played a different role in the 2017 and 2019 general elections. This was true both in terms of how parties politicised the issue, making it a significant element in the electoral campaign as well as how voters perceived party positions with regard to Brexit and closely related issues such as immigration (for the Leave camp), and access to the Common Market (for the Remain camp). Johnson's slogan for the 2019 general election was "Get Brexit done". Leadership clearly played a role in the greatly asymmetric personalisation of Brexit by the leaders of the two main parties, that is, very assertive and investing all on this topic in the case of Johnson, yet much more uncertain and vaguer for Jeremy Corbyn.

In 2017, the apparent return of two-party politics was however

> due to tactical voting on behalf of supporters of the smaller parties. Liberal Democrats and Greens tended to vote Labour if their own candidate had little chance of winning, while UKIP supporters frequently voted Tory. In this way, the Conservatives aggregated the vote of voters who had voted to leave the European Union.
>
> *(Wheatley 2019, 17)*

This was less the case for Labour. The electoral campaign also played an important role. While May had very poor performance (Wring *et al.* 2019; Berz 2021), Corbyn significantly reduced the gap compared to the polls of six weeks earlier, bringing Labour back to percentages not seen since 2001. While Ipsos Mori monthly polls showed the continued relevance of Brexit as "the most important issue facing Britain", other issues were also relevant.

Moreover, after the referendum – while party identifications remained low – the two main parties followed different paths in an attempt to win over the voters who had voted to stay in or leave the EU. The Conservatives united in the pursuit of an exit (even at the cost of a no-deal), while Labour was more divided. According to various estimates, (the differences between the polls of YouGov, Ipsos Mori, and Lord Ashcroft are irrelevant, in the order of one or two percentage points), the voters of the two parties who voted "Leave" in 2016 were respectively about 58 percent among the Conservatives and 37 percent among Labour. Although many polls following the referendum had shown a slight shift in the electorate in favour of staying in the EU, the country remained split in two up to the end of the exit process (Curtice 2020b).

Already in 2017, voters had stronger identities regarding Brexit than party affiliations (Evans & Schaffner 2019). In 2019, the percentage of leavers voting Conservative increased from 65 to 74 percent, while Labour lost votes among the Remainers (from 55 to 49 percent) (Ipsos Mori 2019). To be sure, the Labour Party was always going to struggle in identifying a proper strategy with regard to Brexit. Some of the party's most faithful voters had voted Leave in 2016, and Corbyn's leadership had by then got embroiled in accusations of antisemitism. The party had also not carefully considered the importance of agreements within the Remain camp, starting from those with the Liberal Democrats and the Greens (see Chapter 6). The crucial question then becomes the following: are these new alignments capable of stabilising? It goes without saying that in order to answer this question with more certainty it is necessary to wait for the next elections.

Regarding identity, existing studies show that the Conservative Party has greatly benefited from its repositioning on Brexit. While the party was split in 2015, and in 2016 the majority of the parliamentary group was still supporting "Remain", however, Cameron's successors – especially Johnson from the summer of 2019 – shifted the party towards radical Eurosceptic positions. In the opposite camp, Labour was in trouble attempting to keep together a variegated electorate, then ending up in 2019 with the loss of most of its traditional bulwarks (the so-called "Red Wall") in working-class constituencies in the north of England. And yet,

> while the red wall may have been breached in 2019, the foundations had been weakening for some time. The surge of Leave voters may be the final element which cracked the brickwork, but the decay, reflected in Labour's weakening relationship with working class Britain, had been setting in over much of the last decade, if not earlier. The 2019 general election was not a critical election that signalled a radical departure from the past, but rather, marked the continuation of longer-term trends in the dealignment and realignment of political loyalties in British politics.
>
> *(Cutts et al. 2020, 21)*

The new Brexit identities "reflect pre-existing – but less politicized – social divisions, such as age and education, which were mobilized in the context of the referendum and subsequently consolidated" (Hobolt *et al.* 2020). According to Sobolewska and Ford (2020), the referendum brought to the surface polarisations between conservative and liberal identities (among Labour). As Evans and Mellon note, Brexit identities in 2019 were a greater predictor of the vote than the social class, "to be middle class or working class no longer matters, what matters is Brexit" (2020, 2; see also Ford *et al.* 2021). Likewise, throughout 2019, "British voters appeared to identify more with one of the two camps of Brexit than with a party" (Curtice *et al.* 2019, 192).[16]

Moreover, recent studies have also shown that Brexit identities still mattered four and a half years after the referendum. While at the end of 2017, 75 percent of the electorate had strong Brexit identities, this was still the case for 65 percent at the end of 2021 (Hobolt & Tilley 2021). To understand whether these identities will further consolidate or not in the medium term, it is important to monitor whether and how European issues can still be played in the electoral arena, despite the formal exit from EU institutions.

At the same time, along with Brexit, the leaders' evaluations were also important in the 2019 election (Ford *et al.* 2021). In particular, while Johnson himself was not more popular than May (ibid.), it was the combination of a very strong unpopularity of Corbyn (Whiteley *et al.* 2021) with a strong belief that only Johnson could "break the deadlock" (Allen & Bartle 2021) that made the difference, especially to attract Labour leave voters, since "Johnson's appeal to some part of the Labour electorate was itself driven by his strong personal association with the cause of Brexit" (Ford *et al.* 2021, 512).

3.5.2 Party system classification

How can we classify the British party system in the Spring of 2022? What kind of change can we detect and what role can we attribute to Brexit in these dynamics? The main innovations in the literature of the last ten years allow an answer to these questions in two steps. First, we face a more qualitative assessment on party system types which, building on Sartori and recent innovations, present a range of possible alternative classifications. Then, moving to the adaptation of Lijphart's framework, we provide more quantitative indicators (Table 3.3, which also adopts the work of Nwokora and Pelizzo (2014)).

Placing alternation alongside the Sartorian dimensions of fragmentation and polarisation, we can put Britain today in the "predominant" category. Why? In Sartori's classification the predominant party system shared with other two types (one-party, and hegemonic) the relevance of one party, which made the question of polarisation trivial. However, these two-party system types can also be found in non-democratic regimes. To be sure, the threshold established by Sartori to locate cases inside this class was three electoral victories in a row. Although once problematically (i.e., with a slim majority, in 2015), and twice without a majority (2010 and 2017), the Conservatives have now won four elections in a row.

This classification suggests two main considerations. First, Britain remains in the same category as the previous 30 years in which alternation was less frequent, after long periods of predominance of the two parties (1979–97; 1997–2010), than in the previous long cycle of the two-party system (1945–70). Second, and related, this suggests the importance of analysing electoral data in more detail to further distinguish between situations which can apparently look similar by ending up in the same cell.

This can be done by integrating Lijphart's work with four other main indicators. The first one requires no explanation, in that the two-party vote gives an immediate image of the number of voters still willing to trust the Conservatives or Labour. Second, volatility, which is also traditionally used in research on voting behaviour, is supplemented here by regeneration. As Emanuele and Chiaramonte explain (2017), "regeneration" indicates the amount of electoral variation due to the entry of new political parties. Last but not least, in SMP systems the composition of the parliament is strictly linked to separate competitions inside each electoral district. While in the past there were many marginal seats (where the Conservatives and Labour were neck-and-neck), this is much less the case today. As we see below, this is all the more crucial given that the country has recently experienced an important increase in territorial party system divergence (Stolz 2019), which echoes different results also in the 2016 referendum.

Table 3.4 identifies four phases. Beyond the classic one (1945–70), we have a long period of growth of smaller parties (1974–2005, phase 2), against the background of the aforementioned two-party dominance – formerly Conservative, then Labour (with, respectively, four and three electoral victories) – and the last two phases of multiple electoral shocks (2010–15, phase 3), and post-Brexit elections (2017–19, phase 4). The two-party index provides the simplest information. If the two main parties remain the same in all four phases, their recent recovery (as compared to the previous two phases) takes place in a context that is very different from that of the first one. This is evident especially from the two successive indices of volatility and regeneration, which concern the aforementioned level of institutionalisation of the party system (Chiaramonte & Emanuele 2017). Total volatility (Pedersen index) captures the aggregate change in the vote from one election to another. The average in the period from 1945 to 2015, at the Western European level, is 10.2 (but growing over the last years, even up to 18.0 in the last two elections before 2015 (ibid.). In the first phase, volatility was very low (4.7, versus a European average of the period of 8.3); then it steadily increases. A similar pattern is found for regeneration, indicating the contribution to electoral change caused by new political parties.

Now, if comparatively the UK remains an electorally stable country (no election – in the period from 1945 to 2015, combines high volatility and high salience of regeneration (Chiaramonte & Emanuele 2017, 383)), the upward trend for both indices (especially compared to phase 1) is very clear. The decline in strong identification is also extremely important for political parties. For Butler and Stokes (1974) the identification with parties was a fundamental prerequisite for electoral stability, one of the pillars on which bipartisanship and alternation were based. Even if the direction of the causal relationship between party identification and electoral behaviour is still debated in the literature, the collapse of strong partisan identities is a clear sign of the opening of the electoral market.

These dynamics have been nicely captured in a long-term comparison on party closure:

> While in calculations that utilize information from the entire timespan [1848–2013], the UK ends up as one of the most institutionalized systems,

after Switzerland and in a virtual tie with Malta and Portugal, and is relegated to the twelfth position, in the post-1990 data the UK is only at the eighth place and Portugal appears among the top performers.

(Casal Bértoa & Enyedi 2021)

Similarly, in a comparative European perspective, the UK displays the third-highest increase in party system innovation since 2010 (Emanuele & Chiaramonte 2018, 481). All this suggests that the basis for classifying the British case look more uncertain. In different ways, the two main parties have adapted, also thanks to the preservation of SMP, to new conditions of political competition.

3.5.3 Multiple party systems?

In this last focus, we necessarily need to be brief for three main reasons. First, we have already focused (Section 3.3 above) on institutional changes that have brought about significant electoral reforms that have increased the multi-level nature of the British party system. Second, after the implementation of Brexit, the UK will no longer take part in European elections, which have represented a key platform for UKIP's success and its crusade for Brexit. Third, Chapter 5 returns to the key territorial dynamics that have affected the various phases of the Brexit process. While mainly concerned with the power struggles between London and the peripheries, that chapter contains more information on how party politics and electoral competition have played out recently. But it is also important to remember that, as far as the sub-state level is concerned, in the 2016 referendum only England and Wales voted for Brexit while in Northern Ireland, and especially in Scotland, the choice to remain was by far the preferred option. Testing a Brexit effect on regional elections is no easy task. First, Northern Ireland has a different electoral calendar. So far, the only post-referendum election in that territory was held in 2017, a period in which, as we have seen, Brexit was certainly a relevant issue, but also less important. As far as Scotland and Wales are concerned, the 2021 regional elections were marked, compared to five years before, by respectively, a substantial continuity (Johns 2021) and by a recovery of the Conservative Party (Awan-Scully 2021), which overtook PC as the second most-voted party. The ghost in the room is clearly a second referendum on Scottish independence, which the new coalition between the SNP and the Greens, elected in 2021, has pledged to hold by 2026.

3.6 The weak bases of the party system

After only two general elections, it remains difficult to distinguish between contingent factors and the possible consolidation of structural Brexit effects on the party system. Over the last decade, the profiles of the voters of the two parties have changed. The electoral predominance of the Conservatives was crucially built on the capacity to attract more Leave voters, while still being voted by a small number of Remainers as well.

As a way to reflect on the new bases of support for the two main parties in the last elections, here we focus on the fall of the so-called "Red Wall" and on the role of the Brexit Party in the 2019 general election. As we have seen, both aspects are important in order to make sense of the effects of Brexit both on the geography of competition (see Section 3.2, above) and on the structure of the political supply (Section 3.4). Furthermore, by looking at how the Labour Party lost some of its core areas, and how the Brexit Party played into the competition, we can examine these important elements regarding the prospects of a possible alternation after the next general election.

To begin with, the geography of support for the Labour Party means that alternation can in all likelihood be difficult unless the party manages to reconquer at least some of the seats in the north of England (in addition to Scotland, see Chapter 5). The term "Red Wall" was invented by Conservative Party activist James Kanagasooriam in 2019 (Mattinson 2020; Kanagasooriam & Simon 2021), to indicate a classic Labour stronghold in the ex-industrial area between North Wales, part of the Midlands, and Northern England. It includes some of the areas where Brexit had the highest margins (on average Leave got more than 60 percent) and where UKIP had already stolen votes from Labour in 2015. Although there is no unanimous classification of the constituencies forming the "wall", those that are most often included in this group include the former industrial areas in the north of England, where the Conservatives had begun to gain votes in 2010. In 2019, in some of these areas, Labour recorded the worst result ever (−12.8 percentage points in the North East compared to two years earlier, −10.1 in Yorkshire, compared to an average decrease in the country of 7.9 points). These are areas where economic vulnerability is associated with the strong presence of the working class, even if they are by no means among the poorest in the country. In terms of employment and income, they are close to the average levels of the seats conquered by Labour in 2019. One of their interesting peculiarities is the decline experienced in economic terms, from 2010 onwards, as well as strong demographic stagnation and low mobility (McCurdy *et al.* 2020). However, the population is no older than the average.

The fall of the Red Wall made a lot of noise, but it was not sudden at all (Goes 2020). Brexit was the straw that broke the camel's back, which accumulated over the years while memories of hostility towards Thatcherism, responsible for deindustrialisation in the 1980s, were fading. Although there have been visible cracks in the wall for years, the Labour Party underestimated the possibility of losing those constituencies, while deciding not to campaign on the ground in 2019 (Surridge 2021), since it had already been absent during the 2016 referendum. Negative sentiments and judgements about the party and the leadership are prevalent, given that they have been abandoned in favour of Johnson's Conservatives. However, the charge of detachment and hostility that emerges from Mattinson's interviews (2020) is striking. Labour is portrayed as paternalistic, in exclusive defence of the interests of the south and in particular of the urban middle/upper class of London. Corbyn is negatively mentioned by virtually all respondents (p. 154).

More specifically on Brexit, by not saying how he would personally vote in a second referendum that his own party was recommending, Corbyn had effectively absented himself from the debate. Voters found this hard to forgive in a national leader (Mattinson 2020, 153).

Experts disagree on the role of the Brexit Party on Johnson's victory in the 2019 election. Some argue that, by not presenting candidates in the 317 seats held by the Conservatives on the eve of the election, the party would have helped Johnson. The Brexit Party vote was enough to assign 20 seats to the Conservatives, "thereby doubling Johnson's eventual parliamentary majority" (Norris 2019). On the contrary, according to Mellon (2021), the pact with the Brexit Party was probably not necessary, considering the already very high number of its voters (from the previous European elections) who were converging towards the Conservatives anyway. A recent work (Curtice *et al.* 2021) confirms this second view, with an estimate of 25 costed to the Conservative Party. However, Johnson was also able to make the best of this peculiar desistence, by refusing to make deals with Farage he kept his hands free while the Brexit Party attracted Labour voters, and while the decline of the latter was stronger in constituencies where Farage fielded candidates (Cutts *et al.* 2020, 9).

In this respect, it can be useful to refer to the scheme proposed in the analysis of the success of anti-establishment parties in Europe by De Vries and Hobolt (2020), based on three possible scenarios. With fragmentation, the challenger parties manage to erode control of the electoral market meaningfully; with substitution they come to replace the parties of the establishment; and while in reinvention the challenged parties readapt to the mutated market conditions by increasing their votes.

As we have seen, the permanence of SMP acts as a powerful barrier in defence of the major parties, making the substitution scenario extremely unlikely. More generally, there is a complex interweaving between party conveniences and the political tradition to guarantee the survival of SMP. In this context, Brexit has so far not exercised any influence in favour of an electoral reform towards more proportional formulae. Indeed, in 2017 the pyrrhic victory of the Conservatives – deprived of a parliamentary majority despite having over 42 percent of the votes, an increase of more than five percentage points compared to two years earlier – has reproposed, a further exception to the capacity of SMP in granting a majority to the winning party.

The second scenario (the major one, fragmentation) would be continuity with the trends of the last decade. Considering the inability of the Liberal Democrats to recover from the consequences of the coalition government, this scenario is based on two main conditions, which are the permanence of Scotland in the United Kingdom and the ability of the Conservatives to manage the implementation of Brexit. While SNP has shown no sign of crisis in the 2021 regional elections – thus reinforcing confirmation of its competitiveness in Scotland's Westminster constituencies – speculating on the future of Britain outside of the EU is a moot point (Table 3.5).

TABLE 3.5 Three scenarios for the party system after Brexit

Factors	Substitution	Fragmentation	Reinvention
Social		Re-politicisation of the European issue; linked to condition b in party factors	Reabsorption of Brexit issue within two-party competition
Party		(a) Lib-Dem comeback (b) a more centrist Conservative leadership (c) continued success of SNP ...	Labour regaining part of seats lost in 2019; fading of territorial cleavage
Institutional	PR electoral reform, combined with other external shocks	... and Scotland remains in UK	SMP still in use

Source: Authors' compilation based on the scheme proposed by De Vries and Hobolt (2020).

3.7 Conclusion: a reaffirmed two-party game, with a very peculiar Conservative predominance

Suppose that in 2017, at the age of 67, the Smiths returned to spend their retirement in the south of England after working for 45 years on a farm in New Zealand, the largest supplier of dairy products to the UK when they left (Bogdanor 2019). In the last elections in which they had participated in 1970, also the last ones before the UK joined the European Economic Community (EEC), the main parties were: Conservatives 46.4 percent, corresponding to 330 seats; Labour with 43.1 percent, equal to 288 seats; while long-distanced and third were the Liberals with 7.5 percent and 6 seats. In 2017, in the first election after the referendum, the distribution of votes and seats was practically the same as 47 years earlier. To believe that nothing has changed in 47 years would be just as wrong as interpreting Brexit as a revolution that has radically changed the face of the British party system. The complicated reality lies between these two extremes.

Building on important innovations of recent research, we have mapped the most important changes during the early years after the Brexit referendum. Brexit has put the British party system under considerable strain. We have shown that Brexit has had mixed effects on the electoral and party dimension. In the short term, the two-party system pattern of political competition has somehow resumed in the post-2016 general elections. Reabsorbing first UKIP's and then the Brexit Party's consecutive challenges, the Conservatives have finally stopped "banging on" about Europe, 15 years after Cameron asked them to do so in his first conference as party leader. At the same time, the effects of Brexit are often not easy to disentangle from other effects. We have to keep this in mind while also reflecting on the different plausibility of future scenarios on the "very peculiar" fragile predominance achieved by the Conservatives since 2010.

In this respect, the part of predominance that was achieved through the "absorption" of Brexit as "an electoral shock", (with former UKIP and Brexit Party voters converging towards the Conservatives in 2019: Evans *et al.* 2021), must also consider that the implementation of Brexit "as a policy" is far from complete. Talks with the EU are still taking place in many crucial sectors such as the Northern Ireland Protocol, fishery policies, and others. As such, the Brexit issue, while seemingly less important than others within public opinion (Ipsos Mori December 2021), is far from gone. No one can seriously rule that future elections will result in the appearance of something like a so-called "real Brexit" party, or anything similar.

If Brexit came about as "the UKIP revolt", today electoral competition takes place in a profoundly different social context from half a century ago. Voters are much more "secular" in their orientation towards parties (with less party identification, less participation, higher volatility, and party switching) and the geography of support is now much more uncertain, thus making any assessment on change more provisional by definition.

As far as the effects of Brexit are concerned, as the authors of the fifth edition of a classic book on electoral behaviour in Britain underline in their preface:

> part of the very powerful Brexit effect in 2019 is likely to die away as the issue slowly recedes, with other issues such as the economy liable to regain importance. On the other hand, part of what looked like a Brexit effect was more a reflection of longer-term trends in the sociology and geography of British public opinion, especially relating to the issue of immigration, and this looks to be potentially a more enduring change.
>
> *(Denver & Johns 2022, VI)*

By reflecting on the possible factors affecting future scenarios, we have sought to provide some instruments to put the Brexit effects on the electoral and party dimension into perspective. We come back to some of these elements in Chapter 6, when we analyse how the implementation of Brexit gets entangled with the Covid-19 crisis. Thus, the findings in this chapter serve as important building blocks for the analysis of the next two in which we move to "institutional games" in the double and equally crucial dimension of the confrontation between government and parliament in London (Chapter 4) and, subsequently, between the government and the Celtic peripheries (Chapter 5).

Notes

1 Notably, the SMP electoral system is also the single most frequently identified attribute of the Westminster Model in comparative politics literature (Russell & Serban 2021, 754).

2 To be precise, between 1912 and 1965 the main centre-right party in Scotland was the Unionist party, which was an independent organisation. However, it was associated with the Conservative party, and took its whip in Westminster.

3 As a multinational state, the UK's constituency design is also subject to the demographic constraints provided by national boundaries. The latter also means that the structure of the political offer is different in the various nations, especially because the nationalist parties only compete within the national borders, which however, only count for a small percentage of the population, and therefore, seats in Westminster. As of December 2019, England had 83.8 percent of the population and 82 percent of the seats in the House of Commons. A boundary commission for England is due to report in July 2023.

4 See Webb and Bale (2021, 54) for more specific figures on "block volatility" which, due to some methodological problems that they explain (ibid., 56–7), we have chosen to not use in this chapter.

5 In 1977–8, the Callaghan government (Labour) was supported by an agreement with the Liberal party, the Lib-Lab pact (Kirkup 2016).

6 See also Pelizzo and Nwokora (2014) on the gap between qualitative and quantitative approaches in the study of party system change.

7 As recently summarised by R. Rose: "Britain's first-past-the-post system is healthy as long as it does what it is supposed to do; placing control of government in the hands of a single party. This enables voters to choose a government rather than having government emerge after weeks of post-election negotiations among politicians. It also enables voters to hold the government accountable at a subsequent election and to exclude from office indefinitely, an opposition party that does not learn lessons from election defeat. On the rare occasions in the past half century in which the system has not given one party a parliamentary majority, the electorate has responded by giving a minority government a working majority at the next election" (2021b, 29). See also Denver and Johns (2022, Chapter 8) for the main arguments for and against the use of SMP.

8 In various contributions, Josep Colomer (most recently: 2018) argues that it is the strategic choices of the major parties that determine the use of a plurality electoral system, rather than the latter being the primary cause of the birth of a two-party system.

9 The contrast is particularly stark with countries, such as the Netherlands or Israel, which use a proportional representation system with a single national constituency in which party competition is homogeneous throughout the territory.

10 Malapportionment is particularly important in this respect, but other factors include turnout and the role of third parties. See Johnston et al. (2021, Chapter 6) for more details.

11 This point has been confirmed to us in Interview 9, with a prominent expert of British elections.

12 An important avenue of research which we cannot pursue here regards the shifting dynamics of intra- and inter-party value differences in the two main British parties. On this topic, which has clearly important implications on how Conservatives and Labour would structure their message in future elections, Wager et al. (2021, 1) find "a considerable disconnect between "neoliberal" Conservative members of parliament and their more centrist voters on economic issues and similarly significant disagreement on cultural issues between socially liberal Labour members of parliament and their more authoritarian voters".

13 Implicitly, our framework is also inspired by a simplified version of the important theoretical work of Stefano Bartolini, which elaborates on four key concepts at the intersect of demand and supply in the relationship between competition, collusion, and democracy, namely: contestability, availability, decidability, and vulnerability (see Bartolini 1999; 2000).

14 Recent studies on issues and volatility reinforce the argument about the difficulty of consolidating collective identities similar to those on which the twentieth-century cleavages were built. For instance, there is a strong volatility in the salience of the issues (Dennison 2020). This is particularly true for valence – as opposed to positional – issues, related to competence, have long been recognised (Denver 2005; Green & Jennings 2017). Moreover, the advantage that a party can build on valence issues and competence is subject to frequent changes in public opinion with respect to the importance of the issues on which parties and candidates are judged by the voters (De Sio & Weber 2014).

15 For sake of brevity, Table 3.2 refers to some of the studies that focus on the elements highlighted.

16 As one of our interviewees put it "people are now shopping around (...) they're to some extent free of their party loyalties, so they're floating and able to move, in some cases quite quickly, to new political homes, if they suit their Brexit predilection" (Interview 42).

4

WESTMINSTER CHALLENGED

The constrained dominance of the executive

4.1 Introduction

In the classic Westminster model, single-party governments are the norm. They command a cohesive majority in parliament, ensuring that legislation – which they introduce, controlling the parliamentary agenda – gets smoothly approved. For Anthony King, the only tools available to the parliamentary opposition are "good reasons, and time" (cited in Russell & Cowley 2018, 19). This stands in stark contrast with the more balanced executive–legislative relationship of consensus models, where cross-party agreement is the norm.

To what extent has the relationship between the executive and the legislature changed over, and because of, Brexit? This chapter seeks to provide a systematic answer to this question. In theory, two rather different outcomes are possible. On the one hand, in the words of a former Brexit minister, withdrawal from the EU was designed to allow "Parliament to take back control of UK laws and policies" (Davis 2017). With the repatriation of policy competences, Parliament would regain its effective sovereignty, taking it back from Brussels. On the other hand, however, it is the Government to be in charge of the negotiations with the EU, the withdrawal process, and the kind of future cooperation in place with the EU post-Brexit.

The early decisions taken after the 2016 referendum provide a clear illustration of the mounting tensions in executive–legislative relationships. EU rules leave it to the departing Member State – "in accordance with its own constitutional requirements" (Art. 50.1) – to decide how to activate the procedure, and the executive led by Theresa May did not consider the involvement of Parliament necessary to start the withdrawal process. This uncertainty about institutional competences had to be resolved by the courts. Eventually, the

DOI: 10.4324/9781003127680-5

Supreme Court ruled that relying on the royal prerogative to start the withdrawal process was unlawful. However, the involvement of Parliament did not stop the Government from (legitimately) fast-tracking a 133-word bill giving the PM the power to notify the UK's intention to withdraw, which Parliament rapidly approved. Given the complexity of the two-level game played by the executive between the EU and the domestic arena, and the need to take rapid decisions in a context of uncertainty, Parliament may be thus relegated to a more passive, or "reactive" – as Mezey (1979, 49) classically put it – role.

In *Models of Democracy* (1999), Lijphart uses average cabinet duration as a proxy for executive dominance. He also considers the share of minimal winning and one-party cabinets. Both measures, which belong to his executive–party dimension, are very useful for macro-comparative analyses *à la* Lijphart, but they appear to be of limited value when studying a single case. In this chapter, in order to capture how executive–legislative relations changed during the Brexit years, we rely on a number of measures and indicators. First, we use the index of opportunity for opposition influence (Powell 2000, 103–9; Matthews & Flinders 2017). This index considers two factors within the legislature enhancing the opposition's clout: the political strength of the government and the nature of the committee system. Its lowest value is for majority governments and a weak committee system (0.1), while the highest score is for minority governments and a distribution of committee chairs among all large parliamentary parties (0.75). In the former scenario, aptly describing the classic Westminster model in countries like New Zealand and the UK, "opposition party representatives may do little more than use the legislature as a forum for mobilising public opinion" (Powell 2000, 103, 106).

While this index provides a first overall picture of the changes (or lack thereof) in executive–legislative relationships, we complement it with other indicators of parliamentary influence, such as the Government's defeats in Parliament and backbenchers' agenda-setting capacity. In addition, while the empirical analysis presented in this chapter mainly focuses on the lower chamber, the role of the upper house – the House of Lords – in the bicameral system should not be overlooked. While Lijphart included a variable, "bicameralism" (V7, cf. Chapter 1) in the federal–unitary dimension – given its strong association with decentralisation or federalism – we consider here the House of Lords as an additional constraint on the action of the Government. Indeed, the Lords has the capacity to significantly delay the approval of legislation which, in a process running under tight deadlines like Brexit, is a valuable one.

Finally, we also placed our analytical focus on some critical case studies, where the institutional strains between the executive and the legislature have prominently come to light. They allow us to appreciate how such tensions unfolded, how they were eventually solved, and which institution was rewarded the most. We selected key legislation and votes on the issue of Brexit. Not only are they likely to provide the strongest evidence of any Brexit effect, but such files characterised the 2017–2019 parliamentary session, lasting (unusually) almost 2 and a half years in order to get the Brexit legislation through. While the majority of parliamentary activity was focused on activities other than Brexit, it has been shown that, beyond Brexit legislation, the government dealt with specific areas of policy rather than broader reforms and major bills (Institute for Government 2020). Indeed, the 2017–19 session has been labelled as "Brexit Parliament" (Lynch *et al.* 2019, 54).

The chapter develops as follows. Section 4.2 reviews the literature on executive–legislative relationships to map the "state of the art" before the 2016 Brexit referendum. Section 4.3 focuses on parliamentary rebellions and the EU issue. Section 4.4 assesses the capacity of Parliament to "take back control". Finally, Section 4.5 discusses the development of executive–legislative relationships as Brexit was formally over and concludes.

4.2 Executive–legislative relationships before Brexit

Executive–legislative relations have changed significantly in the last few decades or so and, *pace* Lijphart, there is robust empirical evidence to assert that Parliament has consolidated its position vis-à-vis the executive. In other words, executive dominance, as presented by the traditional Westminster model, would no longer accurately capture the essence of the UK political system as it works today.

Executive dominance is, in British constitutional history, intertwined with the principle of "parliamentary sovereignty" (cf. Chapter 2). In Albert V. Dicey's words (1885):

> Under all the formality, the antiquarianism, the shams of the British Constitution, there lies latent an element of power which has been the true course of its life and growth. This secret source of strength is the absolute omnipotence, the sovereignty of Parliament … Here constitutional theory and constitutional practice are for once at one … It is, like all sovereignty at bottom, nothing less but unlimited power.

This "unlimited power" of Parliament – which does not have any constraint in the form of a written constitution or an external check on the "constitutionality" of legislation, at least until the UK membership in the European Economic Community (EEC) in 1973, when such a role was taken up by the Court of Justice of the EU – means in actual practice executive dominance, through the "close union, nearly complete fusion" (Bagehot 2001 [1867], 11) of the executive and legislative powers. In the classic Westminster model, the capacity of Prime Ministers to control "their" party in Parliament is the "efficient secret" guaranteeing its smooth functioning and performance. The executive power to introduce legislation, together with the cohesion of the majority parliamentary party, allows the Government to implement the election manifesto and the pledges endorsed by the electorate. Through a careful use of a consolidated systems of punishments and rewards, like the allocation of governing posts, suspending the whip, or threating the deselection of MPs, the PM normally ensures that backbenchers toe the party line. It is therefore not a coincidence that, in traditional descriptions of policymaking in the UK, the role of Parliament is either ignored or under-valued (Russell & Cowley 2016, 122–4).

Yet, in the last decade or so, this characterisation of Parliament as servient vis-à-vis the executive has been challenged. As recent scholarship has argued and demonstrated, Parliament is neither weak nor further in "decline" (cf. Flinders & Kelso 2011).

First, empirical research has shown that Parliament exercises "preventive influence" (Russell et al. 2017) and, albeit not formally controlling its own agenda – which is mostly set by the Government – it is able to somewhat affect what the government proposes or does not propose. Indeed, knowing that a legislative proposal will stand little chance of being approved by Parliament, the Government may find it convenient to postpone or withdraw it.

Furthermore, while most of the amendments made by Parliament to the bills introduced by the Government fail, this figure hides more complex dynamics. Analysing 4,361 tabled amendments to 12 bills throughout the different steps of law-making, Russell and colleagues (2017) have shown that several substantive changes are compromised between Government and Parliament before the bill reaches the plenary (Russell & Gover 2017).

In addition, recent reforms in the committee system, in particular the election of the majority of select committee chairs by their fellow MPs, has strengthened Parliament. Elected chairs have gained visibility and recognition within the House of Commons, and they have generally embraced a more independent standing vis-à-vis the Government (Kelso 2016; Matthews & Flinders 2017; Russell & Cowley 2016, 130–2).

As select committees are designed to scrutinise the work of government departments and do not enjoy legislative powers, their role in law-making has often been overlooked. Once more, however, the detailed analysis on amendments of Russell et al. (2017) demonstrates how their findings and the evidence they gather are often used by the other actors. Moreover, another study on the influence of seven committees shows how about half of their recommendations had been implemented, in totality or at least in a substantial part, by the Government. Finally, the need for government ministers to explain and justify their choices before a select committee may set limits to action (Benton & Russell 2013).

Governments face increasing rebellions from backbenchers. The pioneering work by Philip [Lord] Norton indicates that, in the first four parliaments after WWII, 90 percent of the votes in the Commons did not record a single rebel within the majority – and governing – party. More recently, however,

Philip Cowley's work (i.e., 2015; Cowley & Stuart 2014) has revealed how rebellions have grown. They reached 28 percent of the votes during the last Labour government (2005–10) and got closer to 40 percent during the Coalition years (2010–15). The largest rebellions belong to these periods, with the vote on the war in Iraq in 2003 (139 rebels in the Labour Party) and the one on EU membership in 2011 (with 81 Tory rebels, and others abstaining)[1] setting new records. Significantly, while no Prime Minister – until Edward Heath in the early 1970s – had lost a vote in Parliament because of a rebellion, debacles of this kind have become more frequent (Russell & Cowley 2016). Facing a larger number of potential rebels, Governments engage more and earlier on with backbenchers, in order to avoid embarrassing defeats or, at least, lengthy and uncertain confrontations in Parliament.

Further research has also shown that reforming the House of Lords – particularly the abolition of the entitlement of most of the hereditary peers to sit and vote, with the exception of 92 hereditary peers, in 1999 – has strengthened the upper chamber and, as a consequence, bicameralism. The end of the traditional Conservative majority has made the outcome of votes more uncertain, with a pivotal role for Liberal Democrats and Independent peers (Russell 2013). During the Coalition, some of the flagship policies of the government were amended by the upper chamber, notwithstanding its Liberal–Conservative majority. The higher participation to the workings of the House of Lords seemingly confirms its enhanced role. The assertiveness of the House of Lords could also boost confidence of the rebels in the lower house. Coordinating across chambers, the rebels may seek obtaining more concessions from ministers (Russell & Cowley 2018).

Such recent changes are at least partly captured by Powell's index of opportunity for opposition influence. As Figure 4.1 shows, the index remained close to its minimum value – meaning strong governments, and weak parliaments – for decades. Barring some limited exceptions, post-WWII single-party majority

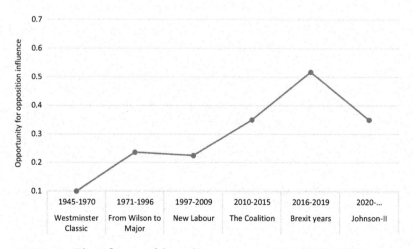

FIGURE 4.1 The influence of the parliamentary opposition (1945–2021)

government is the norm. The establishment of select committees in 1979, and then the reform of the committee system under the Coalition – notably the election of committee chairs – pushed the index up. Due to the latter reform, Matthews and Flinders (2017) assigned the score of 0.35 to the 2010–15 period.

In the Brexit years, the index reached its peak, due to the combination of (supported) minority governments (May II and Johnson I) and a robust committee system. Incidentally, the single highest score is assigned to the first government led by Johnson which, despite the confidence-and-supply agreement with the DUP, failed to command a majority in the Commons.

4.3 Rebellions and government defeats in the House of Commons

4.3.1 Rebels and the EU issue

For British political parties, the EU issue is, as the former Tory leader William Hague put it, "a ticking bomb" (cited in Lynch & Whitaker 2013, 337). While in continental Europe it was the signing of the Maastricht Treaty (1992) to symbolically mark the end of the "permissive consensus" on European integration – opening the era of the "constraining dissensus" (Hooghe & Marks 2009) with rising contestation and politicisation of the EU – British Euroscepticism is much older and dates back to the early 1960s, when membership in the EEC started being considered. The debate on membership – on joining the six founding Member States of the Community – was bitterly divisive, and the parliamentary approval of the *European Communities Act* (1972) was a particularly thorny issue for the Labour Party, internally divided between its Eurosceptic left wing and a more moderate and pro-European component which, in 1981, would contribute to the formation of the Social Democratic Party. Indeed, opinions on what EEC membership meant for the "sovereignty" of Parliament were very heterogenous, with some MPs considering it a "surrender" to Brussels and others appreciating, instead, the new opportunities of "sharing" sovereignty (Bogdanor 2019; Gee Young 2016; Norton 1975; cf. Interview 26).

Thus, parliamentary votes on Europe have historically represented – well before the Brexit years – a compelling test for the capacity of the two main parties to manage their internal dissent. The "Maastricht rebels" represented a thorn in the side for John Major's government which, eventually, ended up losing its Commons majority. In the third reading of the Maastricht Bill, there was a peak of 41 MPs voting against the Tory whip and 71 against the Labour leadership. Ultimately, however, the Conservative Party managed to secure a robust majority even after the rebellion, as most Labour MPs abstained. During Blair's governments, conflict on the EU issue remained for the most part underground – although it featured prominently in the competition for leadership of the Conservative Party (Baker 2002, 324–6) – and, in the votes on the ratification of the Treaty of Lisbon, there was a maximum of 28 rebels within Labour ranks and 20 among Conservative MPs (Baldini *et al.* 2020, 223–4).

Because of the referendum lock introduced in 2011 by the Coalition (cf. Chapter 2), any new amendment to the Treaty of Lisbon would have required to be confirmed by a referendum. While the EU treaties were eventually not further amended, the EU issue nonetheless gained prominence during the premiership of David Cameron. The Coalition undertook a "review of the balance of competences" with the EU, whose recommendations – for the disappointment of the Eurosceptics – could not be taken by the Government to start renegotiating the terms of membership with the EU.[2] As is well known, however, pushed by the Eurosceptic wing in his own party and because of the growing electoral threat represented by UKIP, Cameron promised a referendum on membership in his Bloomberg speech (January 2013). Following the unexpected Conservative majority in the 2015 general election – and the end of the Coalition with the pro-EU Liberal Democrats – Cameron found himself in the position to have to implement the referendum pledge. Indeed, as the Conservative manifesto put it, after a renegotiation with Brussels UK membership in the EU would depend on the outcome of a "straight in–out referendum … by the end of 2017" (The Conservative Party Manifesto 2015, 30).

Immediately after the 2015 elections, the Eurosceptic wing of the Conservative Party asked Cameron to keep his word and implement the referendum pledge. On 28 May 2015, the Government presented the European Union Referendum Bill. Cameron was confident that the swift approval of the legislation on the referendum, and the renegotiation of the terms of membership with the EU, would allow him to keep his grip on the party and put the EU issue to rest. Unfortunately for him, events followed a rather different trajectory. Through the different parliamentary readings, the approval of the EU Referendum Act provided a clear illustration of the conflicts featuring inside the Conservative Party on Brexit. Although on 9 June 2015, at second reading, the bill was supported by a large majority of MPs – with only the Scottish nationalists in opposition – key differences between Eurosceptics and pro-EU MPs emerged during the long parliamentary debate, such as on the extension of the franchise to the age of 16 (as in the referendum on Scottish independence), the timing of the referendum and, especially, the (lifting of) purdah rules, with ministries asked not to disclose information provided by the government departments during the referendum campaign.

Yet, it was at the third reading of the bill, on 7 September, that the internal splits in the Tory party came most prominently to light, as a difference of opinion turned into rebellious votes. On a Tory-promoted amendment on the Government influence in the referendum campaign, 37 Conservative MPs rebelled. The list also included four former ministers who served in cabinet with Cameron and the chairman of the 1922 Committee. In the run-up to the third reading, Cameron and his team engaged in protracted negotiations with the Tory Eurosceptics to avoid a defeat in the Commons. On 2 September, David

Lidington, the minister for European affairs, met with both Labour MPs and Conservative rebels to discuss changes to the bill. The Government had already agreed to rephrase the question of the referendum (bringing explicitly in the option "to leave" the European Union) and offered a compromise on the purdah rule to restrict its own use of the Whitehall apparatus during the referendum campaign. Notwithstanding this offer, several Eurosceptic members still believed that the purdah period was an issue.

To appease the rebels, the Government further accepted an amendment by a Conservative backbencher, requiring it to give a four-month notice before fixing the date of the referendum. This amendment ruled out having a "snap" referendum – which, it was believed, favoured the Government and the Remain option – and was a costly choice for Cameron. As Lidington stated in the House of Commons: "in the interest of trying to secure as great a consensus as possible, [...] of bridge-building, I am prepared to accept the amendment" (HC Hansard 7 September 2015). Notwithstanding the concessions, when the Government brought forward its own version of the purdah rule to a vote,[3] 37 Tory rebels joined a united opposition, causing the first defeat of the Cameron II government in the Commons on a piece of legislation (Bennet 2016).[4]

Once the EU Referendum Bill passed through the Commons, the Government faced the House of Lords where, on 18 November 2015, it was defeated on the extension of the franchise to the age of 16. Although this amendment was, ultimately, rejected by the Commons, where it was deemed to be inadmissible, generating financial costs for the administration,[5] this case illustrates that the House of Lords was not afraid to oppose the executive.

The difficult approval of the EU Referendum Bill reveals the strength of the internal party opposition led by Eurosceptic backbenchers. Their principled opposition to the EU made them unwilling to compromise and to accept the concessions that the Government was ready to make.[6] Cameron's failure to appease the most Eurosceptic wing of his party was a feature of his last year in office. On 24 June 2016, as the UK chose to leave the EU, Cameron stepped down, ending his premiership and political career. In his resignation speech, the departing PM acknowledged that leaving the EU and negotiating a new relationship with it would have required "strong, determined and committed leadership". It was for the new PM, Theresa May, to succeed displaying such skills.

4.3.2 After the Brexit referendum: the beginning of the withdrawal process

The first ten months in office were, for Theresa May, relatively void of conflict, at least in Parliament, despite the uncertainty of the post-referendum period and the lack of preparation of the civil service on Brexit (no contingency plan on Brexit had been prepared). From July 2016 to May 2017 the Conservative majority was cohesive, with very few defections in parliamentary divisions; on the other hand, the Labour leadership faced huge issues in managing backbenchers.

Indeed, the Labour parliamentary party was experiencing a particularly pronounced "MP-versus-constituency" disconnection on the EU issue. According to Whitaker (2020), only ten of Labour's 232 MPs in 2016 voted Leave in the referendum, while estimates indicate that in 148 constituencies where the 232 Labour MPs had been elected there was a majority for Leave.

The main difficulty for the Prime Minister was of procedural nature and centred on the power (or lack thereof) of the executive to trigger Art. 50 of the TEU without the prior authorisation of Parliament. May's government was forced to introduce a bill in Parliament following a judgement of the Supreme Court on 24 January 2017, ruling that the executive could not trigger Art. 50 relying on the royal prerogative over foreign affairs. Thus, the EU (Notification of) Withdrawal Bill was introduced to the House of Commons, for its first reading, on 26 January 2017 and fast-tracked to allow the PM to invoke Art. 50 before the (self-imposed) end-of-March deadline. The official position of the Labour Party was not to oppose the bill – thus endorsing the Government's position – issuing a three-line whip to contain opposition within its own ranks. The Labour Party also accepted the bill to be fast-tracked, despite diffuse dissatisfaction among its MPs for the limited time set for parliamentary scrutiny.

The second reading of the bill took place in the Commons on 31 January and 1 February. The bill passed its second reading by a large majority of 384, with both the Conservative and Labour Parties backing it. Opening the debate, however, the shadow minister for Brexit, Keir Starmer, confirmed that Labour accepted the outcome of the referendum and would not block the Prime Minister from triggering Art. 50, but he also explicitly recognised that "for the Labour Party, this is a very difficult bill" (HC Hansard 31 January 2017). Among Tory backbenchers, there were some isolated expressions of discontent, but the "Father of the House" Kenneth Clarke eventually cast the only rebellious vote. On the contrary, it was the Labour Party which, despite the three-line whip, could not contain defections among its members. A few days before the second reading vote, Corbyn received the resignation letters of two members of the shadow cabinet who intended to vote against triggering Art. 50.[7] Later, another shadow minister resigned, while two other shadow ministers voted against their party, together with several frontbenchers.[8] Overall, about one-fifth of the parliamentary Labour Party rebelled. This was the largest rebellion on the EU for Labour since the third reading of the Maastricht Bill.[9] With no less than 16 frontbenchers rebelling, Jeremy Corbyn had to reshuffle the shadow cabinet. However, the leadership of the party decided to be "flexible" (*The Guardian* 2 February 2017) and no disciplinary actions were taken.

In the third reading of the bill in the Commons, which took place on 6–8 February, not only did the Labour rebellion not recede, but it increased in strength – 52 Labour MPs, with an increase of five from the second reading, defied the whip.[10] The leadership of the party, fearing even more problems, did not take any decisive action, with rebels simply receiving a written warning.

The approval of the EU (Notification of) Withdrawal Bill clearly shows that the early steps of Brexit have been more difficult for the (official) opposition, which was divided among members rejecting the referendum outcome and a more pragmatic component that, albeit often equally opposed to Brexit in principle, did not believe that Parliament should resist withdrawal from the EU (but was keen to define *how* and *which* Brexit should occur).[11]

4.3.3 From the 2017 general election to the end of May's premiership

The event that fundamentally changed executive–legislative relationships, significantly weakening the government, was Theresa May's unexpected decision – based on very favourable opinion polls[12] – to call a snap election in June 2017. Her gamble backfired: with only 48.8 percent of the seats controlled by the Tories, the PM needed the "confidence and supply" of the ten Members of the Democratic Unionist Party (DUP) to form a minority government. The agreement with the DUP ensured a majority of six – and a working majority of 13 – which became progressively smaller as some MPs seated on the Tory benches crossed the floor and quit the Conservative Party.

A minority government in itself is a significant deviation from the Westminster model. It suffices to note that this was only the fourth minority government in post-WWII history: Harold Wilson led a minority government after the 1974 elections, while in two other cases – James Callaghan in 1977 and John Major in 1996 – the slim majority was lost during the term. Yet, May was not only leading a minority government. Her party was also fundamentally divided over Brexit. Therefore, the two conditions that Lijphart identified as necessary for "strong cabinet leadership" (1999, 12) were missing. As Table 4.1 shows, comparing different periods starting with the Labour government in 2005, a high proportion of significant rebellions – with ten or more MPs voting against the Conservative whip – characterised the

TABLE 4.1 Rebellions and defeats for the governments in the HoC (2005–19)

	Labour government 2005–10	*Coalition government 2010–15*	*Conservative (majority) government 2015–17*	*Conservative (minority) government 2017–19*
Percentage of rebellious votes (at least one rebel)	Lab: 37 Cons: 15	Cons: 37 Lab: 16	Cons: 26 Lab: 15	Cons: 35 Lab: 38
Percentage of rebellious votes (at least ten rebels)	Lab: 10 Cons: 2	Cons: 9 Lab: 2	Cons: 2 Lab: 3	Cons: 15 Lab: 5
Government defeats (No.)	6	4	2	PM May: 28 PM Johnson: 12

Sources: Slapin *et al.* 2018; Institute for Government 2020; The Public Whip (www.publicwhip.org.uk).

2017–19 parliament, boosting the number of defeats for the government (28 for May alone, all but one in her second year of minority government).

A senior clerk of the House of Commons (Interview 14; cf. Interview 15) recalls the importance of the electoral outcome for executive–legislative relationships:

> Raw arithmetic made a big difference there. And I think part of that was because, although you had a Government going from a majority into a minority, in many ways it still continued to behave like it was a majority government. In terms of its attitude towards select committees, in terms of its attitude towards the whole process. It was very much 'the Government negotiates, Parliament has a straightforward approve/not approve role'.

An interpretation underscored by another clerk of the House of Commons (Interview 25):

> Parliament is not designed to work with a minority government; it is not the default mode of governments in the UK to function with a minority in Parliament. What that means is that the instinct is always to try to win on as narrow a basis as possible. We can see that in the way the Government has been very reluctant to reach out to Labour, and others, to try to get some of their policies through.[13]

A clear illustration of the difficulty of working with a minority government is effectively provided by the attempt of the Government to maintain a majority on bill committees, in order not to have its bills – particularly the Brexit bills – heavily amended at committee level. As the Commons Leader Andrea Leadsom put it, the Selection Committee nominating MPs to committees should "interpret paragraph (2) of Standing Order No. 86 (Nomination of general committees) in such a way that where a committee has an odd number of members the Government shall have a majority".[14] Normally, a norm requiring party proportionality is in place, meaning that the majority party has a majority of MPs in committees. However, this is obviously not the case in periods of minority government. The (ultimately successful) attempt to stack key committees with Tory MPs was condemned by the opposition leader as an "unprecedented attempt to rig parliament and grab power".[15]

The bill to incorporate all existing EU legislation into British law – the EU (Withdrawal) Bill, also known as "the Great Repeal Bill" – was the first key test for the new government. The vote on the second reading took place on 11 September 2017, it was won by the Government by a majority of 36, and the only defectors were seven Labour backbenchers, mainly representing Leave constituencies, voting with the Government. The first parliamentary test for the new minority government led by Theresa May was, therefore, at first sight easily passed. Yet, the situation behind the cohesive votes of the Conservative Party was, in reality, more complex. A group of Conservative MPs, large enough to create more than a headache to the Government, made clear ahead of vote that its support for the bill was all but unconditional. In order to support it, it demanded reassurances that significant changes to the bill would be introduced before third reading.

What worried some MPs the most were the so-called "Henry VIII powers", which were regarded as a "grab" of parliamentary competences. The government advocated for itself the power to take rapid decisions without parliamentary scrutiny since, it was argued, the incorporation of the entire corpus of EU legislation into British law required more efficient decision-making procedures. The former Attorney General, Dominic Grieve, led the criticisms of the bill.[16] As this controversy centred more on the institutional (in)balance of power between the executive and the legislature, rather than on the EU as such, support within the ranks of the Tory backbenches was broader than it usually was.

The Government avoided an embarrassing and possibly life-threatening rebellion – in a context where the leadership of Theresa May was called into question[17] – carefully negotiating a compromise with the critics. It promised to take on board the observations made on the Henry VIII powers and amend the bill accordingly. It also agreed to expand the timing for the scrutiny of the bill and confirmed its willingness to "discuss" the points raised by MPs "on both sides of the House" (HC Hansard 11 September 2017). At the second reading, the threat of a large rebellions was therefore avoided.[18]

It did not take long, however, before the May government lost his first vote in the House of Commons. On 13 December 2017, an amendment tabled by Dominic Grieve to give Parliament a "meaningful vote" on the withdrawal agreement was supported by 12 Tory backbenchers. This remained the only defeat of her government on the EU (Withdrawal) Bill in the House of Commons. After the Lords introduced its own amendments to the bill (Thimont Jack 2020; cf. further below), the EU (Withdrawal) Bill – which had been debated for 272 (!) hours overall – finally received royal assent on 26 June 2018.

It was only after the UK and the EU had agreed on the text of the withdrawal agreement – on 28 November 2018 – making Brexit appear in sight, that the Government started to regularly lose votes in the House of Commons. On 4 December 2018, the Government lost three times, including on an amendment to give Parliament more control over Brexit. The vote featured 26 Tory rebels – the largest rebellion up to that moment – and cross-party support. The size of the opposition (including from a large section of the Tory parliamentary party) mounting against the withdrawal agreement pushed the PM to make a last-minute move to postpone the final vote, which was eventually rescheduled for the new year. The PM admitted to the House that she was postponing it because otherwise the Government would have lost it by "a significant margin", mainly due to dissatisfaction – by the DUP and Tory backbenchers – around the institutional arrangements on the so-called Irish backstop.

TABLE 4.2 Defeats on the EU issue by the governments led by PM Theresa May

Date	Division	No. Tory rebels	Outcome of the vote
13 December 2017	Amendment (Cons: Dominic Grieve) on the *EU (Withdrawal) Bill*	12	309 vs 305
17 July 2018	Amendment (Cons: Phillip Lee) on the *Trade Bill*	12	305 vs 301
4 December 2018	Government amendment on the contempt motion	2	307 vs 311
4 December 2018	Contempt motion in publishing of legal advice	2	311 vs 293
4 December 2018	Amendment (Cons: Dominic Grieve) on the motion on the withdrawal agreement	25	321 vs 299
8 January 2019	Amendment (Lab: Yvette Cooper) on the *Finance (No. 3) Bill*	20	303 vs 296
9 January 2019	Amendment (Cons: Dominic Grieve) on the motion on the withdrawal agreement	17	308 vs 297
15 January 2019	Vote on the withdrawal agreement or *meaningful vote I*	118	432 vs 202
29 January 2019	Amendment (Cons: Caroline Spelman) on May's declaration on the withdrawal agreement	17	318 vs 310
14 February 2019	Government motion on withdrawal from the EU	5	303 vs 258
12 March 2019	Vote on the withdrawal agreement or *meaningful vote II*	75	242 vs 391
13 March 2019	Amendment (Cons: Caroline Spelman) on the motion on the withdrawal of the UK from the EU	9	312 vs 308
13 March 2019	Amended motion on the withdrawal of the UK from the EU	17	321 vs 278
25 March 2019	Amendment (Cons: Oliver Letwin) on the motion on the next steps in the Brexit process	30	329 vs 302
27 March 2019	Amendment (Cons: Oliver Letwin) on the motion that confers to the House of Commons control of its business	33	331 vs 287
29 March 2019	Vote on the withdrawal agreement or *meaningful vote III*	34	286 vs 344
1 April 2019	Amendment (Cons: Oliver Letwin) on the motion that confers to the House of Commons control of its business	28	322 vs 277

(Continued)

TABLE 4.2 Continued

Date	Division	No. Tory rebels	Outcome of the vote
3 April 2019	*European Union (Withdrawal) (No. 5) Bill* known as "*Cooper-Letwin Bill*" – motion on the business order	14	312 vs 311
3 April 2019	*European Union (Withdrawal) (No. 5) Bill* – second reading	14	315 vs 310
3 April 2019	*European Union (Withdrawal) (No. 5) Bill* – amendment (Cons: George Eustice)	15	304 vs 313
3 April 2019	*European Union (Withdrawal) (No. 5) Bill* – third reading	14	313 vs 312

However, her desperate attempt to buy time did not affect the outcome: on 15 January 2019, the Government lost the "meaningful vote" by an unprecedented margin (230 votes), the largest ever defeat for a British government in the democratic era. Reacting to the vote of the House, the statement by the PM acknowledged defeat, but it was also keen to point out that Parliament fell short of providing any indication on what Brexit (if any) it really wanted:

> The House has spoken and the Government will listen. It is clear that the House does not support this deal, but tonight's vote tells us nothing about what it does support; nothing about how, or even if, it intends to honour the decision the British people took in a referendum that Parliament decided to hold.
>
> *(HC Hansard, 15 January 2019)*

The next two votes on the deal (the latter on the withdrawal agreement only) were also lost, with a reduced majority of 149 and 58, respectively (see Table 4.2 for an overview of Government's defeats). As a result, Brexit was postponed well beyond the originally scheduled date of 29 March 2019, bringing May's premiership to a premature conclusion.

4.4 Taking back control: Parliament and the strains of Brexit

4.4.1 The interpretation of the standing orders and parliamentary procedure

The attempts of Parliament – that is, a cross-party coalition composed by the opposition and Conservative backbenchers – to "take control" of the Brexit process, or at least to meaningfully constrain the actions of the Government, were conducted through a non-conventional interpretation of the parliamentary rules of procedure. As the *Institute for Government* documents in its *Parliamentary Monitor 2020*:

During the 2017–19 session alone, over 1,000 points of order were raised by MPs in the Commons [...] roughly 44 hours of the Commons' time were spent on points of order – more time than was spent debating several pieces of legislation that were passed during the session. This illustrates that the increased salience of concerns over process came to dominate debates more than concerns over policy.

(Institute for Government 2020a, 34)

These developments unambiguously show that "procedure matters" (Norton 2001, 24). Procedures have consequences, they can be constraints as well as creating opportunities for political action and, notwithstanding the difficult institutional context for opposition parties, backbenchers can use procedure as a weapon in agenda-setting and to exert influence over the policy process.

Conflict on the interpretation of the parliamentary rules became prominent towards the end of 2018, when the conclusion of the withdrawal agreement with the EU made Brexit a very concrete outcome. In January 2019, the Speaker John Bercow selected an amendment to a motion on the business of the house, proposed by the Conservative backbencher Dominic Grieve, which eventually changed the "Brexit timetable". The EU Withdrawal Act compelled the Prime Minister, in case of a parliamentary rejection of the negotiated deal with the EU, to make a statement within 21 calendar days, and then to allow a vote within seven sitting days. The Grieve amendment, instead, compelled the government to table a motion outlining a "Plan B" within three sitting days.

To understand why the Speaker's decision to select the amendment sparked a heated debate in the House, it is necessary to go back to the early days of December 2018, when the House of Commons approved the business of the House motion put forth by the Government to update the Brexit debate, stating:

No motion to vary or supplement the provisions of this Order shall be made except by a Minister of the Crown; and the question on any such motion shall be put forthwith.

(HC Hansard 4 December 2018)

The key reference text on the interpretation of the parliamentary rulebook – Erskine May – explains that "forthwith" means "without debate and usually without the possibility of amendment" (Erskine May 2019, Part 3, par. 20.45). Yet, about a month later, Bercow selected the Grieve amendment, thus prioritising "what he perceived to be the 'will of the Commons' over the existing rules as they stood at the time" (Simson Caird 2019).

The Speaker's decision was strongly contested within the ranks of the Conservative Party. On the one hand, several MPs vocally condemned his decision to select the amendment. Mark Francois, a prominent Brexiteer, expressed incredulity about the subversion of tradition: "I have been here for 18 years and I have never known any Speaker to overrule a motion of the House of Commons" while another Eurosceptic MP, Andrew Percy, warned that the public would be encouraged "to believe that there is a conspiracy and a procedural stitch-up taking place by a House of Commons which is grossly out of touch with the referendum result" (HC Hansard 9 January 2019).

Bercow stood with his decision. He acknowledged the importance of precedent, but strongly underlined that "precedent does not completely bind [...] If we were guided only by precedent, manifestly nothing in our procedures would ever change. Things do change". It was ultimately for Parliament to take a decision, voting for or against the amendment. He further added that there is a responsibility for the Speaker "to stand up for the rights of the House of Commons, including the views of dissenters on the Government Benches [...] and to defend the rights of opposition parties" concluding that his job was "not to be a cheerleader for the Executive branch" (HC Hansard 9 January 2019). In any case, a borderline interpretation, allowed by the Speaker, has been used to change – according to the critics, frustrate – the Brexit process.[19]

4.4.2 Controlling the business of the House of Commons

In early 2019, after the massive defeat of the government in the vote on the withdrawal agreement,[20] Conservative backbenchers and the opposition attempted to take control of the parliamentary agenda by suspending Standing Order 14, which reads:

> Save as provided in this order, government business shall have precedence at every sitting

It also lists some specific and limited exceptions, such as the Fridays dedicated to Private Members Bills, 20 days allocated to opposition parties and 35 days for debates chosen by the Backbenchers' Business Committee. In all other circumstances, it is the Government which decides what is debated, and when. Despite some attempts to limit executive control over the parliamentary agenda – i.e., the recommendations of the Wright Committee on Reform, (see Russell & Paun 2007) – the executive still very much controls it.

However, on 25 March 2019 a successful amendment to the government motion, tabled by the Conservative backbencher Oliver Letwin, set aside time for the House to hold a series of "indicative votes" (non-binding) on various Brexit options. Standing Order 14 was therefore suspended, and the House of Commons took control of its own agenda.

Unsurprisingly, this conduct of parliamentary business has been harshly criticised by Eurosceptic MPs. The suspension of Standing Order 14 was labelled as a "constitutional revolution" by the veteran MP Bill Cash, while another Tory MP, Bob Seely, described it as "parliamentary insurgency". On the other hand, the proponent of the amendment, Oliver Letwin, evoked the principle of "exclusive cognisance" – a corollary of parliamentary sovereignty – because of which it is Parliament, and Parliament alone, interpreting, judging, and determining its own procedure (Evans 2017). As Letwin put it in the debate:

> the Order Paper of the House of Commons is governed by the Standing Orders of the House of Commons, and those are the property of the House of Commons and nobody else. They are the property not of the Executive but of the House of Commons. [...] That principle goes back not to 1906 when the Government—in my view, improperly—instituted Standing Order 14 in its current form, but way back into the origins of Parliament. From the very beginning, Parliament sought to establish its right, through the Speaker and otherwise, to control its own proceedings, which is a very proper thing for Parliament to do.
>
> *(HC Hansard 27 March 2019)*

Whatever the veracity of this historical account – speaking in support of the Government, Jacob Rees-Mogg claimed that "it is a principle of the greatest antiquity that the business of the House is guided by those representing the sovereign in Parliament" (HC Hansard 27 March 2019) – what matters here is that Standing Order 14 gives the edge to the executive on determining the parliamentary agenda, constituting a backbone of the "Westminster model" in Parliament. The suspension of this widely accepted norm is therefore a huge procedural innovation which, for its critics, impacts on the way government (should) work.

Controlling its own agenda, the House of Commons held several indicative (non-binding) votes on 27 March and 1 April 2019, testing the existence of a majority supporting any Brexit option. Ultimately, however, the House failed to endorse any of the available options and, at the end of the last day of voting, it was clear only that the House rejected a no-deal Brexit. MPs had the possibility to vote a straight "yes" or "no" to any of the alternatives, rather than using more complex procedures such as the single transferable vote or any ranked choice voting system. The rules themselves did not favour building a compromise, as "some MPs preferred not to support proposals that they probably considered better than a hard Brexit or May's deal, to increase the probability of a better relative positioning of their preferred option" (Giuliani 2021b, 8). Thus, a clear alternative to the plans of the executive did not emerge, showing the limits of parliamentary initiative. As an analyst of Parliament observed:

> We saw the limits in the ability of the Commons to act proactively in our system. They were very reactionary, but with a limited ability to actually put forward constructive proposals that garner consensus. Even if the Government was politically weak, institutionally I think it could have had a much rougher ride.
>
> *(Interview 15)*

On the other hand, Parliament has been resolutely opposed to "no deal", forcing the Government to postpone the Brexit deadline by approving, in less than a week, a Private Member's Bill (PMB) – the EU Withdrawal (No. 5) Bill – sponsored by the Labour MP Yvette Cooper.[21] Thanks to the Letwin's business motion, this PMB was considered in what would have normally been government time – i.e., on a Wednesday rather than on a Friday, the day normally reserved for PMBs – and was therefore debated and voted by the whole House.

The success of PMBs is normally very low. While the number of successful PMBs was not exceptional in the 2017–19 session – as 15 of them were approved (3.8 percent), while 8 (4.6 percent) were supported by MPs in the shorter 2016–17 session (Hansard Society, 2019) – it was noteworthy that backbenchers voted twice to take control of the House of Commons, and twice – in March and September 2019 – they compelled the Government to request an extension of the Brexit deadline to Brussels (Institute for Government 2020, 43–4).

4.4.3 The role of the House of Lords

An additional constraint for the Government came from the House of Lords. The lack of a Conservative majority in the upper house – the Conservative Party currently holds less than a third of the seats, having lost a majority following the 1999 reform – coupled with the pro-EU attitude of most peers (including several Conservative peers), made it even more difficult for the Government to pass legislation (Smith 2019). In addition, the very existence of the Salisbury convention – according to which the House of Lords does not oppose the bills implementing the election manifesto – is debatable during a minority, or a coalition, government (House of Lords 2017).

The upper house has frequently opposed the Government on Brexit. Starting with the EU Referendum Bill, the Lords have attempted to amend – often in a substantial way – the bills voted by the lower house. In the case of the EU Referendum Bill, the Lords approved amendments to extend the franchise to the age of 16 and to British citizens resident in an EU Member State by more than 15 years. However, when the bill made its return to the lower house – due to the so-called "ping pong" among chambers – all the Lords' amendments were defeated. Eventually, the Lords did not press further on its amendments and approved it. As a Tory peer told us: "this House has an ability to repair chaotic situations in legislation quite effectively" (Interview 11). Yet, when the Government does not back its amendments, the House of Lords normally retreats.

A revealing case is, once more, that of the EU (Withdrawal) Bill. The bill received extensive scrutiny by the Lords – about five months passed between the first and the third reading – and the Government lost 15 times. Eventually, the Government accepted one of the Lords' amendments and made concessions on eight of the remaining 14 (Institute for Government 2018). The most prominent concession was on the amendment prescribing that if either the House of Commons did not approve the deal with the EU, or the Government did not meet the deadlines set by Parliament, the executive would follow "any direction" indicated by a parliamentary resolution. The executive did not accept being so constrained by Parliament. A compromise was eventually found and, in the case of rejection of the deal, a minister would have made a statement in the House of Commons, with the latter voting on a motion "in neutral terms" (that is, emendable at the Speaker's discretion).

Interestingly, the Lords' amendment had already been tabled in the House of Commons (Simson Caird 2018) – incidentally, by MP Dominic Grieve – showing that the upper chamber may cooperate closely with the lower chamber in what is, effectively and not only formally, a bicameral system, albeit unbalanced (cf. Russell & Cowley 2018). At the same time, it has to be stressed that it is not easy for the Lords to work in a politically charged environment: the influence of the upper chamber is judged to be "inversely proportional to the political excitement of the situation" (Interview 11). When the changes made by the Lords are more political than technical, and conflict with the executive and the lower chamber becomes more heated, the very legitimacy of the Lords can be brought into question, with demands for its reform, or even abolition, by the media and elected politicians. True, situations where the government has the urgency to pass legislation quickly – i.e., because of an upcoming Brexit deadline – give more prominence to the "power to delay" of the Lords.[22] Ultimately, however, in the super-politicised context of Brexit there existed clear limits for the policy influence of the unelected chamber, which tends to operate best "in the shadows" and when it has the opportunity to offer its technical scrutiny of bills (Interview 21).

4.4.4 Johnson's government and the final battle with Parliament

The conflict between Government and Parliament reached its climax when Boris Johnson, PM since July 2019, "prorogued" Parliament, which was not expected to meet from 9 September until 14 October 2019. Johnson claimed that a fresh start was necessary, as the parliamentary session had lasted far too long. For the opposition, such a lengthy prorogation was deemed unnecessary, and was being instrumentally used by the PM to avoid scrutiny on his Brexit agenda.

Following the announcement of prorogation of Parliament, on 3 September 2019 the House of Commons scheduled an emergency debate – based on Standing Order 24 – which was, in turn, followed the day after by a new suspension of Standing Order 14 on the business of the House. These actions were triggered by the need to compel the Government to request an extension of Art. 50 to avoid a "no deal" scenario. No deal was then effectively ruled out by the EU Withdrawal (No. 2) Act, also known as Benn Act from the surname of the MP sponsoring it, the Labour chair of the Brexit Select Committee Hilary Benn, which was approved in a single day in the House of Commons and two in the upper house.

The successful attempt by the House of Commons to take control of its own agenda led to another heated debate, and to the expulsion from the Conservative Party of 21 rebels. The most contentious issue was the interpretation of Standing Order 24, reading as follows:

> a Member rising in his place at the commencement of public business may propose, in an application lasting not more than three minutes, that the House should debate a specific and important matter that should have urgent consideration.

The procedural controversy centred around the fact that the emergency debate was used to table a substantive motion. On the one hand, Jacob Rees-Mogg – then Leader of the House – argued that, by allowing an emergency debate on a substantive motion, the Speaker authorised something "constitutionally irregular". In particular, he criticised the Speaker of holding inconsistent views on Standing Order 24 – on 19 April 2018, in light of two emergency debates on the UK's decision to take military action in Syria, Bercow had ruled that, to allow for the tabling of a substantive motion in a situation of emergency, the Standing Orders would need to be amended – and to attempt to frustrate the outcome of the referendum:

> Sovereignty in this House comes from the British people. The idea that we can overrule 17.4 million people is preposterous, and the idea that our rules do not exist to protect the people from arrogant power grabs is mistaken. Those rules are there for the protection of the people [...] The motion would allow a designated Member—or a few of the Illuminati who are taking the powers to themselves—to give notice of the presentation of this Bill on the first day of a new Session.
>
> *(HC Hansard, 3 September 2019)*

People's sovereignty is here opposed to parliamentary sovereignty and, importantly, the former is deemed superior to the latter. According to Rees-Mogg – speaking in his capacity as the Leader of the House, and therefore officially for the Conservative Party – disregarding the will of the people, through disregarding the procedural rules – means "stretch[ing] the elastic of our constitution near to breaking point". It is not only a right, but a duty of the executive to control the parliamentary agenda, precisely in view of implementing the people's mandate.

On the opposite side, although still seated on Conservative benches (but he and other MPs would lose the party whip after their "rebellion"), Kenneth Clarke made a plea for a different role for Parliament. He applauded the Speaker's decision on Standing Order 24 as it gave Parliament the possibility to "assert itself". In his view, what should guide members is the pursuit of the "national interest" which, in the specific circumstances, meant avoiding a no-deal Brexit. The onus to act is on Parliament (and its MPs across benches) who, in order to minimise damage and avoid an outcome not supported by any majority, "must seize its own agenda" (HC Hansard 3 September 2019).

In reality, prorogation was not as lengthy as the Government imagined it to be. The issue escalated to the Supreme Court, which found prorogation unlawful as it effectively curtailed "without reasonable justification, the power of parliament to carry out its constitutional functions as a legislature and as the body responsible for the supervision of the executive" (The Supreme Court 2019). The Supreme Court, as it had done at the start of the Brexit process, protected the constitutional role of Parliament which, on 24 September, could reconvene again.

Before the conflict between the Johnson government and Parliament could make it manifest again in the House, the Prime Minister announced to the Conservative Party conference his new slogan "Get Brexit Done". Implementing the referendum became the key (if not the only) objective of the Government. A new and mostly unexpected agreement with the EU – with a new solution, opposed by the DUP, on Northern Ireland – was due to be voted by the House of Commons on 19 October 2019, unusually on a Saturday.[23] Yet, the House of Commons voted an amendment – tabled by MP Oliver Letwin – which postponed the vote on the agreement until the approval of legislation on its implementation – i.e., the Withdrawal Agreement Bill. After a few days, as the business motion on its (quick) approval was also rejected, Johnson concluded that "enough was enough". He decided to place the Brexit vote on hold and, with the decisive support of the Labour Party,[24] called a snap election, to be held on 12 December 2019.

4.5 Conclusions: the 2019 general election and the role of Parliament post-Brexit

From the general election of June 2017 to November 2019, the Conservative minority government, weakened by frequent rebellions and occasional alliances across parties in the two chambers, did not manage to implement its Brexit plans. Yet, in the 2019 general election, the Tories took control of the 56.1 percent of the Commons seats, holding a comfortable majority of 80. In addition, Johnson controlled a relatively cohesive parliamentary party on the EU, having deselected most pro-EU MPs who had previously rebelled against his government. With such a majority, the PM was back in the driving seat and the rapid vote on the withdrawal agreement – which had ended the tenure of Theresa May – offered proof that, ultimately,

> the deal that we have, that Parliament is able to vote on, was negotiated by the executive: we can see the extent to which the executive was in control of that process by the degree to which it came up with something the Parliament didn't like.
>
> *(Interview 23)*

Brexit was finally done on 31 January 2020 and, as the former chancellor Philip Hammond – incidentally, one of the most prominent Tory rebels who had the whip removed by Johnson – observed "all of the things that we've got very excited about ... will be completely irrelevant, because a government with a majority can decide everything" (interviewed by Guerrera 2019). Or, as an expert of the British constitution put it: "Parliament has won a series of minor battles, but the executive is continuing to win the war" (Interview 21).

With a substantial majority in the House of Commons and an overall cohesive party on the EU issue, it may be argued that the conditions for a power-hoarding executive are back in place. However, Parliament has become – with a process starting well before Brexit made its appearance on the political agenda – structurally stronger than it used to be. For instance, the system of select committees, and the elections of their chairs in particular, has contributed to make backbenchers more assertive and less controllable by the Government (Kelso 2016; Matthews & Flinders 2017; Interviews 24 and 27). Moreover, the confrontation between the executive and Parliament over the Brexit years could have socialised a new cohort of MPs to new dynamics and behavioural norms, making them less easily well-disposed to quietly follow the Government's lead (Interview 14). Whatever the government majority, executive–legislative relations cannot be "back" to the heyday of the Westminster model.

The Brexit years have brought to the fore the importance of parliamentary procedure. Some important nodes of the Brexit process were managed by a speaker – John Bercow – who strongly emphasised the need to "[frame] everything as giving parliament a voice and backbenchers a say … consulting every single party and giving every party the same opportunity to do things like putting amendments to a vote" (Interviews 24, 41, and 44). As Bercow himself stated – defending his actions from the attacks coming from the Eurosceptic wing of the Conservative Party – it is responsibility of the speaker "to stand up for the rights of the House of Commons, including the views of dissenters on the government Benches […] and to defend the rights of opposition parties" (HC Hansard 9 January 2019). With the end of Bercow's tenure in November 2019, the newly elected Speaker, Lindsey Hoyle, promised to put in place a new system for handling situations where precedent or traditional interpretations do not stand. In such situations, where the Speaker has to take a divisive decision, clerks will be able to place a statement of their views in the Commons library. Incidentally, on the interpretation of "forthwith" (cf. above), Hoyle expressed his disagreement with Bercow.

The impact of the referendum and the complex developments in the Brexit process have brought further and significant tensions onto a political system which, already before Brexit, had experienced relevant institutional changes. Several conventions and parliamentary norms have been tested, first and foremost relating to agenda control. The Brexit years have been characterised by a very intense conflict between Government and Parliament, with Parliament using to the utmost its powers to challenge the traditional dominance of the executive on parliamentary business. This new assertiveness may eventually lead to a reform of the Standing Orders (Interviews 24, 25, and 44). On the other hand, however, the reluctance, or rather incapacity, of Parliament to move beyond its opposition to "no deal" shows that the Westminster model maintains an enduring validity, and in more normal circumstances, it is difficult to imagine Parliament remaining as central in British politics as it has been from the referendum to the accomplishment of Brexit.

Notes

1 The Tory rebels defied a Government three-line whip to support a motion to grant a referendum on membership of the EU. Ultimately, the motion was also opposed by Liberal Democrat and Labour MPs and was thus easily defeated.
2 The review has produced 32 policy reports (Foreign and Commonwealth Office 2014).
3 The Government accepted that purdah should be in place, but with the exception that it would allow ministers "to communicate a position on the referendum in restrained and moderate terms".
4 Although this was not the first defeat for the Cameron II government in the House of Commons as, in July, there had been a former one on an urgent motion. A third defeat came in March 2016 when the Government was defeated on an amendment on Sunday trading hours on the Enterprise Bill.
5 Because of financial privilege, only the House of Commons can legislate on financial matters, such as taxes or public spending.
6 A prominent example is the suspension of the "principle of collective responsibility" in the referendum campaign. Cameron allowed members of the Cabinet to speak up against the official policy (i.e., Remain in the EU) (The Prime Minister 2016).
7 They were Rachael Maskell MP and Dawn Butler MP.
8 Jo Stevens MP, Catherine West MP, and Daniel Zaichner MP.
9 Larger rebellions within the Labour parliamentary party occurred on the Trident nuclear programme – both under the leaderships of Jeremy Corbyn in 2017 and Tony Blair in 2007 – and on military intervention in Iraq in 2003. In this latter case, two rebellions – of, respectively, 120 and 138 MPs – have been the largest since the middle of the 19th century (Cowley and Stuart 2014).
10 They included Clive Lewis MP, the shadow business secretary, who consequently resigned.
11 The House of Lords introduced two amendments on the bill, on the legal status of EU citizens residing in the UK and on the parliamentary vote on the withdrawal agreement between the EU and the UK. Both amendments were then rejected by the House of Commons, and the Lords gave way (Lang *et al.* 2017).
12 As new elections had been scheduled, the Tory party was leading Labour by about 20 percentage points. The last polls before the vote instead gave a smaller margin, of about eight percentage points, to May's party (Financial Times Poll of Polls 2017).
13 While Labour was also reluctant to engage "seriously" in cross-party talks (Quinn *et al.* 2022).
14 See House of Commons, Session 2017–19, *Order of Business*, 12 September 2017. https://publications.parliament.uk/pa/cm201719/cmagenda/fb170911.htm?ncid=newsletter-ukThe%20Waugh%20Zone%20080917. See also Russell 2017 for an analysis of the challenges of minority government.
15 *The Guardian*, Opposition condemns government's Commons committee "power grab", 8 September 2017.
16 In an opinion piece published on *The Evening Standard* on 6 September 2017, Dominic Grieve recognised the need to ensure the continuity of the regulatory framework post-Brexit, incorporating EU legislation into British law. Yet, at the same time, he strongly criticised the bill as it had been tabled by the executive, because "it seeks to confer powers on the Government to carry out Brexit in breach of our constitutional principles, in a manner that no sovereign Parliament should allow".

17 A few days before the vote, a leaked letter signed by Eurosceptic Tory MPs warned the PM to stick to the "original plan for Brexit" and revealed the high levels of tensions inside the Conservative Party (BBC 7 September 2017).

18 Concessions were not sufficient to persuade Kenneth Clarke MP, who finally abstained.

19 More broadly, it has been empirically shown that, since his election to the role of Speaker of the House of Commons in 2009, John Bercow "consistently attempted" to provide more opportunities for backbench MPs to scrutinise the work of ministers, for instance through urgent questions (Bates *et al.* 2018, 180–1). This was also the case through the Brexit process, with the Speaker offering all opposition parties the chance to speak in debates on the floor of the House or selecting contentious backbenchers' amendments (Thompson 2018; Institute for Government 2019).

20 At the same time, underscoring the contradictions in the Brexit process, the motion of no confidence tabled by the opposition leader Jeremy Corbyn was defeated.

21 Tellingly, Bill Cash MP declared that the bill "is to be rammed through the Commons in defiance of established centuries-old procedures in order to delay and reverse Brexit by Act of Parliament. It is outrageous" (3 April 2019).

22 For a similar argument, in a different context, see Kardasheva 2009.

23 It is very unusual for the House of Commons to sit on a Saturday. In the past, this rare occurrence happened four times: on 2 September 1939, for the outbreak of WWII; on 30 July 1949, the last sitting before the summer break; on 3 November 1956, for the Suez crisis and, lastly, on 3 April 1982, for the Falkland/Malvinas war.

24 Because of the Fixed Term Parliament Act (2011) – repealed in March 2022 – snap elections can be held in two circumstances only: (i) a motion on early elections is voted by at least two thirds of MPs or (ii) a no-confidence vote in the government is not followed by the formation of a new government within 14 days. Before the December 2019 elections, Johnson had failed to obtain the necessary qualified majority in three occasions (4 and 9 September, 28 October 2019).

5

WESTMINSTER REASSERTED

A unitary but disunited state

The June 2016 Brexit referendum saw the four components of the UK – England, Scotland, Wales, and Northern Ireland[1] – express different preferences. England and Wales returned majorities in favour of *Leave* and, due to the demographic weight of England, determined the overall UK-wide result. By contrast, Scotland and Northern Ireland expressed clear majorities in favour of *Remain*. Yet, successive Conservative governments have not only merely considered the UK-wide result, thus ignoring the opposing preferences coming from the constituent parts of the UK, but they also interpreted the response of the British people as a mandate to pursue a "hard Brexit", with little apparent awareness (at least initially) of how deeply devolution was embedded in EU membership (Keating 2018). Against this backdrop, pre-existing tensions that had been boiling down the centre–periphery cleavage for decades were reignited and exacerbated during the Brexit process. Indeed, devolution had different and complex effects across the three "Celtic" peripheries. The creation of a power-sharing system of self-government in Northern Ireland significantly contributed to placating political violence and bringing peace (Coulter & Murray 2008), but only within the wider provisions of the Good Friday Agreement which took EU membership of both the Irish Republic and the UK as a given. In Scotland and Wales, devolution turned out to be more a process than a single reform (Bradbury & Mitchel 2005), with escalating demands and negotiated concessions driven by two distinct dynamics: the electoral growth of nationalist (pro-independence) parties, especially in Scotland; and the determination of (non-independentist) Welsh governments to try and catch up with Scotland's self-government achievements. This process led to the territorial constitution being in a state of continuous evolution and increasingly open to contrasting interpretations (Gamble 2006; Hazell 2007), as well as the holding of an independence referendum in Scotland in September 2014. The victory of the unionist forces in the independence

DOI: 10.4324/9781003127680-6

referendum appeared to have defused the risk of disintegration, but Scottish voters made their choice under the assumption of EU membership.

The results of the Brexit referendum and the way Brexit has been pursued by UK governments have reopened the "Pandora's box" of centre–periphery relations in both legal/institutional and political terms. The legal/institutional aspect is analysed through the lenses of Lijphart's framework, particularly by the unitary–federal variable, measured through the index of federalism (see Chapter 1). Actually, Lijphart's variable (and the relative index) conflates two interlinked subdimensions: *self-rule* and *shared-rule* (Hooghe *et al.* 2010). The former refers to the range and importance of policy areas in which devolved administrations can legislate autonomously. The latter taps directly into sovereignty issues, as it concerns the degree of devolved administrations' involvement in state legislation, with particular reference to constitutional change (up to holding veto powers). Brexit has impacted both subdimensions, bringing about an alteration of devolved *self-rule* and a clarification on devolved *shared-rule*. The political aspect of centre–periphery relations during the Brexit process concerns the high tensions and clashes between the UK Government, on the one side, and devolved governments and/or peripheral nationalist parties, on the other. Independently of the level of success reached with the Brexit settlement – satisfactory for Northern Ireland's peripheral nationalism vs unsatisfactory for Scotland's and Wales's nationalists – the political system has witnessed a certain growth of separatist sentiments in all Celtic peripheries.

The first part of the chapter presents the structure of national identities in the UK (Section 5.1.1), focusing on the levels of compatibility/incompatibility between the UK state-national identity (British) and the national identities linked to specific regions of the UK – English in England, Irish and Northern Irish in Northern Ireland, Scottish in Scotland, and Welsh in Wales. It then reviews how centre–periphery politics based on these identities transformed the UK territorial constitution before Brexit: prior to devolution (Section 5.1.2) and after devolution (Section 5.1.3). The second part of the chapter summarises the positioning of the most relevant actors – such as the UK Government, devolved governments, political parties in Westminster, and in the devolved legislatures – vis-à-vis the Brexit referendum (Section 5.2.1). In order to assess the effect of Brexit on the self-rule of devolved administrations, Section 5.2.2 analyses the implications of specific measures contained in the EU Withdrawal Act (also known as the Great Repeal Act) 2018. As far as the constitutional clarification on devolved *shared-rule* is concerned, Section 5.2.3 analyses the rulings of the Supreme Court on the so-called *Miller Case* (2017) and *Scotland Continuity Bill case* (2018), as well as the outcome of the UK-Ireland/EU negotiation, which has led to a special agreement for Northern Ireland. Section 5.2.4 brings together the analysis on devolved self-rule and shared-rule for a comprehensive reflection on (and an assessment of) the post-Brexit territorial constitution. Finally, the centre–periphery political dynamics triggered by the unfolding of the Brexit process are analysed in the third part of the chapter, by looking at the positions adopted by institutional leaders and political parties; with special attention to the disintegration dynamics in Scotland (Section 5.3.1), Wales (Section 5.3.2), and Northern Ireland (Section 5.3.3).

5.1 Ethnonational identities, party politics, and institutional reforms before Brexit

5.1.1 "Anglo-Saxon" centre and "Celtic" peripheries

The United Kingdom is the result of a thousand-year process of polity formation and restructuring, marked by subsequent conquests/unions and separations of different peoples and territories across the islands of Great Britain and Ireland. As well as creating a state-national British identity (Colley 1992), this historical process has also preserved important substate (regional) national identities: English, Irish, Scottish, and Welsh (Crick 1991). These regional-national identities find themselves in very different relationships vis-à-vis the state-national (British) identity.

Historically, the UK can primarily be considered as the result of English expansionism in and across the two islands of Great Britain and Ireland (Bulpitt 1983). In addition, England is (and has always been) by far the dominant component of the UK state: demographically, territorially, economically, and politically. As a consequence, English and British identities have been largely compatible, if not equivalent and interchangeable (Langlands 1999; Henderson & Wyn Jones 2021). Indeed, 66 percent of people living in England identify as both English and British, while 16 percent identify as "English only" and 8 percent as "British only" (Denham 2018). This Anglo-British promiscuity is also reflected outside the UK, where it has been rather common to refer to the UK with the term "England" or to the British people with the term "English".

By contrast, the three "Celtic peripheries" of Northern Ireland, Scotland, and Wales host regional-national identities (Irish/Northern Irish, Scottish, and Welsh) which are less at ease with the state-national (British) identity (Table 5.1).

In Northern Ireland, the community that identifies as "Irish" – arguably the descendants of the Catholic population that inhabited Ireland before the protestant Plantation of the early seventeenth century – does not see British identity as compatible at all: only 0.66 percent of the population identifies as "Irish and British", and only 1 percent identifies as "Irish, Northern Irish, and British" (Census 2011a: p. 15). The population in Northern Ireland is still primarily divided between an exclusive "British identity" (40 percent) and an exclusive "Irish identity" (25 percent). However, it is important to consider that a growing number of people reject these two conflicting identities, embracing a common "Northern Irish-only" identity (21 percent) (ibid.).

In Scotland, the Scottish and British identities are not fully incompatible but the overwhelming majority of people identify as "Scottish only" (62 percent), while 18 percent identify as both Scottish and British, and 8 percent as "British only" (Census 2011b).[2] Similarly, in Wales, 57 percent of the population identify

TABLE 5.1 National identities in the UK (Census 2011)

UK constituent units	Regional-national identities	Share of exclusive regional-national identities[a]	Share of exclusive state-national identity[b]	Share of dual national identities[c]
England	English	16%	8%	66%
N. Ireland	Irish	25%	40%	0.7%
	Northern Irish	21%		6.2%
Scotland	Scottish	62%	8%	18%
Wales	Welsh	57%	34%	7.1%

Source: Census 2011a; Census 2011b; Census 2011c.

a Percentages of respondents declaring that they identity with a regional-national identity only.
b Percentages of respondents declaring that they identify as "British only" or (in the case of Wales) "Anglo-British".
c Percentages of respondents declaring that they identify both with a regional-national and the state-national identity.

as "Welsh only", while only 7.1 percent of the population identify as both Welsh and British, and 34 percent as "Anglo-British" or "British only" (Census 2011c). The main peculiarity of Wales is that the population identifying as "Welsh only" is culturally divided between native Welsh speakers (concentrated in western Wales) and native English speakers (concentrated in south Wales).

5.1.2 The rise and consolidation of centre–periphery politics (1969–99)

Interestingly, the centre–periphery cleavage in the UK began to gain salience at the time of UK accession to the EEC. There were two main sources of political attention for territorial politics. First, from 1969 onwards, political violence (later known as the *Troubles*) erupted in Northern Ireland (Munck 1992), pushing the (Conservative) UK government to adopt a series of convulsive institutional reforms. These peaked in the period 1972–4, with the suspension of the Parliament of Northern Ireland (1972), the holding of a Border Poll (March 1973), the establishment and election of a new Northern Ireland Assembly (May/June 1973), the parallel abolition of the suspended parliament (July 1973), and the eventual abolition of the Assembly too (July 1974), which opened the way to many years of direct rule from London. The second source of attention for territorial politics was represented by the electoral breakthrough of the Scottish National Party (SNP) in Scotland and, to a much lesser extent, of Plaid Cymru in Wales. Plaid went from 4.3 percent of Welsh votes and 0 MPs elected in 1966 to 10.8 percent and 3 elected MPs in October 1974; while the SNP rose from 5 percent of Scottish votes and 0 MPs elected in 1966 to 30.4 percent and 11 elected MPs in October 1974 (Brand 1978). This second territorial shock was also followed by an agenda of institutional reforms, adopted by (Labour or Labour-led) UK governments in the 1974–9 parliamentary term. However, plans to establish elected self-governing institutions in Scotland and Wales were halted by the negative results of (and/or low participation in) the respective 1979 referendums (Balsom & McAllister 1979; Bochel & Denver 1981).

After several terms dominated by Conservative centralism, a new wave of electoral growth for nationalist parties in Scotland and (less so) Wales materialised during the 1990s. As shown in Table 5.2, the SNP obtained 22 percent of Scottish votes in the 1997 general election (10 points up from the 1983 election nadir); while Plaid obtained 10 percent of Welsh votes in the same election, up from its single-digit percentage performances throughout the 1980s and early 1990s. Although these two regions remained Labour electoral strongholds – with the Conservatives losing all their seats in 1997 – the electoral pressure exercised by minority nationalist parties (particularly the SNP) increased substantially.

In the same period, in Northern Ireland, the electoral hegemony of the Ulster Unionist Party (UUP) declined progressively, especially in terms of vote share. By 1997, a four-party system had emerged, formed by two main (UK) unionist parties – UUP and the Democratic Unionist Party (DUP) – and two main (Irish) republican parties: the Social Democratic and Labour Party (SDLP) and Sinn Fein (SF) (Tilly *et al.* 2008). The only non-sectarian party that aimed at transcending traditional communal affiliations – the Alliance Party of Northern Ireland (APNI) – remained a minor force, as the conflict between the two communities (and between the republican forces and the UK military/police forces and institutions) continued until the summer of 1998. However, the two sociopolitical blocs (Protestant/unionist vs Catholic/(Irish) nationalist) were electorally dominated by moderate parties, the UUP and the SDLP, which had an established relationship with the main British parties, Conservative and Labour

TABLE 5.2 Results of the 1997 general election in Northern Ireland, Scotland, and Wales

Parties	Northern Ireland percentages (and number of MPs)	Scotland percentages (and number of MPs)	Wales percentages (and number of MPs)
Conservative Party/UUP[a]	32.7% (10)[a]	17.5% (0)	19.6% (0)
Labour Party/SDLP[a]	24.1% (3)[a]	45.6% (56)	54.7% (34)
Lib-Dem Party (LD)/APNI[a]	8% (0)[a]	13% (10)	12.4% (2)
Scottish National Party (SNP)	–	22.1% (6)	–
Democratic Unionist Party (DUP)	13.6% (1)	–	–
Sinn Fein (SF)	16.1% (2)	–	–
Plaid Cymru (PC)	–	–	10% (4)

a For practical reasons, some Northern Irish regional parties have been associated with the respectively closest state-wide party: the Ulster Unionist Party (UUP) with the Conservatives, the Social Democratic and Labour Party (SDLP) with Labour, and the Alliance Party of Northern Ireland (APNI) with the Liberal Democrats. Figures in the first three rows of the second column (Northern Ireland) refer to regional parties, not state-wide parties.

respectively (Evans & Duffy 1997). In addition, several attempts to bring about a ceasefire from 1994 onwards slowed down the pace (if not the tragic severity) of violent attacks, thus creating a more favourable context for peace-building initiatives.

The combination of a window of opportunity to bring peace to Northern Ireland and the need to neutralise growing electoral pressure by the SNP in Scotland pushed the first New Labour government to adopt a reformist agenda. The late 1990s devolution reform marked a watershed in the UK territorial constitution (Bogdanor 2001), as it consisted of an international (UK-Ireland) treaty – the Belfast (or Good Friday) Agreement 1998 – and three main pieces of legislation (all passed in 1998) establishing elected self-government institutions in Northern Ireland, Scotland, and Wales.[3] Although the reform was proposed and enacted by the UK (Labour) government, it succeeded because it represented a response to a consolidated minority nationalist (bottom-up) pressure from the "Celtic" peripheries. Indeed, the devolution legislation was legitimised and reinforced by the results of three pre-legislative regional referendums in Northern Ireland, Scotland, and Wales.[4] By contrast, the top-down project to extend devolution to various English regions – beginning with the northern ones (Regional Assemblies Act 2003) – failed miserably at the first (and only) attempt: in the 2004 North-East England referendum, in a 48 percent turnout, 78 percent of voters rejected the establishment of an assembly (Bradbury & Mitchell 2005).

The overall structure of the devolution settlement (devolution as an event) rests on the political dynamics triggered by the underlying ethno-territorial identities that shape centre–periphery politics in the UK. Some important differences across regional self-government institutions – e.g., strict power-sharing arrangements in Northern Ireland vs no formal requirements in Scotland and Wales – were dictated by the specific conditions and needs of the three "Celtic peripheries"; while others (e.g., the different electoral systems) were the result of rational calculations by the governing Labour Party. Overall, devolution was more the result of political dynamics than an academically discussed and designed project. Similarly, the subsequent changes to the devolution settlement (devolution as a process) were also shaped primarily by party politics.

5.1.3 Devolution as process and the contested territorial constitution (1999–2015)

While the late 1990s devolution reform succeeded in bringing peace to Northern Ireland, it clearly failed to weaken regional nationalism in Scotland and Wales. The establishment of devolved elections provided the SNP and Plaid with an opportunity to compete on level ground with the regional branches of the British state-wide parties and to nurture ambitions for accessing power at the regional level. The oscillating results obtained by the two nationalist parties between the general and devolved elections are testament to the favourable institutional environment provided by devolution. Lower levels of turnout in regional elections (vis-à-vis general elections), a disproportionate participation by minority nationalist voters and "dual voting" – i.e., a tendency by some voters to support Labour in general elections and SNP/Plaid in regional elections – meant that both nationalist parties performed much better in devolved than in general elections (Wyn Jones & Scully 2006; Hough & Jeffery 2006). For instance, at the first regional election (1999), exploiting fierce divisions within the Welsh Labour Party, Plaid gained over 30 percent of votes (Trystan et al. 2003): an unimaginable result in the pre-devolution context and an incredibly high score compared to those of the previous (10 percent) and subsequent (14.3 percent) general elections. After the 2007 devolved elections, both the SNP and Plaid went into the office, albeit with the crucial difference that the SNP emerged from the election victorious and formed a single-party minority government, while Plaid renounced its role as main opposition party and joined a Labour-led government as a junior partner.

Arguably, the independence referendum held in Scotland in September 2014 represented the most dramatic effect of (or episode in) the overall devolution process, as it represented the most powerful challenge to the integrity of the UK (since 1921). The referendum originated in both the 2011 Scottish election, which produced an SNP single-party majority government, and the accommodating stance of the Con-Lib Dem coalition government, which gave a green light. For the unionist front, consisting of all state-wide parties, the referendum struggle proved to be harder than expected, with promises of further devolution of powers being made in the last part of the campaign with a view to warding off a negative outcome (Mitchell 2016; Keating & McEwen 2017). Eventually, the unionist front obtained a victory by a 10 percent margin (55 vs 45), apparently removing Scottish independence from the agenda for at least a generation. However, the campaign and the aftermath of the referendum saw a tremendous upsurge in popularity and membership of the SNP, which was able to approach the 2015 general election with the wind in its sails.

While Scottish and Welsh politics remained centred on debates regarding further transfers of powers to the two regions (as well as party competition for a reputation as good administrator), politics in Northern Ireland was primarily focused on making the complex power-sharing institutional system work. Political competition at the regional level became immediately as important as in general elections, with levels of turnout very similar in the two types of elections. However, it proved very difficult for political parties to adjust to power-sharing politics. Lack of trust between political forces led to a very weak regional executive, which collapsed several times and sometimes remained inactive due to party boycotts even when it was formally sitting. In such a context, the electoral preferences of some voters progressively shifted from the moderate parties of the two ethno-political communities – UUP for unionists and SDLP for Irish nationalists – to the radical ones. In the 2007 regional election, the DUP and SF obtained over 30 and 26 percent of votes respectively, while the UUP and SDLP got around 15 percent of votes each (Wilford 2010). At a systemic level, this electoral-political development had both negative and positive consequences.

On the one hand, rather than focusing on the adoption of socioeconomic policies that could be beneficial to the whole population, Northern Irish politics remained stuck in ethno-sectarian competition for the control of public policies at the implementation level and, more in general, for the distribution of public spoils and resources (Murtagh & Shirlow 2012; Horgan & Gray 2012). On the other hand, the electoral growth of the DUP and SF was preceded (Mitchell *et al.* 2001), as well as followed, by a moderation process of these political forces. Having become the protagonists of Northern Ireland politics, the two radical parties began to bear most of the responsibility for making devolution work. This pushed them to accept the power-sharing system of government and to develop a pragmatic bargaining attitude vis-à-vis their ethnic counterpart, while still presenting themselves as the most robust advocates of their respective group's identity and interests (Mitchell *et al.* 2009). The success of devolution in establishing peaceful cohabitation between the two ethnic communities in Northern Ireland has also created room for the electoral consolidation of the non-sectarian Alliance Party. The APNI, loosely connected to the British Liberal Democrats (Driver 2011), remained a minor force in Northern Ireland, but it stabilised its vote share and seat share in the regional Assembly, while winning its first MP in the 2010 general election (Mitchell 2018).

The strengthening of minority nationalism in the three "Celtic peripheries" meant that devolution (particularly in Scotland and Wales) became an ongoing and open-ended process (Mitchell 2006), which has progressively transformed the UK territorial constitution. Continuous reforms were adopted by different British governments: Labour (1997–2010), Con-Lib Dem coalition (2010–15), and pre-Brexit Conservative governments (2015–16). In particular, Welsh devolution was enhanced in 2006, 2011, and 2014; while Scottish devolution was further strengthened in 2012. In addition, the unfolding of the devolution process in Scotland and Wales created an "English question" (Hazell 2006), commonly called the "West Lothian question". Given the unpopularity of devolution in England, a solution to the "English question" was not adopted by law. Devolution for England – the so-called "English Votes for English Laws" (EVEL) reform – was *de facto* carried out in a residual form and approved with a mere revision of the House of Commons Standing Orders in October 2015 (Gover and Kenny 2018).

Important reforms – the Scotland Act 2016 and the Wales Act 2017 – continued in the early Brexit period, though initiated before Brexit.[5] These laws seemed to introduce limits to parliamentary sovereignty in two ways: first, they apparently transferred any decision on the removal of devolved institutions from Westminster to the peoples of Scotland and Wales (who would have to express their choice in referendums); and secondly, they appeared to constitutionalise the so-called Sewel Convention, by which "it is recognised that the Parliament of the United Kingdom will not normally legislate with regard to devolved matters without the consent of the Scottish Parliament" (Scotland Act 2016, Part 1, Art. 2).

As a consequence, the unitary character of the UK appeared to be in question. In contrast to the majoritarian dynamics of the Westminster model, devolution has introduced more proportional/coalitional politics (in Scotland and Wales), and even compulsory consensual politics (in Northern Ireland), thus creating a bi-constitutional setting (Flinders 2010). More importantly, the putative limits to parliamentary sovereignty in favour of apparent constitutional guarantees for devolved administrations have pushed authoritative scholars not only to high-light the presence of both unitary and federal elements (Gamble 2006) but, in the context of a federalising dynamic (Keating 2018, 61), to consider the UK as a *quasi-federal* political system (Hazell 2007; Matthews & Flinders 2017).

The process of devolution has certainly made the territorial constitution of the UK a contested field. On the one hand, parliamentary (Westminster) sov-ereignty and the flexible constitution entail the persistence of a unitary political system. On the other hand, this constitutional position is challenged by two factors. First, devolution has represented a visible and institutionalised recogni-tion of the multinational character of the state, which has become a consensus view. This has led scholars and institutions[6] to increasingly prefer the use of more ambiguous labels – such as *union state*, *pluri-national union*, or *state of unions* (McLean & McMillan 2005; Keating 2001; Mitchell 2006; 2010a), rather than the standard comparative concept/label of unitary state. Secondly, devolution has contributed to the (re)proposition of the Celtic peripheries' perspectives on the constitution, which see sovereignty not necessarily residing in Westminster (or with the British people as a whole), but rather contestable and negotiable amongst the UK nations (MacCormick 1998; Tierney 2005; Keating 2021). In short, on the eve of Brexit, the UK was already characterised by an ongoing aca-demic, juridical, and political struggle over the territorial constitution (Gordon 2016, 337; Bickerton 2019, 896). The following paragraphs analyse the impact of Brexit on centre–periphery politics and the territorial constitution.

5.2 The impact of Brexit on the centre–periphery dimension

This second part of the chapter aims to analyse if and how Brexit has increased pre-existing centre–periphery tensions; whether and how it has influenced the redistri-bution of competences between the centre and devolved administrations (regional self-rule); whether and how it has brought about clarification on the territorial aspects of sovereignty (regional shared-rule); and what were the main political reactions to changes in self-rule and shared-rule of the devolved administrations.

5.2.1 The Brexit kick-off: a dis-United Kingdom (2015–16)

As mentioned above, the SNP entered the 2015 general election with the wind in its sails due to the political capital gained during (and in the aftermath of) the independence referendum campaign. Indeed, the election marked a "sea change" in Scotland, with the nationalists increasing their vote share from 20 to 50 percent and their seat share from 10 to 95 percent (56 out 59 seats), virtually wiping out all the other parties (Mitchell 2015). The Scottish electoral results also meant that the SNP became, for the first time, the third parliamentary party in Westminster (Thompson 2017). In addition, like in Northern Ireland, where the election confirmed the consolidation of the four-party system, the UKIP performed very poorly compared to the UK average (1.6 percent in Scotland; 2.6 percent in Northern Ireland). The only electoral trend that Scotland shared with the rest of the UK was the collapse of the Lib-Dems, already evident in the 2011 Scottish election. By contrast, in Wales, electoral results were a mix of "things as usual" – i.e., a dominant Labour, Conservatives as runner-up, Plaid Cymru in its usual electoral trail – and UK-wide new trends: a dramatic increase of support for UKIP and the collapse of the Lib-Dems.

In this context, the SNP represented the main political force to question the legitimacy of a Brexit referendum from a multinational perspective, denouncing that it was brought forward by a government majority that represented England well (319 out 533 seats), but included only 11 MPs (out of 40) from Wales, only 1 MP (out of 59) from Scotland and 0 – or 2 if we count the UUP's MPs – (out of 18) from Northern Ireland. When the referendum bill was presented in Westminster, the SNP challenged its content from an implicitly federalist perspective. Indeed, it presented an amendment to stop the proposed legislation, primarily on the grounds that "the Bill does not include a double majority provision to ensure that no nation or jurisdiction of the UK can be taken out of the EU against its will" (House of Commons Debates 9 June 2015, c1067). However, that amendment was rejected, gathering support only from SNP, Plaid Cymru, and SDLP MPs.

The failure of this amendment can be considered as the first episode of a series of constitutional clashes that, during the Brexit process, provided clarification on the territorial constitution in favour of a unitary state. This episode is undoubtedly eminently political. Yet, in the context of a "political constitution" (Griffith 1979), the fact that an overwhelming majority of parliament (including the government and main opposition party) did not deem it necessary to consider any referendum result other than the UK-wide one demonstrates that, for British political elites, the acknowledged multinational nature of the state does not alter its unitary character.

In early May 2016, less than two months before the Brexit referendum, devolved elections took place in the three "Celtic peripheries". Overall, these elections confirmed previous results, though bringing about some changes in government formation. In Northern Ireland, the new executive was much less inclusive than the previous ones, though maintaining its mandatory power-sharing character: the moderate parties refused to join the regional government, leaving only the DUP and SF in office. In Scotland, the SNP lost an absolute majority but remained, by far, the hegemonic party, and formed a minority government. Finally, in Wales, a Labour-Lib Dem coalition replaced the previous Labour single-party government.

These elections were also an occasion for parties to clearly position themselves on the upcoming Brexit referendum. As shown in Table 5.3, important differences can be observed across the three devolved administrations. First, the biggest parties in Scotland and Wales, the SNP and Labour respectively, were pro-Remain, whereas the biggest party in Northern Ireland, the DUP, was pro-Leave. Similarly, Scotland and Wales had pro-Remain governments, whereas the Northern Irish executive (DUP-SF) was deeply split on the issue. It should not come as a surprise that the Northern Irish executive collapsed in the early stages of Brexit (January 2017) and remained vacant, despite an early election in March 2017, until January 2020.

In terms of vote shares obtained by pro-Leave and pro-Remain parties, Northern Ireland and Wales showed similar results, whereas Scotland appeared as a consensually pro-Remain polity.

Combining the data of Table 5.3 with those of Table 5.4, the picture of the stances adopted by the three Celtic peripheries on Brexit is complete. Scotland

TABLE 5.3 Party position on Brexit and Party vote shares in the 2016 devolved elections

Parties[a]	Northern Ireland	Scotland	Wales
Conservative Party/UUP	Remain (12.6)	Remain[b] (22.9)	Leave[b] (18.8)
Labour Party/SDLP	Remain (12.0)	Remain (19.1)	**Remain (31.5)**
Lib-Dem Party (LD)/APNI	Remain (7.0)	Remain (5.2)	Remain (6.5)
UK Independence Party (UKIP)	Leave (1.5)	Leave (2.0)	Leave (13.0)
Greens	Remain (2.7)	Remain (6.6)	Remain (3.0)
Democratic Unionist Party (DUP)	**Leave (29.2)**	–	–
Sinn Fein (SF)	Remain (24.0)	–	–
Traditional Unionist Party (TUP)	Leave (3.4)	–	–
People Before Profit	Leave (2.0)	–	–
Scottish National Party (SNP)	–	**Remain (41.7)**	–
Plaid Cymru (PC)	–	–	Remain (20.8)
Abolish the Welsh Assembly	–	–	Leave (4.4)
Leave parties (L) vs Remain parties (R)	**36.1 (L) vs 58.3 (R)**	**2.0 (L) vs 95.5 (R)**	**36.2 (L) vs 61.8 (R)**
Devolved executive	**Split (DUP-SF)**	**Remain (SNP)**	**Remain (Lab-LD)**

Source: UK Electoral Commission.

a For practical reasons, some Northern Irish regional parties have been associated with the closest state-wide party, although they do not (any longer) have formal agreements: the Ulster Unionist Party (UUP) with the Conservatives, the Social Democratic and Labour Party (SDLP) with Labour, the Alliance (APNI) with the Liberal Democrats. The label "Greens" refers to the Green Party of NI, the Green Party of England and Wales (for Wales) and the Scottish Greens.

b The Conservatives were (also) divided in Scotland and Wales. However, the leadership of the Scottish Conservatives was pro-Remain, whereas the leadership of the Welsh Conservatives was pro-Leave.

TABLE 5.4 Brexit referendum results across the UK[a]

	Results (%)	Max pro-Brexit (%)	Min pro-Brexit (%)	Difference
England	53.4 (L) vs 46.6 (R)	West Midlands 59.3	London 40.1	19.2
Northern Ireland	44.2 (L) vs 55.2 (R)	North Antrim 62.2	Foyle 21.7	40.5
Scotland	38.0 (L) vs 62.0 (R)	Moray 49.9	Edinburgh City 25.6	24.3
Wales	52.5 (L) vs 47.5 (R)	Blaenau Gwent 62.0	Cardiff 40.0	22.0
United Kingdom	51.9 (L) vs 48.1 (R)	England 53.4	Scotland 38.0	15.4

Source: UK Electoral Commission.
a The table does not include data on Gibraltar.

emerges as the only polity in which both the people and the government are united in an anti-Brexit position. This condition is strengthened by the stance adopted by the whole political establishment and by the homogeneity of the referendum results across Scotland: even the most pro-Brexit area (Moray) returned a pro-Remain majority, albeit a very marginal one. In addition, regional office is held by the nationalist/independentist SNP, which has a natural confrontational posture not only vis-à-vis the central government, but also vis-à-vis the whole British political establishment. From the outset, therefore, Scotland has had all the necessary political resources to lead the peripheries' struggle against Brexit. By contrast, the anti-Brexit Welsh executive (Labour-Lib Dem), despite having an anti-Brexit main opposition party (Plaid), had to come to terms with the results of the referendum, which saw a pro-Leave majority. Finally, Northern Ireland returned a clear pro-Remain majority, but this "response" could not be effectively advocated by a divided regional government, which collapsed and remained vacant throughout the Brexit process. The extreme territorial variance in referendum results (see Table 5.4), reflected opposing orientations across the two ethnic communities. Therefore, the referendum results contributed to reigniting the sectarian division, as the political debate in Northern Ireland immediately focused on the extremely controversial issue of the border (Gormely-Heenan & Aughey 2017).

Confronted with contrasting referendum results and the divergent positions of political forces across the UK constituent jurisdictions, the UK Government reacted by adopting a discourse that, despite some ambiguities and contradictions, was clearly aimed at reasserting its superiority over devolved administrations on Brexit. On the one hand, the new PM Theresa May acknowledged the multinational character of the state, and paid lip service to the devolution settlement, stressing the need for the central and devolved administrations to cooperate on the UK Brexit policy. On the other hand, and somehow contra-dictorily, she also referred to the UK "nation" (singular) or "people", whose will – expressed in the UK-wide response of the referendum – represented a political mandate for the Government, and no one else, to negotiate with the EU as one UK and to leave the EU as one UK (Wincott *et al.* 2021, 1532).

Evidently, in the aftermath of the Brexit referendum (or even on the eve of it), all the ingredients for a new centre–periphery clash were present. It was also clear that the domestic political struggle would primarily revolve around the opposition between the UK (Conservative) Government and the Scottish (SNP) government, whereas the issue of the Irish border, due to the lack of a univocal institutional voice speaking for Northern Ireland, would have a predominantly international connotation. Finally, the potential role of the Labour Party, which since 2010 was relegated to hold office only in Wales, was an enigma. In theory, the Labour Party could represent a (weak) buffer between peripheral nationalism and the growing Anglo-British nationalism of the Conservative Party (Gamble 2016). However, its capacity to regain electoral strength and its will/determina-tion to adopt a substantively different stance on the territorial constitution (vis-à-vis the Conservative government's) remained a moot point.

5.2.2 Brexit and devolved self-rule: between expansion of powers and (temporary) recentralisation

If there was an aspect of Brexit that could play in favour of devolved adminis-trations, this certainly was the perspective of widening their legislative/regu-latory competences with the repatriation of a considerable number of powers from Brussels. Indeed, the devolution legislation – including the original Acts adopted in 1998 – formally assigned a series of powers that, in fact, had already been transferred to the EU (or were to be transferred to the EU with the Lisbon Treaty in 2009) to the devolved administrations. Therefore, in the wake of the UK withdrawal from the EU, these powers should theoretically flow from Brussels to Belfast, Cardiff, and Edinburgh. In this respect, Brexit could have represented another step in the long process of devolution, which has seen the competences of devolved parliaments/assemblies (particularly in Scotland and Wales) progressively enhanced by subsequent transfers of powers.

However, the British government deemed it necessary to maintain central control over some of these devolved and about-to-be repatriated policy areas. The need was justified based on seven objectives: enabling the functioning of the UK internal market; ensuring compliance with international obligations; ensur-ing that the UK can negotiate, enter into, and implement new trade agreements and international treaties; effectively managing common resources; administer-ing and providing access to justice in cases with a cross-border element; and safeguarding the security of the UK (Paun *et al.* 2020). As such, the main piece of domestic legislation adopted to leave the EU – the so-called European Union (Withdrawal) Act 2018, also known as the Great Repeal Act – included measures

(Section 12) that empowered Westminster and Whitehall to legislate/regulate UK-wide common approaches and frameworks on several repatriated areas that intersect devolved competences.

When the EU Withdrawal Bill was first presented, in summer 2017, the reaction of the (Scottish and Welsh) devolved administrations was fury, also because the initial proposal provided for repatriating all powers to Westminster and then gradually releasing some of them to the devolved administrations (Interview 34). First Ministers Nicola Sturgeon and Carwyn Jones released a joint statement attacking the bill as "a naked power grab" and "an attack on the founding principles of devolution" (*The Guardian* 14 July 2017). In the following months, negotiations between the central and devolved governments, within the Joint Ministerial Committee for EU Negotiations (JMC-EN), carried on trying to identify immediately the policy areas to be retained in Westminster and the ones to be directly assigned to Belfast, Cardiff, and Edinburgh. However, in the first months of 2018 negotiations stalled.

Given the impossibility of obtaining substantive concessions in the intergovernmental negotiations, the devolved administrations of Scotland and Wales tried to put pressure on the UK Government by raising the level of institutional confrontation. As the two devolved administrations prepared to withhold consent on the EU Withdrawal Bill, in March 2018, the Scottish Parliament and the Welsh Assembly hastily approved the so-called Continuity Bills: the Scotland Continuity Bill 2018 and the Wales Continuity Bill 2018. Playing with time, Scotland and Wales tried to secure retention of their full set of devolved powers, as prescribed by the devolution legislation, and prevent the restrictions envisaged in the (still to be approved) EU Withdrawal Bill.

It is worth noting that the confrontational strategy chosen by Scotland and Wales cannot be ascribed to independentist nationalism for two reasons. First, while Scotland was led by an independentist party (the SNP), Wales was not. Secondly, the Continuity Bills were approved by all parties except the Conservatives and, in the case of Wales, the UKIP (BBC News 20 March 2018). However, it is also worth noting that not all Labour politicians agreed on the narrative of London's "power grab" plot, and the dramatisation of political confrontation, especially by the Scottish executive (Interview 35). Indeed, the widespread approval of the Continuity Bills was probably an attempt to strengthen the bargaining powers of the two devolved administrations, with the understanding that they would be repealed once an agreement was reached with the UK Government.

The reaction of the central Government was two-fold. On the one hand, it promptly appealed against the Continuity Bills before the Supreme Court, thus blocking the royal assent. On the other hand, it proposed some concessions, such as a temporal limit to the retention of repatriated devolved powers in London (up to two years to legislate common frameworks and up to five years of application of such frameworks), a guarantee that frameworks would not favour England over Scotland and Wales (or Northern Ireland) and a pledge to legislate on frameworks in agreement with devolved administrations. The Government's move had the effect of dividing Scotland and Wales.

In April 2018, the Welsh executive accepted the compromise offered by London, promising consent on the EU Withdrawal Bill and a repeal of the Wales Continuity Bill (Welsh Cabinet Secretary for Finance, letter to the UK Minister for the Cabinet Office, 24 April 2018). The Welsh Assembly passed the legislative consent motion in mid-May and then, a few months later, it scrapped the Continuity Bill (BBC Wales 2018). By contrast, Scotland denied its consent (with the same wide majority approving the Continuity Bill) and kept its Continuity Bill, preparing itself for a judicial clash before the Supreme Court. Although this was a substantive battle for *self-rule* (i.e., concerning the width of legislative powers assigned at the level of devolved administrations), the true nature of the judicial struggle has more to do with devolved *shared-rule* (i.e., the power of devolved administrations to concur with or veto UK-wide law-making). Therefore, while it is important to state here that the Supreme Court's ruling did not stop the "power grab", the content and implications of the judicial case are reported in the next part of this chapter.

Here, it is of greater interest to discuss the factors that led the two devolved administrations to part ways in this important negotiation with the central government. A Plaid Cymru MP whom we interviewed imputed Carwyn Jones's choice to lack of nationalism in the Welsh executive: "If Welsh Labour had chosen Plaid, rather than the Lib-Dems, as a partner for government, we would have followed Scotland on that occasion" (Interview 5). According to another interviewee, one of the most authoritative scholars of devolution, the different reaction of the two devolved executives reflects the different strengths of devolution in Scotland and Wales:

> the Welsh government are quite happy with that outcome, because they said, "Well, at least they took us seriously, at least they talked to us", which they normally don't. The Scottish government says, "They've always talked to us, but they override us anyway".
>
> *(Interview 34)*

Direct protagonists of that negotiation, from the Welsh side, confirmed that the decision was based on a change of attitude by the UK Government and on a positive (albeit barely satisfactory) evaluation of the extracted concessions (Welsh Cabinet Secretary for Finance, letter to the UK Minister for the Cabinet Office 24 April 2018; Interview 72).

The position adopted by the Welsh administration undoubtedly contributed to legitimising the Government's approach, showing that it was not incompatible with the devolution settlement, both politically and institutionally. The press conference following the agreement was an occasion for the central Government to celebrate the "significant achievement that will provide legal certainty, increase the powers of the devolved governments and also respect the devolution settlements", while stigmatising the position of the Scottish executive: "It is disappointing that the Scottish government have not yet felt able to add their agreement to the new amendments that Ministers and officials on all sides have been working on very hard over recent weeks" (Cabinet Office, press release 25 April 2018). In any case, the rigid opposition by Scotland proved to be ineffective. Indeed, in June 2018 the EU Withdrawal Act was approved and sealed with royal assent, without receiving the Scottish consent. This was the first time that Westminster legislated on the (re)assignment of devolved competences was passed without the consent of a devolved administration; and it did so by amending the 1998 devolution Acts in a more restrictive direction.

More precisely, the UK Government identified a total of 154 areas of EU law that intersected devolved competence in Northern Ireland, Scotland, or Wales (UK Government, Frameworks Analysis September 2020). These included 12 policy areas whose competence is contested by the centre, which considers them as reserved, and the Celtic peripheries, which see them as devolved. In any case, the most important issue was to identify which policy areas could be directly and fully assigned to the devolved administrations, and which needed the adoption of common frameworks by central institutions. Initially, only 49 areas were to be directly assigned to the devolved administrations (UK Government, Frameworks Analysis 9 March 2018). However, this number grew to 115, including virtually all areas pertaining to the departments of the Home Office, Justice, Work and Pensions, Health, Transport, Public Housing, and Local Government (UK Government, Frameworks Analysis September 2020).[7] The number of areas in which non-legislative frameworks were needed dropped from 82 to 22; while those requiring legislative frameworks went from 24 to 18. These numbers show that the central Government, in collaboration with the devolved administrations, has tried to increase the areas that could be immediately transferred to the devolved administrations as much as possible. Indeed, most of the academic experts that we have interviewed, including those most critical of London's management of the issue, hold that there was no purposeful intention by the central Government to use Brexit to restrict devolved powers.[8]

Nonetheless, the powers retained by London are not of trivial importance for the devolved administrations, as they predominantly pertain to the policy areas of Agriculture and Fisheries, the Environment, and Energy. The Celtic peripheries were amongst the main beneficiaries of EU funds in the UK and, as such, devolved policies were deeply shaped by the incentives provided by EU policy frameworks. This was particularly the case with environmental and energy policies, about which devolved administrations have raised concerns in relation to how far the new UK frameworks will deviate from the EU's (McEwen & Remond 2019). In the area of agriculture, in which England's organisation of the sector and policy approach have always been different (particularly on subsidies) from those of the Celtic peripheries (Keating 2019), there were strong concerns (expressed particularly by Scotland) about adopting a common framework that would fit the preferences and needs of all jurisdictions.

In conclusion, Brexit has impacted on devolved self-rule through a contested process, centred on specific parts of the European Union (Withdrawal) Act 2018. The outcome, on the formal Brexit Day (31 January 2020), can be interpreted in two opposing ways. On the one hand, devolved self-rule has *de facto* been widened considerably, with the Celtic peripheries acquiring the power to rule autonomously over a large number of specific areas (111 in Northern Ireland, 73 in Scotland, and 35 in Wales). On the other hand, the devolved powers identified by the devolution legislation have, *de jure*, been restricted in 40 specific areas, which will remain under central control for the adoption of legislative (18) and non-legislative frameworks (22). Unquestionably, the reduction of devolved self-rule has occurred only on paper, as the subtracted powers were previously held by Brussels, not by the devolved administrations. In addition, the restriction of devolved self-rule is expected to be only temporary: up to seven years. Yet, some of our interviewees[9] have raised concerns about how (initially) temporary measures can become stable and entrenched in actual policymaking. More importantly, the devolved administrations have denounced the attitude and decision-making process adopted by central institutions in dealing with their requests and grievances. The question of the legitimate and appropriate institutional process, however, pertains to the constitutional issue of sovereignty and, therefore, to the dimension of devolved shared-rule.

5.2.3 Brexit and devolved shared-rule: a constitutional clarification

From the very early stages of the Brexit process, a centre–periphery struggle invested the most crucial question of the territorial constitution: whether sovereignty belongs (undivided) to the people of the UK and to the institution that represents it (the House of Commons in Westminster); or, rather, it is somehow shared amongst the several nations of the UK and their respective parliaments/assemblies. As mentioned above, traditional pillars of the UK institutional system and of British Political Tradition (BPT), particularly the flexible constitution and parliamentary sovereignty, clearly point to the persistence of unitary and undivided sovereignty, residing in Westminster. However, devolution has partially changed or, at least, muddled the picture. First, it has divided legislative competences between Westminster (as the UK Parliament) and Cardiff Bay, Holyrood, Stormont, and restricted-Westminster (as an England-only parliament). In addition, it has generated a convention – the Sewel Convention – whereby the Parliament legislates neither on devolved policy areas nor to change the set of devolved policy areas without the previous consent of devolved parliaments/assemblies. In this respect, it is worth remembering that, before Brexit, the Sewel Convention had always been respected, and it had been explicitly inserted in the Scotland Act 2016. Secondly, devolution has further institutionalised the recognition of the multinational character of the state, enhancing awareness of the negotiated/consensual origin of the UK – particularly as far as Northern Ireland

and Scotland are concerned (Tierney 2004). The latter aspect is not trivial, as it opens some space for the recognition of different legal/constitutional traditions in the UK, while reconnecting with foundational principles of the BPT, such as the Lockean insistence on "consent" and "freedom of association" as bases for legitimate political obligation (Hoff 2015). The Brexit shock, therefore, intervenes at a time in which the UK territorial constitution is both in flux and open to both academic and political controversies.

From the perspective of the Celtic peripheries, the question of sovereignty translates into the level of shared-rule that they hold vis-à-vis central institutions on UK-wide law-making and constitutional reforms. If their consent was recognised as a judiciable right, particularly on constitutional matters affecting devolved powers, then they would reach a level of constitutional guarantees that substantively equates to that of federal systems. During the Brexit process, the devolved administrations clashed repeatedly with central institutions, both politically and judicially, to claim such a right.

The first and most important judicial clash occurred between late 2016 and early 2017, in what came to be known as the *Miller Case*. The case began as a controversy about whether the UK Government could formally initiate the Brexit process (i.e., triggering Art. 50 of the TEU) without a vote by Westminster. As the High Court of England ruled that an Act of Parliament was needed to start the process in November 2016, the UK Government appealed before the Supreme Court. At that stage, the devolved governments (Scotland and Wales) joined the constitutional case, claiming that a consent vote by devolved legislatures was necessary too. Clearly, this judicial bid entailed some (perhaps too many)[10] risks. Indeed, the Scottish First Minister appeared to count more on general principles than on judiciable norms:

> I believe that as a matter of politics and as a matter of fairness and respect to the devolution settlement, before we even get into matters of law which are not for me to determine, then it is inconceivable that the UK Government would try to ignore or not seek the approval of the Scottish Government.
>
> (The Independent *08 November 2016*)

Yet, no matter how remote the possibility of a favourable sentence was, the potential rewards (i.e., obtaining a historical constitutional victory and a chance to stop Brexit) made the endeavour worth attempting.

Scotland was represented in the case by its senior law officer, the Lord Advocate, who appealed to the Sewel Convention to claim that, given the manifold implications of Brexit for devolved powers, a formal vote of consent by Holyrood was a prerequisite for triggering Art. 50 (UKSP, 2016/0196, Written case of the Lord Advocate, 4–5). The position of the Welsh legal representative – the Counsel General for Wales – substantively reflected the Lord Advocate's, whereas the Attorney General for Northern Ireland took the UK Government's side. However, some independent lawyers joined the case to advocate the rights and guarantees of Northern Ireland. They claimed a special status for Northern Ireland, making explicit references to the Northern Ireland Act 1998 – particularly its first section "Status of Northern Ireland" – and to the overall settlement of the Good Friday Agreement, which took the common EU membership of the UK and the Irish Republic for granted.

The verdict of the Supreme Court, released on 24 January 2017, represented a heavy defeat for all the devolved administrations (McHarg & Mitchell 2017). First, the Court noted that the devolution legislation does not restrict Westminster's sovereignty over any policy area and vis-à-vis any devolved administration:

> The [Sewel] convention was adopted as a means of establishing cooperative relationships between the UK Parliament and the devolved institutions, where there were overlapping legislative competences. In each of the devolution settlements the UK Parliament has preserved its right to legislate on matters which are within the competence of the devolved legislature.
>
> *(UKSP, Judgement, 24 January 2017, 44)*

Secondly, as far as the decision to leave the EU is concerned, the Court did not detect any exceptionality for Northern Ireland. The provision allowing Northern Ireland to choose between the UK and the Irish Republic "neither regulated any other change in the constitutional status of Northern Ireland nor required the consent of a majority of the people of Northern Ireland to the withdrawal of the United Kingdom from the European Union" (UKSP, Judgement 24 January 2017, 44). Thirdly, according to the Court, the Sewel Convention concerns cases in which UK law impacts directly on devolved matters, not cases where the effect on devolved powers is an indirect result of a law that pertains to reserved (UK) powers, such as relations with the EU and Foreign Policy:

> legislation which implements changes to the competences of EU institutions and thereby affects devolved competences, such as the 2008 Act which incorporated the Treaty of Lisbon amending the TEU and the TFEU into section 1(2) of the 1972 Act, has not been the subject of legislative consent motions in any devolved legislature.
>
> *(UKSP, Judgement 24 January 2017, 44)*

Finally, the Court clarified the political, rather than juridical, nature of the Sewel Convention, despite its inclusion in recent devolution legislation. As such, the question of its application is considered to lay beyond the remit of the Court itself:

> Judges therefore are neither the parents nor the guardians of political conventions; they are merely observers. As such, they can recognise the operation of a political convention in the context of deciding a legal question...

but they cannot give legal rulings on its operation or scope, because those matters are determined within the political world ...

The evolving nature of devolution has resulted in the Sewel Convention also receiving statutory recognition through section 2 of the Scotland Act 2016 ...

... the UK Parliament is not seeking to convert the Sewel Convention into a rule which can be interpreted, let alone enforced, by the courts; rather, it is recognising the convention for what it is, namely a political convention, and is effectively declaring that it is a permanent feature of the relevant devolution settlement.

The Sewel Convention has an important role in facilitating harmonious relationships between the UK Parliament and the devolved legislatures. But the policing of its scope and the manner of its operation does not lie within the constitutional remit of the judiciary, which is to protect the rule of law.

(UKSP, Judgement 24 January 2017, 47–9)

In other words, the Supreme Court judges affirmed that Westminster remains sovereign. It is up to Westminster to judge if a situation can be considered as normal, thus requiring a legislative process that fully respects the Sewel Convention, or exceptional, therefore legitimising a legislative intervention by the central Parliament on devolved policy areas with or without consent. Indeed, according to an expert of the UK constitution, Brexit constitutes an evident situation of exceptionality that justifies, in principle, a direct intervention by Westminster, independently of consent from devolved legislatures (Interview 21). At the same time, another interviewee wondered whether two more decades of normal politics (without Brexit) would have institutionalised the Sewel Convention into a constitutional rule (Interview 34). In any case, the ruling of the Supreme Court reaffirms the political nature of the UK constitution (Griffith 1979; Interview 40). As far as the territorial constitution is concerned, the Court decision has clearly restated – beyond any doubt, nuance, or political forcing – the unitary character of the UK, based on parliamentary sovereignty.

A second court case, on the so-called Scotland Continuity Bill, provided a further strong restatement of Westminster sovereignty. As explained in the previous section, the UK Government appealed against Scottish legislation that aimed to preserve the full set of devolved powers, as assigned by the Scotland Act 1998, in contrast to the temporary restrictions prescribed by the EU Withdrawal Act 2018. On 13 December 2018, the Supreme Court ruled on all the specific questions related to the case.

The overall subject of the Bill was found to be within the competences of the Scottish Parliament, as (contrary to the UK Government's claims) the main content did not intrude on reserved matters, such as "observation or implementation of obligations under EU law" or "relations with the EU". In addition, some parts of the Bill were found to be unconstitutional only because, in the time interval between the passing of the Bill (March) and the Court's ruling (December), the coming into force of the EU Withdrawal Act 2018 (June) had changed the competences of the Scottish Parliament – amending the original Scotland Act 1998.

The Scottish government, in particular through its Cabinet Secretary for the Constitution, Europe and External Affairs – Michael Russell – emphasised this part of the Court's sentence, presenting the latter as absolutely favourable to Scotland and accusing the UK Government of having "changed the rules of the game midway through the match", thus making recourse to "an act of constitutional vandalism" (Holyrood 13 December 2018). This political polemic catalysed attention on the timing (of law-making), giving the impression that the prevalence of Westminster law was exclusively based on the "trick" of blocking royal assent for the Scottish Continuity Bill while bringing the EU Withdrawal Act into force.

However, the Court considered specific provisions of the Continuity Bill unconstitutional, not only because in contrast with the (intervened) EU Withdrawal Act 2018, but also with the preceding Scotland Act 1998. More crucially, some parts of the sentence clearly distinguish the issue of timing (which piece of legislation entered the statute book first) from the question of sovereignty and, therefore, from constitutional hierarchy. Early in the sentence, the Court restates that "The Scottish Parliament is a democratically elected legislature with a mandate to make laws for people in Scotland … But it does not enjoy the sovereignty of the Crown in Parliament" (UKSP, Judgement 13 December 2018, 24–5). Then, in discussing a sub-question related to the putative infringement of Westminster's reserved matters by Section 17 of the Continuity Bill – though arguing against such alleged infringement – the Court could not be clearer in restating parliamentary sovereignty and, therefore, the unitary character of the UK:

> Nor are we persuaded that section 17 impinges upon the sovereignty of Parliament. Section 17 does not purport to alter the fundamental constitutional principle that the Crown in Parliament is the ultimate source of legal authority; nor would it have that effect. Parliament would remain sovereign even if section 17 became law. It could amend, disapply or repeal section 17 whenever it chose, acting in accordance with its ordinary procedures.
>
> The preferable analysis is that although section 17, if it became law, would not affect Parliamentary sovereignty, it would nevertheless impose a condition on the effect of certain laws made by Parliament for Scotland, unless and until Parliament exercised its sovereignty so as to disapply or repeal it.
>
> *(UKSP, Judgement 13 December 2018, 24–5)*

Having said that, the Brexit process did not only provide a clarification on the legal aspects of the territorial constitution. It also led to a new territorial settlement that marks a further divergence between the *de facto* status of Northern

Ireland, on the one hand, and that of Scotland and Wales, on the other (Keating 2021). Indeed, in negotiating the Brexit Withdrawal Agreement, the UK government has had to come to terms with some EU's red lines, including the maintenance of a borderless Ireland – a request clearly advanced by the EU to protect the interests of the Irish Republic. Therefore, to avoid the establishment of a physical/visible border within the island of Ireland, the Northern Ireland Protocol (a key component of the Withdrawal Agreement) provided for the *de facto* maintenance of Northern Ireland within the EU customs union and the free circulation of goods. Clearly enough, this specific Brexit outcome galvanised the republican/Catholic community of Northern Ireland and dismayed the unionist/Protestant community, who saw the establishment of a *de facto* customs border in the Irish Sea – i.e., between Northern Ireland and Great Britain. However, the point that matters here is that, while the legal clashes before the Supreme Court provided a clarification that confirmed the unitary nature of the UK, the actual territorial settlement at Brexit Day (31 January 2020) has pushed Northern Ireland in a different direction vis-à-vis Scotland and Wales. To be sure, the ever more special status of Northern Ireland is not formally enshrined in basic principles of the (domestic) UK constitution. It, rather, originates in – and finds its protection from – international agreements. Yet, the guarantees provided by these agreements appear to have been strengthened by the Brexit test.

5.2.4 Brexit and the territorial constitution: "unitary and decentralised"

The impact of Brexit on the breadth of devolved powers (self-rule) remains controversial. On the one hand, Brexit legislation has restricted the range of competences assigned by devolution legislation to devolved parliaments/assemblies. In this respect, the Brexit effect could be seen as one of formal recentralisation. On the other hand, these restrictions are meant to be temporary, while the repatriated competences already reassigned to the devolved administrations have, in fact, widened the scope of devolved powers. Overall, up to Brexit Day (31 January 2020), the Brexit process does not seem to have had a clear and univocal effect on devolved self-rule.

By contrast, Brexit has produced a clear effect on the issue of sovereignty, i.e., on devolved shared-rule. Nearly 20 years of devolution had made the territorial constitution undefined and contested, leading some authoritative scholars to consider the UK as a quasi-federal system (Matthews & Flinders 2017), or a system on a federalising course (Keating 2018). In Lijphart's index of federalism, this evaluation corresponded to a "2.5" value, pointing to an intermediate position between "unitary and decentralised" ("2") and "semi-federal" ("3") (Matthews & Flinders 2017). While we share this evaluation, we also think that the Brexit process has had an important impact, which requires tracing the constitutional relationship of the Celtic peripheries with the UK by distinguishing between Northern Ireland, on one side, and Scotland and Wales, on the other.

The formal constitution of the UK has proved to be still unitary in nature. First, the negotiation between central and devolved governments in the relevant Joint Ministerial Committee has confirmed the lack of formal devolved powers in that specific venue (McEwen 2018). Secondly, the exceptionality of Brexit generated an overwhelming test for the solidity of the Sewel Convention, which was indeed disregarded (for the first time) by the UK Government and, as a result, emerges as an extremely weak form of guarantee for all the Celtic peripheries. Finally, two legal clashes brought before the Supreme Court put a stop to claims or hopes that devolution had substantively changed the unitary character of the UK. Yet, the Brexit process and outcome (up to Brexit Day) has also shown that Northern Ireland is not entirely subject to the unitary UK constitution. Rather, its *de facto* constitutional condition is crucially affected (and protected) by international agreements that determine its special status.

Therefore, referring to Lijphart's conceptual map and indicators, we think that in light of the Brexit process, the UK should be "demoted" to the category "unitary and decentralised" (value "2"), in respect to its relationships with Scotland and Wales; while it should be "upgraded" to the category "semi-federal" (value "3") of the index of federalism, in respect to the status of Northern Ireland (see Figure 5.1).

In particular, the "demotion" of the UK formal constitution to "unitary and decentralised" (as far as Scotland and Wales are concerned) is justified by the gap between the level of devolved self-rule and shared-rule, as already pointed out in comparative studies (Bolleyer *et al.* 2014, 376). This gap emerges very clearly from the latest dataset of the Regional Authority Index (RAI), which includes

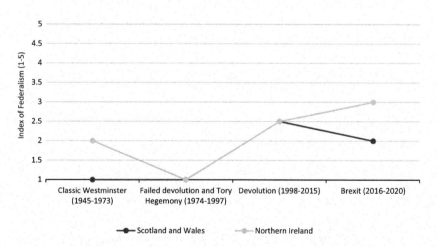

FIGURE 5.1 Longitudinal changes in the Index of Federalism Source: Matthews and Flinders (2017) for scores related to Scotland and Wales until 2015. Authors' assessment for Northern Ireland (throughout the period) and for Scotland and Wales in the Brexit period.

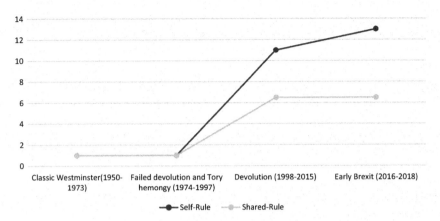

FIGURE 5.2 Longitudinal change in devolved self-rule and shared-rule for Scotland and Wales Source: Hooghe *et al.* (2021) – Regional Authority Index (RAI) scores: RAI–MLG zip file.

data up to 2018 (Hooghe *et al.* 2021). As shown in Figure 5.2, the UK's Celtic peripheries score relatively high in self-rule, but relatively low in shared-rule.

Just to provide some terms for comparison, in Spain, which is usually considered a quasi-federal system, Catalonia and the Basque country score respectively 9.5 and 10.5 in (RAI measured) shared-rule. When Belgium undertook a constitutional transition from a regionalised to a federal system, the (RAI measured) shared-rule scores of the Flemish and Francophone communities rose from "6" in 1988 (very close to the latest available score of Scotland and Wales) to 11 in 1996 – virtually the same score as the *Länder* of the German federation. Indeed, low shared-rule is identified as the classical feature of unitary systems, including the Westminster model. In the UK, the level of shared-rule of the devolved administrations has grown considerably with devolution but is in no way near the values found in semi-federal or federal systems.

5.3 Brexit, secessionist backlashes, and ethno-territorial tensions

Brexit has further polarised UK politics on the centre–periphery cleavage. On one side, the leading political force in the Brexit process, the Conservative Party, has become (or is back to being) a catalyst and advocate of Anglo-British nationalism and hyper-unionism (Gamble 2016).[11] These ideological connotations and (constitutional) policy orientations have become more evident with Boris Johnson's leadership, but they were clearly present in May's approach to Brexit from the outset (Wincott *et al.* 2021). Needless to say, the Conservative Party is flanked by the unionist parties of Northern Ireland, each bringing its own specific shade of unionism and British nationalism. On the other side, secessionist nationalist parties in the three Celtic peripheries opposed the Brexit process but were neither able to stop it nor to shape/steer it to accord with their preferences, with the partial exception of the Irish nationalists (SF and SDLP), who could count on the support of the Republic of Ireland and the EU. As a consequence, these political forces were naturally inclined to use Brexit as a trigger (or an additional reason) to pursue their preset secessionist projects.

A complete picture of centre–periphery politics in the UK, as shaped by the Brexit process, should also include the intermediate position between hyper-unionism and separatist peripheral nationalism. This political space is occupied by important political forces, primarily the Labour Party and the Liberal Democrats. However, during the Brexit process, they were rather ineffective in presenting a clear alternative vision between the two poles (Andrews 2021). The electoral/institutional weakness of these two parties, which held power only in Wales, has certainly constituted a structural limit on their capacity to steer the debate and policy outcomes. Yet, aside from outright opposition to both Tory nonchalance about devolution and (peripheral) nationalist secessionism, they were rather timid and hazy in their proposals. The Labour Party hid behind the idea of an open Constitutional Convention that would gather the preferences of the public. As far as the territorial constitution is concerned, it did not go beyond stating a "preferred option for an elected Senate of the Nations and Regions" and a vague commitment to "safeguard the future of a devolved UK, reforming the way in which it works, to make it fit for the future" (Labour Party, Manifesto 2019, 81–2). As for the Lib-Dems, they adopted a similarly ambiguous position in 2017 (Liberal Democratic Party, Manifesto 2017, 89–94), before finally committing to a fully-fledged federal reform in the run-up to the 2019 general election (Liberal Democratic Party, Manifesto 2019, 83).

The positioning of these two parties vis-à-vis the UK's territorial settlement represents an important element for speculating on the possibility of finding more stable and less divisive constitutional arrangements in the long run. After all, Labour still represents the main alternative to Conservative governments. Yet, during the Brexit period – as well as in the subsequent "Brexit and Covid" period (see Chapter 6) – the importance of their programme formulation remained rather marginal. By contrast, the initiatives taken by peripheral nationalist parties attracted a lot of attention, as the capacity of the UK to hold together appeared to be in question.

This third and last part of the chapter, therefore, synthetically analyses secessionist backlashes in the three Celtic peripheries, starting with Scotland and Wales, before looking at the more complex case of Northern Ireland.

5.3.1 Scotland: struggling for a second chance

In Scotland, the battle lines on Brexit and its link with the potential reopening of the independence question (less than two years after the September 2014 referendum) were already drawn in the campaign for the 2016 devolved election. On that occasion, it was clearly stated that Brexit would inordinately change the context on which Scottish voters had based their judgement in September 2014. As a consequence, especially if Scotland's vote on Brexit differed from the UK-wide result, it would be fair and necessary to hold a second referendum on independence (Indyref2).

Indeed, the astonishment sparked by the results of the Brexit referendum met a prompt response by the Scottish government. Speaking the day after, Nicola Sturgeon declared that she regarded the prospect of Scotland "being taken out of the EU against our will" as "democratically unacceptable", and (in line with a 2016 manifesto pledge) that "the option of a second referendum must be on the table. And it is on the table". (BBC 24 June 2016). Apparently, the shock and bold reaction ignited an independentist flame, captured by three surveys conducted by different pollsters for different newspapers – the *Daily Record*, the *Sunday Times*, and the *Scottish Daily Mail* – between 25 and 28 June 2016. Excluding the undecided, the three polls returned an average support for independence of nearly 53 percent (see Figure 5.3). Yet, as the situation regarding Brexit – and what type of Brexit would be pursued – remained uncertain, public endorsement for independence quickly returned close to the levels of the 2014 referendum.

In March 2017, as the UK government triggered Art. 50 of the TEU to start the withdrawal process (Allen 2018), Sturgeon made the first formal move. After securing a mandate from the Scottish Parliament, she sent an open letter to the PM requesting the start of talks to reach an agreement on a second independence referendum (*The Financial Times* 31 March 2017). It is interesting to note that that first request was expressed rather ambivalently. Indeed, the Scottish government

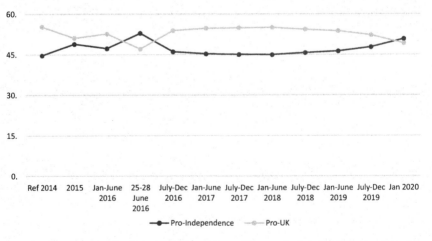

FIGURE 5.3   Support for Scottish independence Source: Authors' elaboration based on all available polls conducted in the period.

presented the independence referendum as a hypothetical event, dependent on the details of both the internal Brexit legislation and the external agreement with the EU; and to be held possibly between late 2018 and spring 2019 (Baldini *et al.* 2022). In any case, Theresa May had dismissed the issue even before Holyrood voted on it, although the answer was as ambivalent as the request: "now is not the time" (*The Guardian* 16 March 2017).

The request for Indyref2 also featured in the SNP manifesto for the 2017 general election (SNP 2017 Manifesto, 29), and the Scottish government, as discussed above, maintained a confrontational approach both regarding the EU Withdrawal Bill and the negotiated Withdrawal Agreement. In particular, as far as the latter was concerned, it denounced the diverse treatment of Scotland and Northern Ireland, in spite of the fact that both devolved administrations had voted against Brexit.

Nonetheless, faced with the UK Government's refusal to even consider talking about Indyref2, the Scottish government preferred not to insist. Clearly, the chaos besetting Catalonia since autumn 2017,[12] reinforced the SNP leadership's determination to avoid any unilateral (and purportedly illegal) approach to independence.

This strategy was maintained throughout 2018, when much of centre–periphery politics was absorbed by the EU Withdrawal Act, and most of 2019. However, in autumn of that year, pressure mounted from the SNP's rank and file for a more resolute approach to independence. Several interviewees confirmed that a lively intra-party debate on Indyref2 had been present since the start of the Brexit process and intensified considerably from late 2018 to late 2019.[13] In the October party conference, the SNP's leadership had to push back on an initiative by a few politicians and many activists to commit to a unilateral declaration of independence, even without holding a referendum (BBC 10 October 2019).

The December 2019 general election triggered a second formal request. The claim was already presented in the party manifesto (SNP 2019 Manifesto, 4), but was formalised a week after the election. A mix of grassroots pressure and encouraging polls (Curtice & Monatgu 2020), on the one hand, and, on the other, the clear victory of a Johnson-led Tory party united behind the battle cry "Get Brexit done", pushed the Scottish government to end the delay. A letter was sent to the PM, with an attached document (*Scotland's Right to Choose*) advocating, with an argumentative but also peremptory style, holding an independence referendum by 2020, with the precise date to be at the discretion of the Scottish parliament (Scottish Government 2019). With Brexit Day approaching fast, the request was followed by a series of initiatives, including Sturgeon's missions to Brussels (in search of political support), and some street demonstrations, such as the march in Glasgow on 11 January 2020, at which around a hundred thousand people were present (*The Guardian* 11 January 2020).

The Scottish nationalist push for a second referendum, however, met the firm opposition of the PM. Just two weeks before Brexit Day, Johnson sent a formal memorandum to Sturgeon, declaring that he "cannot agree to any request …

that would lead to further independence referendums", and that "The people of Scotland voted decisively on that promise to keep our United Kingdom together … The UK Government will continue to uphold the democratic decision [made in 2014]" (Foreign Policy 14 January 2020). From an instrumental point of view, the UK Government's outright opposition to a second referendum is well justified by poll data, which show a growth of pro-independence preferences and, in January 2020, a tiny margin of advantage vis-à-vis preferences for the union.

Yet, given the strategic choice made by the Scottish government not to step beyond the limits of UK constitutional procedures, the struggle for Indyref2 was postponed to the subsequent devolved elections (see Chapter 6), in which the SNP hoped to gather enough support to further legitimise its request, thus breaking the deadlock.

5.3.2 Wales: firmly in the UK

For several interconnected reasons, anti-Brexit separatist opposition was much less intense in Wales than in Scotland. First, support for independence has traditionally been very low in Wales (see Figure 5.4). Secondly, during the Brexit process, the devolved administration was governed by non-nationalist parties, namely Welsh Labour and the Welsh Lib-Dems; or, if Welsh Labour is to be considered a Welsh nationalist party,[14] by non-independentist parties. Therefore, in contrast to Scotland, there was no chance that Welsh devolved institutions would use – or threaten to use – the independence card in their potential confrontations with the UK Government. Finally, in the Brexit referendum, Wales voted to leave the EU. As a consequence, there was a limit to the extent to which the Welsh executive could oppose the UK's Brexit policy.

In fact, the Welsh executive remained very critical of Brexit in principle and the type of Brexit being pursued by the UK Government, not to mention the

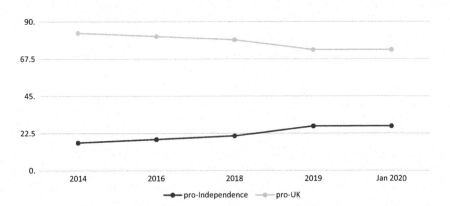

FIGURE 5.4   Support for independence in Wales Source: Authors' elaboration based on all polls conducted in the period using the standard question ("Should Wales be an independent country?").

Brexit implications for devolution. Yet, Welsh Labour could not ignore the (pro-Brexit) preferences of a considerable portion of its own voters and the post-referendum (re)positioning of UK-Labour. Indeed, the first reaction was to adopt a rather low-profile strategy (IWA 27 July 2016). As mentioned above, the Welsh executive expressed significant opposition to the "power grab" envisaged in the EU Withdrawal Bill, but (differently from the Scottish executive) then reached a compromise with London.

By contrast, the pro-independence Plaid Cymru was in a position to voice its outright anti-Brexit stance and to link it to highly confrontational anti-UK politics. In this case, there were no trade-offs between advocating the party (nationalist-independentist) ideology and opposing Brexit, as their electoral strongholds (the Welsh-speaking areas of west Wales) had returned pro-Remain majorities in the Brexit referendum. As a consequence, Plaid Cymru pushed for Wales to follow the antagonistic approach of the SNP Scottish executive (Interview 20). However, Plaid Cymru had also to come to terms with the Wales-wide vote on Brexit and low support for secession from the UK.

Indeed, from the start of the Brexit process, the independence option could only be framed in very weak terms, *de facto* relying on a possible domino effect of any potential Scottish path to independence: "This is not an attempt to say that Wales is in the same position as Scotland. We are not. We didn't vote to remain", yet "If other nations are advocating this [i.e., independence] path, why would we in Wales not even be debating it as an option?" (Plaid Cymru's leader Leanne Wood, quoted in *The Guardian* 29 June 2016).

Throughout the Brexit process, Plaid brought back the issue of Welsh independence as a reflex to Scottish initiatives. While Scottish nationalists were requesting a referendum, their Welsh counterparts were still conducting a background battle to build a culture of independence. When, in March 2017, Sturgeon issued her first request for a Scottish referendum, Plaid politician (and future leader) Adam Price penned an essay that urged his fellow nationals to decide whether Wales wanted to be more like Scotland or Cornwall (WalesOnline 18 March 2017). Similarly, during party conferences in autumn 2019, when the SNP was discussing a more daring approach to independence for 2020, Price set out his objective of obtaining a Welsh independence referendum by 2030 (BBC 4 October 2019).

Nonetheless, Plaid's cultural work on Welsh national self-confidence did produce some results. During the Brexit process, support for independence rose by ten percentage points: from nearly 17 percent in 2014 to nearly 27 percent in January 2020 (see Figure 5.4).

5.3.3 Northern Ireland: between republican galvanising and loyalist anxiety

The reaction of the main political forces to the Brexit referendum – both UK-wide and in Northern Ireland – varied not only across the British unionist–Irish nationalist divide, but also between moderate and radical parties. The moderate parties on both fronts (UUP and SDLP) reacted with a mix of preoccupation and pragmatism. The UUP insisted on the legitimacy of the UK-wide result, in spite of the contrary response in Northern Ireland, and the need to find practical solutions to the manifold and thorny implications of Brexit (BBC 24 June 2016). The SDLP immediately occupied the "winning position" – i.e., the one that proved to be closest to the outcome of the UK-EU/Ireland negotiation on the Irish border. The party refrained from using Brexit to pursue Irish reunification but, at the same time, claimed that the referendum results in Northern Ireland sanctioned the impossibility of re-establishing a physical border in Ireland (ibid.).

By contrast, the two radical parties tried to exploit the referendum results to blatantly voice their opposing nationalist projects. Ignoring the Northern Irish results, the DUP welcomed the pro-Brexit UK-wide response as a first step to redefining the destiny of the "nation state" (ibid.). With this spirit, they decided to support (and prod) the UK Government in the Brexit enterprise after the June 2017 general election (Tonge 2017). Unrealistically, they hoped that Brexit could be used to partly undo the Belfast agreement (*Belfast Telegraph* 3 October 2018). However, given the inclusion of the Northern Ireland Protocol in the Brexit agreement, they came out as the main losers of the Brexit gamble. When it became clear that the renegotiated (by the Johnson government) agreement was setting Northern Ireland apart from Great Britain, the DUP came under fierce criticism from the other unionist parties. They were accused of committing a "catastrophic miscalculation", which had left Northern Ireland on the "window ledge" of the UK (*The Guardian* 17 October 2019).

At the opposite end of the spectrum, Sinn Fein hoped that Brexit could be used to move decisively towards Irish reunification. Immediately after the Brexit referendum, they launched the option of a Border Poll (*The Independent* 25 June 2016). The hard-core Irish nationalists gradually moved from a discourse that presented reunification as a reaction against the potential dangers of Brexit (especially the re-establishment of a hard border in Ireland), to one that projected reunification in the non-distant future, building on the favourable outcome of Brexit (Coakley 2022). It was the latter mechanism – i.e., galvanising for a positive Brexit outcome whetting appetites for reunification – that appears to have been at work amongst Irish nationalist voters.

As shown in Figure 5.5, support for a united Ireland grew only marginally as a consequence of the initial shock in 2016, remaining stable in the following two years. However, as the final Brexit agreement became certain and Brexit Day loomed, support for Irish reunification reached a historical maximum of 42.5 percent. To be sure, the pro-UK majority in Northern Ireland seems still firmly in the lead. Yet, in comparison with Scotland and Wales, the Brexit process has left peripheral nationalism in Northern Ireland considerably more satisfied and more optimistic. Needless to say, this course might trigger tensions within (and reactions by) the unionist side.

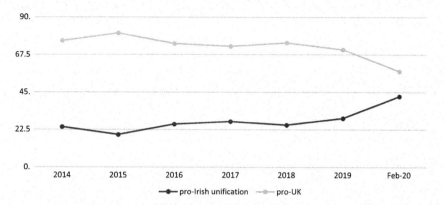

FIGURE 5.5   Support for Irish unification in Northern Ireland Source: https://www.ark
.ac.uk/nilt/results/polatt.html#conpref (for the years 2014–19); https://
www.reuters.com/article/uk-britain-nireland-poll/poll-shows-northern
-ireland-majority-against-united-ireland-idUKKBN20C0WF?edition
-redirect=uk (for February 2020).

5.4 Conclusions: a unitary but disunited state

The different national identities present in various constituent units of the UK
and their different relationships with the state-national (British) identity have
constituted the socio-cultural context for an active centre–periphery cleavage,
which has increased in political salience since the late 1960s. In the late 1990s,
devolution represented the main institutional response to the various claims and
demands emerging from the three Celtic peripheries. However, contrary to some
expectations, devolution did not undermine peripheral nationalism, which kept
growing, particularly in Scotland. Yet, with the outcome of the 2014 Scottish
independence referendum, the territorial integrity of the state appeared to have
been not only secured but also placed beyond political contestation, at least for
a generation.

As largely anticipated (Minto *et al.* 2016), Brexit has reignited all the political
and constitutional tensions within the centre–periphery cleavage, bringing the
survival of the UK back into question. While a certain degree of centre–periphery conflict was inevitable, given the diverging results of the Brexit referendum
and the contrasting positions of governments across the UK jurisdictions, the way
in which the process was conducted intensified the confrontation. Indeed, in line
with our third working hypothesis (cf. Chapter 2), the pro-Brexit Conservative
Government showed little patience with the established inter-governmental
practices linked to devolution, proceeding rather unilaterally in disregard of the
Sewel Convention. More importantly, the Government exploited the opportunity to restrict, albeit temporarily, the range of powers devolved to the three
Celtic peripheries, particularly some of those that had been exercised by the

EU. In fact, it is difficult to ascertain whether the whole operation amounted to recentralisation or not, as many powers repatriated from Brussels did go to the devolved administrations. However, both the pro-independence Scottish government and the pro-union Welsh government denounced the Brexit legislation as a "power grab" by the central Government. The peripheral reaction was led by Scotland, the only Celtic periphery governed by a secessionist party, the SNP. This reaction led to repeated judicial and political clashes.

The judicial clashes – *Miller Case* 2016–17 and *Scotland Continuity Bill case* 2018 – have produced a confirmatory clarification on the territorial constitution. The authoritativeness of the Supreme Court, which included judges from the different territorial jurisdictions of the UK, appears to have settled disputes arising from alternative interpretations of the constitution. In particular, what emerges from the rulings of the Supreme Court is that Westminster's sovereignty and, therefore, the unitary form of the state is fully preserved, in spite of devolution and in spite of the acknowledged multinational character of the UK's people. The central Parliament maintains the prerogative to intervene with its legislation both to alter devolved powers and to directly affect policies in devolved areas. From the point of view of the devolved administrations, this clarification confirms the absence of any judiciable constitutional guarantee for their self-government. However, in this respect, Northern Ireland constitutes a *de facto* exception, as its status is regulated by international treaties – the 1998 Belfast Agreement and (with Brexit) the 2020 UK-EU Withdrawal Agreement – that constrain the intervention of Westminster. In other words, constitution-wise (as well as domestic market- and custom-wise), the Brexit process has set Northern Ireland further apart from Great Britain. The latter emerges as a unitary system, in legal-constitutional terms, while it is evidently divided in political terms, with governments of different colours in London, Cardiff, and Edinburgh.

The Scottish government has already engaged in arm wrestling with London to obtain the green light for a second independence referendum. With about half of Scottish voters steadily in favour of independence, the UK Government is firmly denying its consent. As it is often the case in UK politics, it will take a political/electoral thrust to overcome the institutional standoff. In addition, in the process, pro-independence attitudes have also grown in Wales and, more conspicuously, in Northern Ireland. In short, it can be easily claimed that the UK, as we have known it since 1921, has never been as politically disunited as on Brexit Day.

Notes

1 For reasons of space, the analysis of the centre–periphery dimension is restricted to the institutional and political relations between the UK and its national components – England, Northern Ireland, Scotland, and Wales – with a particular focus on the last three "Celtic peripheries". Important effects of Brexit on territorial politics, such as the rural-urban divide (Brooks 2020) or Northern England's regionalism (Giovannini 2016; 2019), are left out of the analysis.

2 Data gathered asking the Moreno question show a greater compatibility between the Scottish and British identities. Respondents declaring to identify equally as Scottish and British oscillated in the range between 21 and 32 percent during the period 1999–2022 (https://whatscotlandthinks.org/questions/moreno-national-identity-5/).

3 The devolution reform also created an elected assembly for the London metropolitan area – Greater London Assembly (GLA) (Travers 2002; Sandford & Maer 2004), led by a directly elected Mayor (Sweeting 2002).

4 In Scotland and Wales, the referendums were held on 11 and 18 September 1997 respectively. Voters supported devolution much more convincingly in Scotland than in Wales, where the pro-devolution campaign also benefitted from the Scottish bandwagon effect (Mitchell 1998; McAllister 1998). In Northern Ireland, the referendum was held on 22 May 1998, simultaneously with a parallel referendum in the Republic of Ireland. The Northern Irish referendum represented an explicit (post-hoc) approval of the Good Friday Agreement (signed in April 1998) and an implicit (ex-ante) acceptance of the 1998 Northern Ireland Act. The overall massive approval (71 percent) came disproportionately from the Catholic/republican community (Hayes & McAllister 2001).

5 The Scotland Act 2016 received royal assent only three months before the Brexit referendum. However, the related bill was presented immediately after the 2015 general election. The proposal for strengthening Scottish devolution drew on the conclusions of the Smith Commission, which was set up immediately after the Scotland independence referendum, and whose report was published in November 2014. The 2017 Wales Act received royal assent at the end of January 2017, but the legislation process began with the presentation of a bill in October 2015.

6 For instance, in 2001 the House of Lords Select Committee on the Constitution defined the UK as a union state (Mitchell 2010a, 86).

7 The exact number of policy areas to be directly assigned to each devolved administration varies as follows: 111 to Northern Ireland, 73 to Scotland, and 35 to Wales (UK Government, Frameworks Analysis, September 2020, 9).

8 Interviews 21, 23, and 34.

9 Interviews 12, 13, and 34.

10 An authoritative scholar advanced some doubts about the strategic opportunity for the devolved governments to meddle in a controversy between Whitehall and Westminster (Interview 24).

11 A recent contribution defined this approach as "muscular unionism" (Andrews 2021).

12 For an analysis of how the Catalan crisis was reported in the UK media and in other European countries, see Perales-Garicia and Pont-Sorribes (2019).

13 Interviews 13 and 22.

14 For a comprehensive reflection on Welsh Labour's ideology before and after devolution, see Carwyn Jones (2004).

6

UNDERSTANDING THE BREXIT STRAINS DURING THE COVID CRISIS

So far, we have analysed the effects of the Brexit process in a period – from the 2015 election to Brexit Day (31 January 2020) – when the traditional patterns of the political system were in many ways being challenged. In doing so, we tried to ascertain the implications of Brexit for the party system and institutional dynamics. Our assessment is clearly provisional, as the consequences of the exit from the EU will no doubt unfold for many years to come. At the same time, we believe that we have identified significant trends across the three selected dimensions, which point in the same direction: back towards the Westminster model.

In this chapter, we look at the main developments following Brexit Day in our three dimensions, when the UK – like the rest of the world – became embroiled in the Covid crisis. Brexit and Covid-19 are clearly intertwined, and the attempt to accurately disentangle their respective effects is a very complex exercise, in itself beyond our scope. However, by discussing what happened after the exit day, we can take a step further in our assessment of how British politics has been changing in these turbulent years, as a consequence of Brexit.

6.1 Political parties in the aftermath of Brexit Day: looking beyond "self-evident truths"

As already remarked, the survival of the SMP electoral system represents a powerful barrier against the rise of challenger anti-EU parties similar to the one Britain has experienced over the last decade. As a radical transformation of the party system remains a very remote prospect, the main parties nonetheless have had to cope with increasing uncertainties, especially after the emergence of the Covid-19 pandemic in February 2020. In this respect, the Covid-19 crisis emerged in a climate already marked by higher electoral volatility (see again Chapter 3) as well as by more volatile opinion polls.

DOI: 10.4324/9781003127680-7

In line with the approach taken in Chapter 3, in order to make sense of the challenges that emerged as the country officially left the EU, we can profitably combine a focus on electoral supply and demand. Hence, the first point regards the ability of the leadership of the two main parties to adapt to a mutating electoral market (Fieldhouse *et al.* 2020). In this respect, a less loyal and more disaffected electorate is clearly prone to follow populist leaders. Yet, rather than looking at the ebbs and flows of a leader's popularity (but see next section), it is perhaps more important to reflect on some elements that are less frequently considered but are more important for our scope. Stressing the need to look beyond self-evident truths (such as the idea that the 2019 general election was *only* about Brexit) and the importance of performative acts evident in the rise of the UK's peculiar form of populism, Flinders underlines that "Johnson's buffoonery and pantomime antics appear not as the behaviour of a political clown but as the carefully calibrated statecraft of a sophisticated politician" (2020, 232). Again, while the public grew increasingly dissatisfied with the way the Johnson Government was handling Brexit in 2021 (Menon 2022),[1] what is striking is that, at least until February 2022, the prospect of (yet another) snap election was linked more to scandals than to party management or strategies.

In April 2020, Labour replaced Corbyn with former shadow Minister for Brexit, Keir Starmer. The leadership turnover took place in a context marked by divisions between the Corbynite and New Labour factions. As Roe-Crines (2021) underlines, the former are too skewed in the perception that Corbyn's defeat was all down to Brexit, while the latter underplays the extent to which it will be more difficult to replicate the 1990s strategies, given that, in contrast to the 1980s, the leftist faction has now been at the helm of the party for several years. And here we are again with the danger of self-evidence. As a matter of fact, "both factions believe their analysis of Labour's route back to power to be self-evidently correct, despite both having lost elections since 2010" (ibid.). Electorally, Starmer's party finds itself in a stranglehold, having lost many votes in the most marginal seats (poor, with lower literacy rates and more critical health conditions) and suffering – on the other hand – the growth of the Lib-Dems in the richest and most educated urban constituencies (Green 2020; Wager *et al.* 2021). Also, party strategists should think twice before drawing too many lessons from by-elections held in 2021. While the recurrent propensity of the British electorate to deliver surprising results was confirmed by several of the by-elections held, some of which were marked by very big swings[2] in comparison with the 2019 general elections (Surridge 2021), the two-party system has already proved resilient to similar shifts in the past.

More in general, we can once again refer to the scenarios sketched at the end of Chapter 3: from the most radical one which sees the "replacement" of traditional parties by the challengers, to "fragmentation", up to "reinvention", fruit of the ability of traditional actors to reabsorb the challenges. In this respect, the prospects for transformation of the first dimension following the definitive exit are linked to the consolidation of identity issues as decisive elements in electoral behaviour. The electorates of the two main parties are increasingly differentiated between "identity liberals" (Labour voters, concentrated also in geographical terms more and more around the main urban areas) and "identity conservatives" (Sobolewska & Ford 2020), mainly clustered in rural areas. As such, it will be interesting to monitor the possible repoliticisation of the European question. But can this really take place?

Given that the EU-UK Trade and Cooperation Agreement has left various sectors un-determined (e.g., finance and – partially – fisheries), the scope for a future repoliticisation of the European issue, even outside the EU, cannot be excluded. For the European question to become salient again, a credible political entrepreneur is, however, necessary. Someone able to campaign on the perception that Brexit has been betrayed. To be sure, Britain already has a sort of "UKIP 3.0", in the form of "Reform UK", led by Richard Tice. However, the party hardly made it to the headlines throughout 2021 (while scoring poorly in opinion polls, 3–5 percent).[3] While this could easily have been said about UKIP's first years of life, the huge difference between then and now is that any anti-EU party in the future will miss the main springboard for its possible resurgence: elections for the European Parliament.

All in all, however, the two-party system dynamics, which were confirmed after the 2019 election, then saw the two main parties alternating at the top of the opinion polls in the following two years. While underlining that Brexit has certainly been the single most important factor in the disruptions experienced by the party system since the 2014 European elections, it is also clear that the Covid crisis has added to the uncertainties that the electoral market had already been experiencing in the previous years, or even decades. In such a context, the Conservative predominance, within a resurgence of the two-party vote comparable to the 2010–15 elections, appears fragile. The Conservatives and Labour will still benefit from SMP to fight future elections as the main adversaries, but the underlying political and social environment is much less clear-cut than it was in the past.

While this last point seems rather easy to predict, Labour's return to power seems to be conditional on the emergence of a "progressive front", possibly in the form of pacts and alliances between parties that opposed Brexit, either in 2016, or during the years following the referendum. The parties that could be involved are those which – already in 2019 – were allied in 60 constituencies in the "Unite to Remain" electoral pact, namely Labour, the Liberal Democrats, the Green Party, and Plaid Cymru.[4] Corbyn's resignation as party leader has strengthened the likelihood of such alliances for two – somewhat related – reasons. First, he was ambivalent towards Brexit, as demonstrated in 2016 when he chose to go on holiday during the EU referendum campaign. Second, his radical positions on economic issues might have alienated centrist voters, as well as some Liberal Democrat leaders, thus discouraging building such alliances on a large scale. There is a third and further reason that might facilitate the emergence of such pacts, namely the alliances already tested between Labour and the Liberal

Democrats in the first years of the devolved administrations of Scotland and Wales. But, of course, it is too soon to predict any kind of realignment in the structure of what will be offered by anti-Conservative parties, which in some circumstances have appeared to be more united about what they oppose than on what they propose.

6.2 Executive–legislative relations: Johnson's difficult leadership amidst the pandemic

The transition year – which began after Brexit Day (31 January 2020) and lasted until the end of the calendar year – almost completely overlapped with the pandemic crisis. Johnson's agenda for 2020 proved to be very different to the one he was expecting. Having achieved his key objective to "get Brexit done", the PM was almost immediately confronted with the spread of Covid-19 and the need to tackle the pandemic crisis. While the next deadline post-Brexit – i.e., the end of the transition period – required that legislation to implement Brexit be approved on time, the policy responses to the pandemic crisis came to dominate the government's agenda (incidentally, not unlike other European states). To be sure, the implementation of Brexit remained an important issue, but it was over-shadowed in terms of public salience by the new crisis.

Despite the strong majority secured with the 2019 elections and a more cohesively Eurosceptic parliamentary party, the Johnson II government had to face several rebellions on the legislation to implement Brexit, such as the Internal Market Bill – regulating the UK internal market post-Brexit – and the Trade Bill – on trade agreements post-Brexit. Starting with the former, the debate in the House of Commons had a broad national and international echo. In particular, the words of the Northern Ireland minister, Brandon Lewis, confirming that some of the provisions in the bill would "break *international law in a very specific and limited way*" (8 September 2020) sparked outrage. Some clauses included in the bill gave ministers the power to decide on state aid and customs procedures in Northern Ireland, thus contradicting the withdrawal agreement between the EU and the UK. At the second reading, 20 Tory MPs rebelled – all of them, except Andrew Percy and Sir Roger Gale – abstaining, while the Government was hit by the resignation of a minister and the head of the Government's legal department. The embarrassment and anger of several MPs – one of whom (Sir Charles Walker) described the relationship between Government and Parliament in the following way: "If you keep beating a dog, don't be surprised if it bites you back" – led the Government to accept an amendment, tabled by the Conservative chairman of the Judiciary Committee, Bob Neill, giving the House of Commons veto power over attempts by ministers to introduce new rules clashing with the withdrawal agreement. In December, after a long scrutiny of the bill and several amendments approved by the House of Lords (Institute for Government 2020), the bill went back to the lower house, where further defections within the Conservative ranks – including that of the former PM, Theresa May – were recorded. The Government compromised and accepted the removal of the most controversial provisions from the text of the bill, which was eventually approved (cf. further below for the implications for devolved administrations).

The emergency measures and the decision to impose tight restrictions on individuals to contain the spread of Covid also became a very divisive issue within the Conservative Party. In October 2020, the vote in the House of Commons on the regulation on health protection featured more than 40 rebel MPs – plus about 20 within the Labour ranks – expressing concerns about the violation of individual rights and the damaging impact of lockdowns on the economy. In December, the subdivision of England into "zones" to limit the spread of the virus was approved only thanks to the abstention of the Labour Party, with 55 Conservative MPs against it and 16 abstaining. Not unlike what occurred in other countries in Europe (Lynggard *et al.* 2022), the Covid crisis has led to a (further) centralisation of power in the executive's hands, with limited (if not absent) parliamentary scrutiny. This situation raised frustration and disappointment among MPs, who vocally expressed their dissatisfaction (Grogan 2020; Schrimsley 2020). The largest revolt happened in December 2021, with the Omicron variant sweeping across the UK and the Government proposing the introduction of Covid passes showing a recent negative test or full vaccination. In the Commons, 99 Tory MPs voted against the Government, with the measure securing approval once again only because of Labour support (incidentally, in the Labour Party there were eight rebels, and a shadow minister resigned).

Not only the lower chamber, but also the upper chamber represented more than a mere headache for Johnson's Government. The House of Lords – which is not controlled by any party – defeated the Government 114 times in the period between December 2019 and April 2021, and a further 35 times in the new parliamentary session starting in May 2021. For comparison, the Government lost 69 times in the House of Lords in the 2017–19 parliamentary session (House of Lords 2022). Although several of the Lords' amendments did not survive the parliamentary "ping-pong", the Government could not afford to ignore the upper chamber, which could use its power to delay the approval of legislation and push the government to compromise.

Despite such difficulties for the Government, legislation implementing Brexit has once again given evidence of its readiness to take full control of the process, attributing broad discretionary powers to the executive through delegation. As the Select Committee on the Constitution of the House of Lords observed: "a distinguishing feature of the Brexit bills was the extent of the delegated powers they contained" (House of Lords 2020, 9). The bills were often drafted in a minimalist way, with little detail on the content of the policy or the nature of the new institutions, giving ministers the powers to create new public bodies or policy regimes post-Brexit. They also often included "Henry VIII" powers – which, as Chapter 4 has shown, constituted the early target of contestation by Conservative backbenchers under Theresa May's government – enabling ministers to amend legislation through statutory instruments (for an in-depth analysis, see House of Lords 2020).

Another indication of the unwillingness of the executive to be constrained by Parliament is provided by the latter's approval of the Trade and Cooperation Agreement. The last-minute deal on the Agreement – on Christmas Eve 2020 – required an extraordinary sitting of Parliament. Given the urgency to vote on it – on 31 December 2020, the transition year would end with the UK "crashing out" of the EU – parliamentary scrutiny was bound to be extremely limited. Exceptionally, in a single sitting day, both the House of Commons and the House of Lords completed their readings. As the Hansard Society (Fowler 2020) notes, this is an extremely unusual procedure as, since 2006, there has been only one precedent. What cannot go unnoticed is that having fought for years to have a say on the Brexit process and for proper scrutiny of the executive, Parliament voted the new regulatory framework on post-Brexit relationships with the EU in less than 24 hours.

The joint effect of Brexit and the pandemic have led to a strong concentration of power in the executive. The Conservative government has not missed the opportunity to broaden its powers by limiting parliamentary scrutiny and through delegated legislation (cf. Cygan *et al.* 2020). While "emergency politics" has provided a strong normative justification for executive action, at least in the most dramatic phases of the pandemic, the Government has certainly not shied away from making good use of the crisis, about which several Conservative backbenchers have also complained. In any case, despite the joint effect of Brexit and Covid strengthening the dominant role of the executive, in both cases Parliament has been much more than a mere nuisance, amending legislation and forcing the Government to compromise. While post-Brexit Day developments seem to provide further evidence on the general validity of the Westminster model still capturing the essence of executive–legislative relationships, they also show that this is a different Westminster system compared to what it used to be in its heyday.

6.3 Centre–periphery relations: recentralisation and contestation

The transition phase was marked by the rise of the Covid-19 emergency, which soon became another fertile terrain for centre–periphery politics, adding to the strains of Brexit in various ways. First, the Covid emergency confirmed the scant regard of the Anglo-British political elites for the devolution settlement,[5] and constituted another occasion for recentralisation, vis-à-vis both devolved and local government (Morphet 2021). Secondly, anti-Covid policy variation across the UK – especially in terms of the timing of adopted measures (Basta & Henderson 2021, 298) – emphasised the role of devolution and strengthened the salience of territorial politics (Morphet 2021, 4; Andrews 2021). Thirdly, public satisfaction with the anti-Covid policies adopted by the UK and devolved governments were deeply shaped not only by party identification, but also by national identities and leave/remain orientations of citizens (Griffiths & Larners 2021). More precisely, satisfaction with the UK Government's responses to Covid were positively correlated to Leave orientations (throughout the UK), as well as to English identity in England and British identity in Scotland and Wales; whereas appreciation of Scottish/Welsh government responses was positively correlated to Remain orientations and Scottish/Welsh identity in the two Celtic peripheries.

This section tries to isolate, as much as possible, the effects of Brexit from those of the Covid crisis on centre–periphery relations post-Brexit Day, with a particular focus on the transition phase (2020). In order to do that, it analyses the adoption of the Internal Market Act 2020; further backlashes from the Brexit process in the Celtic peripheries; and the state of the debate on reforming the territorial constitution.

6.3.1 The Internal Market Act 2020: Brexit against devolution?

If the devolved administrations had the impression that UK governments used Brexit legislation (the EU Withdrawal Act 2018) as an opportunity to push back devolution, such an impression was definitively reinforced during the transition phase, especially with the proposal of the Internal Market Bill in summer 2020. In line with the Queen's speech delivered in the aftermath of the November 2019 general election, the stated purpose of the bill was not only to preserve but also to strengthen the UK internal market in the post-Brexit scenario. The proposed legislation centred on two key principles that were meant to guarantee internal uniformity in trade: "mutual recognition" and "non-discrimination" (Thimont Jack 2020). The former forbids devolved administrations to enact additional requirements for products or services that are legally sold/provided in other constituent parts of the UK; while the latter prevents them from taking measures that, directly or indirectly, make the selling/buying of products or services from other parts of the UK more difficult or less appealing. The bill betrays the UK Government's impatience with the consensual method for the identification of common frameworks established with the EU Withdrawal Act 2018. In addition, it represents an acceleration of the re-establishment of a UK public funding regime, under a planned "UK Shared Prosperity Fund", which is meant to replace the EU structural funds (Nice 2021). Indeed, the Internal Market Bill enables the UK government to finance any project/activity, including in devolved areas.

Moreover, one part of the bill implied unilateral changes to the terms of the Northern Ireland Protocol and, therefore, to the EU Withdrawal Agreement. More precisely, the proposed legislation allowed UK ministers to enact secondary legislation aimed at removing checks for goods travelling from Northern Ireland to Great Britain, even if such legislation did not comply with domestic legislation or international agreements, including the EU Withdrawal Agreement. As stated by the PM, the aim of the UK Government was to try and preserve unrestricted access to Great Britain's market for Northern Irish businesses, thus defusing anxieties within the unionist parties and community of Northern Ireland about the emergence of a significant border in the North Sea:

> My job is to uphold the integrity of the UK but also to protect the Northern Ireland peace process and the Good Friday Agreement ... And to do that, we need a legal safety net to protect our country against extreme or irrational interpretations of the Protocol, which could lead to a border down the Irish Sea, in a way that I believe would be prejudicial to the interests of the Good Friday Agreement and prejudicial to the interests of peace in our country. And that has to be our priority.
>
> *(PM Boris Johnson, reported in BBC 9 September 2020)*

Indeed, the DUP was the only parliamentary party of the opposition that (cautiously) supported the bill. All other parties strenuously opposed it. In addition, the unilateral withdrawal from specific norms of the Northern Ireland Protocol sparked an international controversy, with the EU and the Irish government joining domestic UK opposition in denouncing the bill as a breach of the rule of law. The law proposal was also met with dismay by the domestic judiciary, including the Lord Advocate of Scotland, who resigned in September 2020 (BBC 16 September 2020).

As far as domestic centre–periphery relations are concerned, the UK Government tried to present the Bill as a power surge for devolution and a balanced approach for protecting peace in Northern Ireland. However, the significant restrictions that the Bill introduced for devolved powers were immediately clear to expert observers (Dougan *et al.* 2020), as well as to the devolved administrations themselves. Nicola Sturgeon defined the proposed legislation as a "full frontal assault on devolution", and the SNP's leader in Westminster, Ian Blackford, described it as "nothing short of an attack on Scotland's parliament and an affront to people of Scotland"; while Wales's Counsel General Jeremy Miles declared: "The UK government plans to sacrifice the future of the union by stealing powers from the devolved administrations" (*The Scotsman* 9 September 2021; BBC 9 September 2020). As for the potential impact of the Bill in Northern Ireland, Sinn Fein's Deputy First Minister, Michelle O'Neill, denounced the nonchalance with which the UK Government was ready to break an international agreement that it had ratified just a few months earlier, and which was agreed to protect the Good Friday Agreement (BBC 9 September 2020).

Eventually, the part of the Bill that was inconsistent with the EU Withdrawal Agreement was scrapped from the final text of the Internal Market Act 2020. The Scottish parliament denied its consent but the parts of the legislation that introduced further limitations to devolved powers were kept with very limited revisions. In January 2021, the Welsh government – through the Counsel

General – tried to initiate a process of judicial review of the Internal Market Act 2020, stating that it unduly restricted the powers of the Welsh legislature, the *Senedd*. The judicial initiative was blocked by the High Court of Justice in April 2021, on the grounds that the appeal was premature (BBC 19 April 2021). In June 2021, the Court of Appeal agreed to examine the case on the grounds that it raised important questions of principle (BBC 29 June 2021). However, the ensuing ruling, issued in February 2022, confirmed the sentence of the High Court of Justice (BBC 10 February 2022).

6.3.2 Further backlashes in the Celtic peripheries

The process for the adoption of the Internal Market Act 2020 made Johnson's Conservative Party's ideological opposition to devolution even more evident. If there was a need for an explicit evaluation of devolution by the PM, this came in mid-November 2020, in the middle of the political polemic on the Bill (and on the management of the Covid crisis). During an online meeting with some MPs from northern England, he said that devolution had been "Tony Blair's greatest mistake", and "a disaster north of the border" (*The Guardian* 16 November 2020). These statements clearly confirm the passage from traditional unionism, characterised by flexibility and indefiniteness (Keating 2021), to what has been labelled as the hyper-unionism or muscular unionism of contemporary UK conservatism (Kenny & Sheldon 2021; Andrews 2021). On the one hand, this kind of discourse can resonate well with Anglo-British nationalist voters and/or with those citizens that simply resented the holding of an independence referendum in Scotland and resent even more the proposal for a second independence referendum. On the other hand, it represents a gift to peripheral nationalism, restricting the space for political forces that adopt intermediate positions, such as the preservation and development of devolution. Indeed, the SNP's immediate reaction to Johnson's statements was a "tweet" by Nicola Sturgeon saying: "independence is the only way to protect and strengthen the Scottish parliament" (*The Guardian* 16 November 2020); while Plaid's leader, Adam Price, defined Boris Johnson as "a great recruiting agent" for the pro-independence cause (*The New European* 29 November 2020).

Polls on Scottish independence showed a marked increase in support for the secessionist option in the second half of 2020 (see Figure 6.1). It is difficult to say if this increase was determined by the Brexit process only – i.e., the debate on the Internal Market Bill and the approximation of the end of the transition – or, rather, whether it was also linked to the difficulties/criticism that the UK Government was encountering in dealing with the Covid crisis. Certainly, the time looked favourable for Scottish nationalists to present a request for a second referendum on independence. However, with the UK Government determined to deny such an option, the SNP could only hope for a further electoral breakthrough at the forthcoming Scottish election, scheduled for May 2021. A huge surge in electoral support for the nationalists would indeed increase pressure on

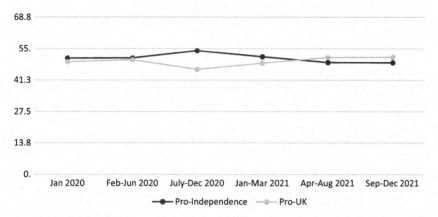

FIGURE 6.1   Support for independence in Scotland Source: Data elaborated by authors on the bases of available polls.

the central Government to negotiate a new referendum or new self-government concessions.

Unfortunately for the SNP, in May 2021 support for independence had already declined and lost the lead (though remaining very close to 50 percent). Indeed, the results of the 2021 Scottish election, while confirming the SNP as the dominant party and returning a pro-independence majority in parliament (SNP + Scottish Greens), did not provide a shock sufficient to break the deadlock (Johns 2021). If anything, the Covid crisis provided the UK Government with an additional argument to shut down new calls for a referendum. In September 2021, the Scottish government declared that, Covid permitting, they wanted to hold a referendum by 2023 and that, should London deny its approval again, the SNP-Green majority in the Scottish Parliament would proceed unilaterally. However, a poll revealed that most Scottish voters disapprove of a unilateral approach to a second referendum (*Herald Scotland* 20 September 2021).

Separatism remained a distant prospect in Wales, where most opinion polls showed a consolidation of support for independence between a quarter and a third of the decided electorate. In the May 2021 Welsh election, Plaid Cymru managed to keep its share of electoral support above 20 percent but lost the position of the second party. It was overtaken by the Welsh Conservatives, who were able to reabsorb most of the votes lost to UKIP in the 2016 election and achieve the best result ever in a Welsh election. Welsh Labour emerged, once again, as the clear winner of the election (Awan-Scully 2021). Again, it is difficult to say if Labour gained support due to its positioning on Brexit-related or Covid-related issues.

As usual, the situation appeared more complex and delicate in Northern Ireland. The failed assault by the UK Government on the negotiated Northern Ireland Protocol reassured the Irish nationalist/Catholic community, and support for Irish reunification remained high, albeit still trailing the unionist option.

By contrast, the unionist/Protestant community started to manifest clear signs of unease with the new situation. In early March 2021, the Loyalist Communities Council, which includes representatives of paramilitary groups, sent an open letter to PM Johnson announcing their withdrawal from the Good Friday Agreement (*The Guardian* 4 March 2021). A few weeks later, violence erupted between groups of young loyalists and the police, followed by limited clashes between loyalist and republican groups (BBC, 14 April 2021). Fortunately, violence was promptly condemned by all political parties in Northern Ireland, as well as by London and Dublin. More importantly, these riots have (so far) remained isolated episodes. In addition, the non-sectarian Alliance Party emerged as the third political force in the May 2022 elections (Murphy, 2022; Tonge, 2022), signalling that a growing portion of Northern Ireland's public perceives competition between the two ethnic groups and the respective constitutional preferences (i.e. belonging to the UK or to the Irish Republic) as something that needs to be overcome and left in the past. Having said that, about four-fifths of Northern Irish voters still support either a unionist or republican party. As such competition based on ethnic belonging and constitutional preferences still considerably shapes the Northern Irish society and party system. In this respect, the fact that *Sinn Fein* came up on top in the 2022 elections (albeit with just two seats more than the DUP) might add to unionist anxiety stemming from the outcome of the UK–EU Brexit withdrawal agreement. Indeed, the DUP refused its collaboration to form the new government until the Northern Ireland Protocol will be amended (Tonge, 2022).

6.3.3 Latest reforms

The Brexit process has seen genuine pro-devolution (Labour) and pro-federal (Lib-Dem) political forces squeezed in the middle, between a hyper-unionist Conservative Party, increasingly captivated by Anglo-British nationalism, and peripheral nationalism which, though interested in incremental concessions of self-government, is ultimately committed to the independentist (or Irish unification) cause. As the Conservative Party remains solidly in office, prospects for institutional reforms that, building on the devolution settlement, move the territorial constitution in a federal direction remain out of question. If anything, the opposite trend is clearly visible. The EU Withdrawal Act 2018 and the Internal Market Act 2020 have primarily moved in the direction of recentralisation and unitarisation. In addition, in the post-Brexit period, the English Votes for English Laws (EVEL) provision, the only one concerning devolution in England, was abolished with the aim of restoring "the beauty and the uniformity of our constitution so that it will work properly" (Jacob Rees-Mogg, Leader of the House, reported by the BBC 13 July 2021).

However, as devolved administrations are probably there to stay, the UK Government needs to find ways to work effectively with them on issues of common interest/competence. In this respect, there appears to be a shared view across the political spectrum that the Brexit process has proved the current system of intergovernmental relations, based on the Joint Ministerial Committees, largely unfit for purpose (House of Commons – Public Administration and Constitutional Affairs Committee – Eighth Report 24 July 2018). Yet, in the passage from analysis to the proposal, the consensus is immediately lost. As explained by McEwen *et al.* (2020, 635), the UK Government and all devolved governments have different interests and approaches. The Labour-led Welsh government seems to be the most interested and proactive in finding a solution that moves decisively in the federal direction. Indeed, it has proposed the establishment of a sort of "UK Council of Ministers", freely inspired by the EU Council of Ministers, with an unanimity or qualified majority decision-making procedure. Such a proposal can be expected to be rather unpalatable to the UK Government, which remains jealous of its hierarchical position and unrestrained (through Westminster) authority. However, the Welsh proposal might not even meet an enthusiastic reception in Scotland, where the SNP government appears reluctant to restrain its space of autonomy and might fear that a stable settlement would undermine independence. Last but not least, as usual, the position of Northern Ireland is split between the (Irish) nationalist side, which is already (and better) protected by international treaties, and the unionist side, which might have an interest in the proposed solution but is ideologically tied to the unitarist conception of the UK. As for the position of England, the scrapping of EVEL testifies to the (non) commitment of the UK Government to insert the biggest nation into a new devolution settlement.

However, these divergent interests and approaches did not stop the Joint Ministerial Committee from starting a review process in March 2018. After nearly four years, a report with very ambitious proposals has come out (McEwen 2022). The Joint Ministerial Committee is to be replaced by a three-tier system of intergovernmental relations (The Review of Intergovernmental Relations 2022, 3–4). The top tier, clearly the most political one, maintains a formal hierarchy, also in name: "Prime Minister and Heads of Devolved Governments Council". The lowest tier, where most technical issues are to be addressed, prescribes regular portfolio-level engagement in "Inter-ministerial Groups" (IMGs). In this tier all governments are to be at the same level. The middle tier is split between a general "Inter-ministerial Standing Committee" (IMSC), where all governments have equal status, and a "Finance Inter-ministerial Standing Committee" (FISC), where the central Treasury maintains a leading role. Clearly, this new system represents an achievement for devolved governments, which might make some progress in *shared-rule*. However, only time will tell if the new procedures will be substantively different from the past and will be consolidated to the point of becoming part of the territorial constitution. At the moment, it is not easy to predict the full implications of this reform, including the interests of which government this new system will serve. Much will depend on how it will work in practice. The UK Government probably hopes that most issues will be solved at a technical level in the IMGs, without escalating to the middle level IMSC, where political issues can still be addressed with a non-hierarchical approach. In any case, should a particularly thorny controversy arise, it could still be brought up to the top tier council.

Notes

1 To give an example, one can refer to a Deltapoll survey where fieldwork was conducted in the last week of 2021. From this survey, it appears that the region showing the highest dissatisfaction with the work of Johnson is the North of England (45 percent thinking he was doing his job very badly, as against a GB average of 35 percent). Two years before, this region had seen a strong Labour-Conservative swing (the highest of all was in the North East: 8.3 percent to Conservative; see Denver 2020, 15). This pattern seems to be matched by the emergence of strong dissatisfaction with the government among the MPs of the former Red Wall, where the politics of "levelling up" (Jennings et al. 2021) is particularly important.

2 In particular, with 34.1 points between the Conservatives and the Liberal Democrats, the by-election held in December 2021 in the constituency of North Shropshire recorded the second biggest swing since 1981 (https://www.theguardian.com/politics/live/2021/dec/17/north-shropshire-byelection-liberal-democrats-boris-johnson-tory-majority-live-updates, accessed 17 December 2021; see also: North Shropshire by-election at: https://www.theguardian.com/commentisfree/2021/dec/17/tories-johnson-lost-north-shropshire-mps-voters).

3 Moreover, voters largely appear to ignore the leadership of Richard Tice (Surridge 2021).

4 Kellner (2020) also notes that, if the road back to power for Labour might depend on its capacity to build a progressive alliance with the Liberal Democrats and the Greens, fielding "unity candidates", this project might well be opposed by the activists of the parties. Incidentally, one could note that such an alliance would resemble the German government formed by Chancellor Scholz after the 2021 federal election, with the significant difference that Angela Merkel's successor was able to build a coalition after the election, rather than form alliances beforehand, particularly necessary – albeit problematic – in order to tear down the "Blue Walls" of Conservative predominance (Wager et al. 2021).

5 For instance, UK ministers and spokespersons regularly failed to clarify when a new measure would apply to the whole of the UK or only to England (Basta & Henderson 2021, 303).

7

CONCLUSIONS

British politics after Brexit

In a recent report of the UK in a Changing Europe programme (Menon 2022), the editors aptly claim that there is no single correct answer to the question "are we really living through a post-Brexit' era in British politics?" Indeed, there are many, and their nature depends on the chosen angle and perspective on such a multifaceted phenomenon. In this book, by focusing on electoral and institutional dynamics we have shown that it is possible to detect a return – at the end of the troubled Brexit process that we have analysed – of some of the traditional attributes of the Westminster model.

In this concluding chapter, we return to the broad canvas on which we painted in Chapters 1 and 2. In doing so, we reflect on three main implications of our analysis. First, we look back at how Westminster changed during the Brexit years. Then, we move beyond the domestic domain, by reflecting on the significance and impact of the repatriation of sovereignty, a key question for the Brexiteers, discussing not only how this has been contested amongst domestic institutions, but also its actual value for an "independent" (yet, clearly still also "interdependent"), United Kingdom. Subsequently, we discuss the peculiarities of Brexit in light of other tensions and crises that emerged in other European countries during the last decade, again across the three dimensions of analysis chosen for our research. In the third and final section we reflect upon the type of political system and the type of democracy that is taking shape in the UK post-Brexit.

7.1 How Westminster changed during the Brexit years

Having added an empirical analysis of the Brexit and Covid period in Chapter 6, we are now able to draw conclusions on the overall impact of the former, from the referendum to the end of the transition, on the UK political system. We do

DOI: 10.4324/9781003127680-8

so, proceeding dimension by dimension, before presenting a more systemic argument. In drawing our empirical conclusions, it is worth referring to the initial working hypotheses, which are reported below:

> *H1: The Brexit process leads to a reduction in party system fragmentation*
>
> *H2: The Brexit process leads to an empowerment of the executive over the legislature*
>
> *H3: The Brexit process leads to an empowerment of central government over devolved administrations*

7.1.1 Elections and the party system

The UK entered the Brexit process with a party system that was clearly under stress. In the general elections of 2010 and 2015, electoral support for the two main parties reached its lowest point, with less than two-thirds of votes: 25 percentage points below the average of the 1945–70 period; and nearly eight percentage points below that of the 1974–2005 period. Indeed, the 2010–15 phase saw party system fragmentation reach its maximum value, driven by volatility and growth of new/small parties. As for party identification, the pre-Brexit phase was characterised by strong continuity with previous periods (since 1974), when the share of voters identifying with a party fell about 30 percentage points below the 1945–70 average.

Against this backdrop, the Brexit process appears to have had a substantive impact on the party system, particularly on the level of electoral support for the two main parties. By contrast, it has left party identification virtually unaltered, while the effect on volatility (i.e., party system structuration) appears to be nuanced and open to interpretation.

The vote share of the two main parties went up 13 percentage points vis-à-vis the pre-Brexit period and five percentage points vis-à-vis the 1974–2005 period. This trend is of primary importance, as the two-party system constitutes one of the pillars of the Westminster model. Therefore, its strengthening is a clear sign of a move in the direction of majoritarian democracy. In addition, the reinvigoration of two-partyism during the Brexit period represents a countertrend in a cross-country perspective. As a comparison, in Spain, electoral support for the two main parties fell from 73.4 percent in 2011 to 48.8 percent in the latest 2019 general election; while in Germany it decreased from 68.2 percent in 2013 to 49.8 percent in the latest, 2021, election.

Of course, unlike most other European countries, the British two-party system remains protected – mechanically and psychologically – by the SMP electoral system. Indeed, plurality rule has represented an institutional anchor to the Westminster model of democracy also in the pre-Brexit period – when some reforms moved the UK system in the direction of consensus democracy. To be sure, SMP is contested by some political forces in the UK, including a component of convinced Brexiteers, among others Nigel Farage. However, both main parties appear to consider the question settled by the 2011 referendum. Certainly, the Conservative governments that guided the Brexit process never called SMP into question. On the contrary, in the 2019 general election, SMP was used to forge a solid and united pro-Brexit parliamentary majority despite an electorate that was split in the middle.

Therefore, in line with our first working hypothesis (H1), the UK came out of the Brexit process with a stronger two-party system: underpinned by SMP and voting behaviour that has rewarded the two main parties considerably more than in the recent past.

However, whether the electoral reinvigoration of the two-party system should be interpreted as a short- or long-term effect of Brexit remains a moot point. Some indicators would clearly point to the former interpretation. The sharp decline in party identification appears to have stopped during the Brexit process, but there is no sign of going back to the values of the 1945–70 period. The score of the Brexit phase indicates substantive continuity with the very low levels of the 1974–2005 and 2010–15 periods. In addition, in the last two elections (2017 and 2019), Brexit identities (*Leavers* vs *Remainers*) appear to have trumped party identities.

Shifts in political identities bring us to the question of the party system structuration or de-structuration, which is overrun by volatility. In this respect, the Brexit process appears to have continued a pre-existing de-structuration trend. Indeed, the average value of volatility was in line with – and actually saw a marginal increase from – the 2010–15 period. However, volatility scores need to be qualified, especially when subsequent elections are analysed. Regeneration volatility (i.e., votes migrating to new parties) declined during the Brexit process compared to the pre-Brexit period; and it remains very low if seen from a cross-country comparative perspective. In addition, it is important to distinguish between dealignment volatility, when voters change their preference after being loyal to a party for a long time; "coming back home" volatility, when voters go back to their usual party preference after defecting in the previous election; and realignment volatility, when voters change their loyalty as a consequence of a shift in political identification and/or relative issue salience.

While volatility in the pre-Brexit period was primarily driven by dealignment, particularly in the 2015 general election (i.e., first-time defectors from the Liberal Democrats; first-time voters of UKIP, Green, and SNP); volatility during the Brexit process, and especially in the 2017 election, was largely driven by the "coming home" of most UKIP voters (especially to the Conservative Party). This indicates a process of partial reabsorption of the 2015 election shock on more traditional patterns of voting behaviour. On the other hand, the realignment provided by the 2019 election was mostly shaped by the Brexit issue. Should this issue gradually fade from the UK political debate in coming years, it would be really challenging for the Conservatives to maintain their 2019 variegated (pro-Brexit) electorate.

Therefore, it is fair to conclude with a note of caution on the substantiation of H1: at the end of the Brexit period, the reinvigoration of the two-party system appears to rest more on the institutional pillar (SMP) than on stable electoral alignments, much less party identification.

7.1.2 Executive–legislative relations

The pre-Brexit parliamentary term (2010–15) was rather exceptional in terms of executive–legislative elections. The UK experienced the longest coalition government since the end of WWII, with clear implications for the unity of the cabinet and the parliamentary majority. In addition, Parliament was empowered by the direct election of committee chairs by MPs and by the Fixed-term Parliaments Act 2011. Moreover, the previous reform of the House of Lords, in 1999, had broken the traditionally conservative orientation of the upper chamber of Parliament, making it a more unpredictable institutional actor in the legislative process. Last, but certainly not least, governments increasingly struggled to control their backbenchers in the Commons. In the four terms which followed the end of WWII, nine out of ten votes did not feature a single rebel within the party holding a majority in the Commons. By contrast, during the Coalition, almost 40 percent of the votes featured at least one rebel in the Tory party. It should be noted that this was not an exception: a similar level of rebelliousness characterised the last Labour government headed by Tony Blair (2005–7). In short, the UK entered the Brexit process with a political system in which executive–legislative relations were still marked by a certain predominance of the executive – especially if observed from a cross-country perspective – but which had moved considerably away from the traditional "elective dictatorship" of the past (cf. Chapter 4).

Against this backdrop, the Brexit process does not seem to have produced a significant (and potentially lasting) institutional impact. Rather, it has brought confrontational relationships between Government and Parliament to unexpected new heights. Such a confrontation – sparked by an incendiary mix of minority governments (June 2017–December 2019) and deep intra-party divisions (on Brexit) – has blatantly manifested itself in different domains: at a political–legislative level, with evident mismatches between governmental and parliamentary preferences; at a procedural level, with repeated controversies on the application of parliamentary rules; and at constitutional–judicial level, with open clashes ending up before the Supreme Court, which protected parliament's role from the executive's attempts to bypass its prerogatives (*Miller I case*) or prorogue it (*Miller II case*).

The very existence of a minority government is, in itself, a significant deviation from the Westminster model. Counting from the end of WWII, the minority government headed by Theresa May was only the fourth: Harold Wilson and James Callaghan led minority labour governments in the 1970s, while John Major's slim majority was lost, due to defections and by-elections, in 1996. The confidence and supply agreement with the DUP allowed May to count on a handful of votes in the Commons, but this was no longer the case with Johnson, who could count on fewer Conservative votes and broke with the DUP on the status of Northern Ireland in the renegotiated withdrawal agreement with the EU. However, as several witnesses of the Brexit process told us, the PM continued to behave in Parliament *as if* there were a Conservative majority. While the Westminster model was under strain institutionally, key actors (and, distinctively, the PM), did not modify their behaviour. We interpret this as a sign of the stickiness of norms of behaviour based on majoritarian dynamics, which actors can be unwilling – or are perhaps unable – to adapt notwithstanding the different institutional context.

Moreover, not only were the May II and the Johnson I governments unable to count on a Commons majority, but the two leaders also faced the daunting task of managing a Conservative Party which was fractured beyond repair on the EU issue. There is one figure that is particularly revealing: between June 2017 and December 2019, 15 percent of the Commons divisions featured at least 10 rebels in the Conservative Party, compared to 2 percent in the Cameron II government and 9 percent during the Coalition. However, figures on the government's defeats in the Commons are even more telling: the minority government led by Theresa May lost 28 times, while Johnson's government was defeated 12 times in less than five months. For comparison, from 2010 to 2017 – that is, including the Coalition – the government failed to command a majority only six times in the Commons. The conflict between the Europhile wing of the Tory parliamentary party and the PM reached its peak on 3 September 2019, when 21 conservative MPs – including the former Chancellor of the Exchequer Philip Hammond and the Father of the House, Kenneth Clarke – lost the Conservative whip following a rebellion. To be sure, tensions on the EU issue are far from new – and the "civil war" inside the Tory party on the process of ratification of the Treaty of Maastricht provides a powerful illustration – but, in this specific case, they at least temporarily impaired the government's Brexit plans.

The parliamentary rules of procedure were also put under strain by the Brexit process. Substantive debates and votes on Brexit were often preceded by long debates on Standing Orders and procedural issues. Erskine May – the reference text on parliamentary procedure – reached an unprecedented centrality and the relationship between the executive and Parliament, as reflected in the conduct of parliamentary business, became the object of bitter and harsh debates on the control of the agenda of Parliament, the use of emergency motions, the possibility to amend a Business of the House motion, among others. A system of written rules and informal norms, which had developed since the end of WWII, to enable the government to implement its election manifesto in Parliament – the "efficient secret" of the British constitution, to use Bagehot's famous expression – did not square well with minority government, a majority of MPs in the Commons opposing Brexit as pursued by the executive and a Speaker, John Bercow, who resolutely stood up "for the rights of the House of Commons, including the views of dissenters on the Government Benches [...] and to defend the rights of opposition parties" (HC Hansard 9 January 2019).

Therefore, for most of the Brexit period – i.e., until the December 2019 general election – Parliament appeared to stand up to typical government assertiveness, making the Brexit process very difficult and, sometimes, seemingly hopeless for the executive, thus subverting the traditional reality of the UK political system. From an *ex post* perspective, it could be argued that this unusual assertiveness of Parliament did not stop the Brexit process or substantively change the course of Brexit. However, it had immediate significant consequences, as it obliged the Government to ask the EU for extensions to the Brexit deadline.

As such, most of the Brexit process does not substantiate our working hypothesis on executive–legislative relations (H2). Quite the opposite. That part of the process was characterised by an exceptionally balanced relationship, with specific episodes in which Parliament appeared to have gained the upper hand. Yet, a closer look underscores how the core argument on which H2 is based holds true. Indeed, throughout the Brexit process, the prerogative to have a final say on the Brexit agreement could only be exercised by Parliament on terms that were negotiated by the Government, following the preferences of the Cabinet. In addition, the presentation of Brexit as a particularly challenging constitutional passage, which conflated the need for legal continuity and the ambition of legal change, was used by Government to extract legislative powers from Parliament through delegation. Although the May minority Government did not get as many delegated powers as it had initially requested in the Great Repeal Bill, it still obtained an exceptional amount.

Last but not least, as in most tales, the end of the story matters. In this respect, the December 2019 general election was the real game changer, as it produced a single-party majority government, totally committed to its maxim, "get Brexit done". Under these new conditions, the Brexit agreement negotiated by government was immediately approved by Parliament. The commitment to accomplishing Brexit was a result of Johnson's deselection of Remainers and soft-Brexiteers as candidates for the election, but the single-party majority government was, once again, a consequence of SMP: less than 44 percent of votes provided more than 56 percent of seats. This observation leads us to restate the importance of the linkage between the variables of the first dimension (voting system and party system) and the variables of the second dimension (type of government and executive–legislative relations). Indeed, after the 2019 election, the Brexit process proceeded in the direction envisaged by Government without further delays. Confrontational episodes between Parliament and the Government certainly did not disappear, even on Brexit-related issues (e.g., the Internal Market Bill). Yet, generally speaking, the relationship between them moved back onto a more familiar track.

7.1.3 Centre–periphery relations

When the UK started the Brexit process, the territorial constitution was in flux and contested. Some aspects of it, such as links with the UK's EU membership were only evident to some observers, whereas other features/trends were widely acknowledged and debated, especially the asymmetry amongst the constituent jurisdictions and the incremental expansion of devolved powers (devolution as a process). Asymmetry reflected the different socio-political and demographic characteristics of England, Northern Ireland, Scotland, and Wales; with obvious implications not only for the level of self-rule attributed to each jurisdiction but, most importantly, on the political-juridical foundations of their self-government. Indeed, Northern Irish devolution was underpinned by an international treaty, acts of parliament and a referendum; Scottish and Welsh devolution by acts of parliament and a (respective) referendum; English devolution (if it could be called that) simply by standing orders of the House of Commons. As for devolution as an incremental process, this concerned primarily Scotland and Wales, which saw their self-rule powers widen considerably in the years before Brexit. However, it also included the adoption of a residual form of self-government for England (EVEL) in 2015, and the apparent establishment of some sort of shared-rule for the three Celtic peripheries. Indeed, the Sewel Convention had always been respected by central institutions in the pre-Brexit period. It was precisely the incremental trend that made the territorial constitution fluxional and – academically, juridically, and politically – contested.

Against this backdrop, the Brexit process seems to have had an important impact. First, as far as shared-rule is concerned, it has provided clarification on the juridical nature of the UK, which maintains the characteristics of a unitary state, typical of the Westminster model. Indeed, the Sewel Convention has proved to be an extremely weak protection for devolved administrations, having been repeatedly ignored during the Brexit process. More importantly, the Supreme Court stated very plainly that sovereignty resides in the "Monarch in Parliament" and, since there are now several parliaments in the UK, it has clarified that it resides in Westminster only. In fact, the inefficient system of intergovernmental relationships, based on Joint Ministerial Committees, has been replaced by a newly devised three-tier system, which promises to provide more voice to devolved governments on issues of intersecting competences or common interest. In other words, the brand new system might provide more shared-rule powers to devolved jurisdictions. Yet, at the moment, no one knows how it will work in practice. In any case, decision-making will ultimately be subjected to the sovereignty of the "Monarch in Parliament" or, more precisely, the "Monarch in the House of Commons". Since the government that can command a majority in the House of Commons is the UK Government only, this will always be superior to (and potentially unconstrained by) devolved governments.

At the same time, the Brexit process has confirmed and reinforced the special status of Northern Ireland as a region where formal UK sovereignty is constrained by (now two) international treaties: the 1998 Good Friday Agreement and the 2020 EU Withdrawal Agreement. Therefore, the territorial constitution has become even more asymmetrical, as the status of Northern Ireland is much more protected (against Westminster's undivided sovereignty) than that of Scotland or Wales. In simpler words, Brexit has clarified the unitary nature of the UK but also specified that, *de facto*, it applies to Great Britain only.

Secondly, the Brexit process has also left the overall system more asymmetrical with respect to self-rule, particularly as far as England is concerned. Indeed, with the scrapping of its already feeble form of devolution (EVEL), the biggest jurisdiction is now fully ruled by the UK Parliament. However, what can perhaps be considered as the most important impact of Brexit on the territorial constitution is the halting and reversal of devolution. To be fair, this is an intricate and controversial point, as devolved administrations have *de facto* expanded their self-rule competences by receiving some of the repatriated powers. Yet, during the Brexit process, for the first time, devolution legislation was significantly amended with a view to restricting rather than extending powers. Although most restrictions are meant to be temporary, the adding of some provisions of the Internal Market Act 2020 to others from the EU Withdrawal Act 2018 appears to have inverted the direction followed by previous devolution reforms. In addition, albeit justified with functional arguments, these restrictive measures (and the scrapping of EVEL) seem to be fully in line with the (Anglo-British) nationalist and hyper-unionist ethos that has characterised the Conservative Party throughout the Brexit process. In this respect, the potential effect of referendums on the UK constitution (cf. Chapter 1), in the sense of making the constitution more rigid, could represent a guarantee against a full-blown attack by the UK government on the self-government institutions created by devolution in 1998.

Based on the constitutional clarification, which restated the unitary nature of the UK, and the halting and partial reversal of devolution, we consider H3 as substantiated.

Indeed, it has been easy for secessionist forces in the three Celtic peripheries – particularly in Scotland and Wales – to present the Brexit process as an assault on devolution. As a result, support for independence (or for Irish unification) has increased across the three Celtic peripheries during the Brexit process, especially during 2019 and 2020. The Scottish Government has requested a second independence referendum several times and is still committed to holding one in the coming years. However, neither the Conservative government nor the Labour opposition are set to concede it. In Wales, the level of support for independence is still far from posing a real challenge, though the Welsh electorate has proved to be potentially capable of important swings, often following the Scottish course. More complex (as usual) is the situation in Northern Ireland, where a referendum is not in sight and the level of pro-Irish unification support still trails (though from a much shorter distance) pro-UK support. However, Northern Ireland is the only jurisdiction that has a formal right to hold a referendum. If we add the significant growth of pro-unification support and the outcome of the withdrawal agreement, there is more than enough to trouble the unionist community and raise some concerns for the stability of the peace settlement.

7.2 Beyond the domestic domain

In the following sections, we move beyond the analysis of internal changes to the UK political system. Placing them in the broader international context, we interpret them, comparatively, in the light of recently occurring developments in other European democracies.

The question "How sick is British democracy?" was recently asked by Richard Rose (2021a), one of the doyens and most distinguished scholars of the international political science community. In his forensic analysis, Rose identified "a mixture of healthy and unhealthy symptoms", ending with "a mixed bill of health for British democracy". In this book, we have taken a more selective approach and, building on Rose's analogy, we looked at several of the key organs of Britain's body politic, as structured in the electoral and party systems and the country's most important institutional articulations. Obviously, our contribution is limited by the fact that we have not analysed other important elements of the political system (such as pressure groups, the civil service, and public policies). However, our research helps to shed light on the "politics" and "polity" consequences of Brexit.[1] In turn, this contributes to understanding the Brexit implications for the state of British democracy.

Issues of sovereignty within the state have been reignited by the Brexit process and will keep haunting the integrity of the UK for some time. However, an equally (if not more) important question posed by Brexit concerns the actual viability of external sovereignty. This question, which might ultimately determine whether Brexit will be judged by historians as a success or a failure, is dealt with in the next section.

7.2.1 Sovereignty and interdependence: taking back control?

As we know (cf. Chapters 1 and 2), British membership of the EEC/EU was marked from the start by harsh conflicts, within and across parties, over the meaning of sovereignty. The nature of such conflicts, however, changed considerably. In the early 1960s, in the run-up to membership, the political debate was on the diminished sovereignty of the UK as a member of a supranational community. The "primacy" of EU law and its "direct effect" – authoritatively proclaimed by the Court of Justice of the EU – stood in stark contrast with the key constitutional principle of parliamentary sovereignty. Critics regarded the transfer of policy competences to Brussels as a "surrender" of British sovereignty to the EEC, while supporters welcomed the "pooling" of sovereignty among European nations (see Gee & Young 2016; Bogdanor 2019).

This conflict pitted a traditional understanding of sovereignty, anchored on the principle of the centrality of parliament as a supreme and unbound decision-making body, against membership of a supranational community, introducing strong external constraints to domestic policymaking. However, as Chris Bickerton (2019) argued, and as the previous empirical chapters have clearly shown, in the UK the conflict – or rather *conflicts* – on sovereignty have played out *domestically* during the Brexit years, placing the "People" against "Parliament", "Number 10" against "Westminster", "London" vs "Holyrood" or "Stormont". Of course, this is not to downplay the importance of the tensions between "London" and "Brussels", which were often very high during the negotiations of the Withdrawal Agreement (2017–19) and, later in 2020, the Trade and Cooperation Agreement (TCA). Yet, the conflicts among domestic actors on the understanding of sovereignty – which, of course, were very consequential for the kind of Brexit being implemented, and future relations with the EU – fundamentally characterised the Brexit years, intensifying (sometimes dramatically) the political and institutional strains in the UK political system.

Over the period investigated in this book, two such conflicts on sovereignty emerged. The referendum on EU membership laid bare the conflict between the "People" and "Parliament" which had already been taking shape well before the referendum. In 2011, the Coalition government approved the European Union Act, which required a referendum for any further transfer of powers to the EU. Parliament chose to bind itself, necessitating the mandate of the people before ratifying any new treaty with the EU. In the (non-binding) referendum on membership, a majority of voters backed the "leave" option, while a majority of members of the House of Commons – about three-quarters of MPs – voted "remain", including a majority within the parliamentary Conservative Party. In addition, a majority of peers in the House of Lords continued to support EU membership. In 2017, 44 percent of MPs who chose "remain" in the referendum were representing a constituency with a "leave" majority (Blick & Salter 2020). This disconnection between voters and elected representatives brought high tensions to both major parties – but particularly to the governing Conservative Party – with repeated calls to deselect "remain" MPs by grass-roots members.[2]

In the campaign leading to the referendum, the key slogans of the "leave" camp were "Take back control" and "We want our country back". Indeed, Boris Johnson – perhaps the most prominent Brexit campaigner and, back then, the mayor of London – explained the importance of backing "leave" this way: "[Remain means] the steady and miserable erosion of parliamentary democracy in this country" (Johnson 2016). However, restoring parliamentary sovereignty with a people's vote could paradoxically be seen as a way to undermine it. As Vernon Bogdanor (2016) argued: "the Brexiters hoped to restore the sovereignty of parliament. Yet that is now undermined not by Europe, but by the people through the referendum".

The non-binding nature of the referendum, in formal/legal terms, is meaningless: politically, the referendum is effectively binding. When the 2017 general election failed to deliver a strong mandate for the government to implement Brexit, the conflict between "Government" and "Parliament" was therefore unveiled (see Chapter 4). This conflict on sovereignty really was a debate between different "constitutional" options, with the government (as mandated by the people through the referendum) or parliament (as the "sovereign" institution) taking control of the process.

As the withdrawal of the UK from the EU was completed, the internal debate was partly put to rest, and the discussion on what sovereignty really entails in today's globalised world (re-)emerged. The executive – which had emerged once again as the most powerful institution in the UK political system – was no longer bound by EU rules and judicial constraints. As PM Johnson, in his foreword to the strategic document *Global Britain in a Competitive World*, wrote:

> having left the European Union, the UK has started a new chapter in our history. We will be open to the world, free to tread our own path, blessed with a global network of friends and partners, and with the opportunity to forge new and deeper relationships.
>
> *(HM Government 2021, 2)*

Clearly, post-Brexit the executive was formally freed from the EU's external constraints. Yet, has sovereignty effectively been regained? Is the executive really unbound?

In a strongly interconnected and interdependent world, de-Europeanisation does not equal full autonomy. Indeed, despite the claims that "no deal was better than a bad deal" with the EU (Theresa May) and that a "hard Brexit" was a real option on the table (Boris Johnson), both PMs engaged in long negotiations with the EU, with Johnson ending up agreeing to a deal regulating post-Brexit relations between the EU and UK in more than 1,200 pages. As Richard Rose put it: "The United Kingdom's freedom from EU regulations as a member state has been replaced by being subject to EU rules applying to countries that are not member states" (2021a, 143). Of course, rules for so-called "third countries" are negotiated *ad hoc* and more freedom of action is gained in those areas not regulated by the treaties. Post-Brexit, the UK has been able to introduce its own (very restrictive) migration rules – a key objective of Brexit since the referendum campaign – and it is now able to independently negotiate trade agreements with other countries. However, in order to obtain tariff-free access[3] to the much larger EU single market (and the UK's biggest export market), it had to accept that EU rules – albeit in the form of national legislation "converging" with EU law – would apply to the UK.

A key (perhaps the key) contentious aspect of the TCA has centred on the "level playing field". Regulatory divergence between the EU and the UK is now possible, but the principle of "non-regression" ensures that the levels of protection on labour, social standards, and the environment are anchored to those in place at the end of the transition period. Dynamic regulatory alignment – i.e., the obligation to catch up with EU regulatory developments in such fields – has been much debated but, at the UK's request, was not included in the final agreement. Yet, as the UK has agreed to abide by EU standards when leaving the EU, it will not be in a position to obtain a competitive advantage by deregulating, as some Brexiteers had hoped. Should there be any violations of the terms of the TCA, the Court of Justice of the EU (CJEU) does not have the power to intervene. Based again on a UK request, a special arrangement – a dispute settlement mechanism – has been introduced and tariffs targeting the non-complying party could be applied. As Brigid Laffan nicely summarises, the UK left the EU's "regulatory space, but not its regulatory orbit" (2021, 251).

Moreover, Northern Ireland – whose status post-Brexit was the real stumbling block in the negotiations – remains bound by EU single market rules to prevent a hard border on the island of Ireland. In October 2019, Boris Johnson's agreement with the EU on this point caused outrage among his former allies in the DUP, showing that the regained sovereignty "was in the end about the sovereignty of Great Britain (GB) and not the whole of the UK" (Laffan 2021, 246–7). Indeed, the novel economic border introduced in the Irish Sea to ensure that Northern Ireland could continue trading with Ireland as if the former were still part of the EU, was a costly choice to make to "get Brexit done". The difficult application of the protocol and the border checks between NI and the rest of the UK have triggered repeated calls for a new deal with the EU. Indeed, while the resignation of the Brexit minister Lord Frost in December 2021 was publicly motivated by his criticism of the coercive measures imposed by the government to tackle the new wave of the pandemic, they were also partly triggered by Johnson's seemingly less hard-line position on the protocol.[4]

Both the need to remain fundamentally aligned to EU standards to gain tariff-free access to the single market, and the differentiated regulatory regime for Northern Ireland show that it is indeed possible to "reverse the gear" of integration, but such reversals face external constrains which, *pace* Brexit, do not entirely free the UK and its executive from Brussels.

7.2.2 Going comparative: challenges to British democracy in perspective

As we saw in Chapter 3, the experts of the BES have recently identified five major electoral shocks in recent British history, of which the Brexit referendum represents the latest (Fieldhouse *et al.* 2020). In many ways, the referendum was a shock, in the literal sense that opinion polls did not predict its outcome. As a matter of fact, even inside the "Leave" camp, few actors really believed they could ultimately prevail. At the same time, Brexit did not come out of the blue. The UK invented the term "Euroscepticism" in the mid-1980s, more than 30 years before the referendum, when the same idea that membership of European institutions could one day shrink, rather than continue to increase, was very difficult to conceive.

Brexit can also be perceived as the consequence of the progressive layering of several social, political, and economic tensions that emerged in the decade or so that preceded the referendum. Some of these tensions were common (or at least similar) to other countries, such as the global recession starting in 2007/08 and the rise of immigration as an electoral issue (Magistro & Wittstock 2021). Others, however, were specifically related to British developments, such as the formation of the first post-war coalition government (in 2010), and the 2014 referendum on Scottish independence. In 2015, the political system also witnessed the emergence of a maverick (also mildly Eurosceptic himself) leader, that is, Labour's Jeremy Corbyn. Taken together, all these transformations significantly changed some of the traditional dynamics of the Westminster model, setting the scenario in which the Brexit play unfolded.

But how can we compare these developments to crises and tensions that emerged elsewhere in Western democracies, and especially in Western Europe, namely the area most similar to the UK as far as the main economic and migration crises are concerned? To be sure, the UK is not the only country to have undergone significant political turmoil over the last 15 years.[5] While space constraints mean we cannot comprehensively overview the dynamics of the crises experienced by other countries in this period, it is interesting to reflect on their general traits, so as to be able to identify at least some UK peculiarities in a comparative perspective. While examining how Brexit fits with the study of populism goes beyond the scope of our work (Freeden 2017), the main point to emphasise here regards the fact that Brexit was a peculiar manifestation of the different varieties of democratic "stresses and strains" experienced throughout Western democracies in the aftermath of the Great Recession.

More specifically, back in 2016, the Brexit referendum was considered – together with the victory of Trump in the US presidential elections a few months later – one of the first dramatic manifestations of political crisis and of the rise of populism[6] (Mudde 2021). While in many countries dissent vis-à-vis the political establishment was normally expressed by the success of new parties (usually both Eurosceptic and populist: Taggart & Pirro 2021; see also Zulianello 2020) or personalities, Brexit is different. In this respect, UKIP's success, even if barely sufficient to obtain one or two seats in parliament,[7] was far more consequential than any other similar tiny (and brief) parliamentary representation of a populist and Eurosceptic party could have been in other countries. However, as we have seen in this book, UKIP's pressure to take the UK out of the EU was only part of the story. As a Eurosceptic, as well as the leader of a party whose working-class electorate had voted "Leave" in great numbers in 2016, Corbyn certainly did not do much to oppose the cause of Brexit. Decisively, the implementation of the 2016 referendum then became possible with the shift of the Conservative Party towards more Eurosceptic positions and Johnson's "riding of the populist wave" (Bale & Rovira Kaltwasser 2021).

In their typology of crisis related to the rise of "European populism in the shadow of the great recession", Kriesi and Pappas pointed out that in 2014 the UK was the only country (among the 17 analysed), to experience a strong impact of the economic crisis and a weak impact of political crisis (2015, 17). The two authors also made another important point:

> In Western Europe, the rise of populism has been a long-term process that had already been well underway at the time of the intervention of the Great Recession. This process has, for some time, been driven by the malfunctioning of representative democracy, especially by the deficiencies of the party system, the main intermediary system linking the citizens to political decision-making.
>
> *(ibid., 2)*

This reminds us of the importance of the political roots of the crisis and the tensions experienced by all democracies in these years. While many other countries went through veritable electoral earthquakes, the SMP electoral system preserved the party system in the UK from the more dramatic derailments experienced in many other democracies. After 2010, most southern European countries, such as Greece, Spain, and Italy, experienced more than one election with very high levels of electoral volatility (sometimes even close to 50 percent, and often higher than 25 percent). To recall from Chapter 3, the UK in this period scored its post-WWII record, in 2015, with 18.2 percent, a figure which clearly appears low when compared to above-mentioned countries. These three countries all have electoral systems that, with different degrees of disproportionality,[8] do not set very high barriers for new parties to enter parliament. As such, challenger parties can sometimes even gain representation at their electoral debut (as did both Podemos in Spain and the Five-Star Movement in Italy, though in both cases with more than 20 percent of the votes). In 2018, Italy went through a short-lived experience of an "all-populist coalition", with the Five-Star Movement-League alliance in a self-proclaimed "Government of change" (Baldini & Giglioli 2020). At the same time, the Italian case has shown the troubles that some populist parties suffer in adapting to government (Giovannini & Mosca 2021).

The situation is radically different in countries that employ majoritarian systems, especially SMP systems, such as the United States and the UK (while the two-ballot majority system used in France is more permeable to new entrants: Knapp 2018). In these countries, challenger parties have a much harder time entering representative institutions. Rather, the way in which the status quo can be challenged is via "internal insurgences", by capturing the leadership or prominent positions inside established parties, which is what Donald Trump and Bernie Sanders did in the US, and Corbyn did in the UK.

Hence, the implementation of Brexit was the result of the combination of the external pressure exercised by UKIP, the internal shift of the Conservative leadership towards more radical positions, and the ambiguities and constraints affecting the actions of the main opposition party, in itself led by an anti-establishment leader, split on the issue and unable to make common cause – in the decisive 2019 general election – with other parties more explicitly siding with Remain.

Elsewhere in Europe, many political crises also emerged in contexts already marked – at least in many cases – by a deteriorating relationship between citizens and the political system, as well as a growing sense of "disenchantment" of the former with the latter. In this respect, while representative democracy has been challenged pretty much everywhere (Alonso *et al.* 2011), the precise nature and meaning of the strains experienced vary from country to country. Centre-right parties adopted tougher immigration policies. But this did not prevent the emergence of radical right parties. Notably, in the second half of the 2010s two countries which had long been exceptional in the European scenario for their lack of populist parties, namely Germany and Spain, also saw the rise of a right-wing anti-immigration party (Alternative für Deutschland 12.6 percent in 2017;

and Vox, 10.3 and 15.1 percent respectively, in the two general elections held in 2019). In many other countries, populist parties have entered government, or come very close to it, often affecting the patterns of political competition (Albertazzi & Vampa 2021), as well as the quality of democracy, especially when they have an exclusionary nature (Vittori 2021).

However, as a recent review on "Populism, Democracy, and Party System change in Europe" reminds us:

> The positions that populist parties on the cultural right and the economic left have taken over the last decade in Europe are profoundly different in many respects – especially in whether they adopt an inclusionary conception of the people or an exclusionary one that trades on scapegoating marginalized groups. What is even more striking is how differently they have governed, indicating that varieties of populism should shape our expectations of what happens when populists rule.
>
> *(Vachudova 2021, 492)*

If placing the Brexit peculiarities in the context of an overall synthesis of the consequences of the rise of populism on party systems remains difficult, what about the other two dimensions analysed in this book? How peculiar was the British case?

In the last decade, the empowerment of the executive vis-à-vis the legislature has been a feature of several European countries (Bolleyer & Salat 2021; Curtin 2014). The sequence of crises affecting EU members – from the economic and financial crisis to Covid-19 – has required swift executive action, limiting parliamentary accountability and influence. Emergencies have been tackled granting special powers to executive bodies, using *ad hoc* emergency clauses in constitutional texts, delegating legislative powers to executive agencies via statutory acts, and limiting judicial review (EPRS 2020). Executives have sometimes made good use of such crises, exploiting them to expand their institutional competences beyond the specific emergency situation (White 2019).

Centralisation and the empowerment of executive bodies have characterised both the EU and the national level. At the EU level, responses to the economic and financial crisis, the migration crisis and the pandemic crisis have required strong activism and assertiveness by the European Council – the EU's intergovernmental executive – with a more limited role for the European Parliament, even where its legal competences granted it an important role in legislative decision-making (see Bressanelli & Chelotti 2019). At the national level, across EU states (albeit to varying degrees) the management of the Covid-19 pandemic has led to a limitation of parliamentary scrutiny and control. In Italy, for instance, it is estimated that by the end of 2020 no fewer than 18 law decrees have been adopted by the Council of Ministers and 17 decrees by the President of the Council of Ministers alone. Parliament was therefore sidestepped and, given that prime ministerial decrees have an administrative nature, they were exempted from the Constitutional Court's review of legislation (Fasone 2021). While the UK has offered a particularly dramatic case of conflict between the executive and the legislative branches of government, during the Covid crisis heated parliamentary debates, rebellions and dissatisfaction vis-à-vis executive empowerment featured in several other countries (i.e., Russack 2021).

Intense strains between the centre and peripheries are not a peculiarity of the Brexit period and are not a UK exception. Even limiting the comparison to Western Europe, we find important challenges to the central institutions of the state in Belgium, France, Italy, and Spain (Alonso 2012). All these countries have had to manage minority nationalism, trying to strike a good balance between accommodation of peripheral demands and maintenance of effective central administration. In the process, these states needed to pursue several objectives at the same time, such as internal peace, democratic legitimacy, and territorial integrity. Amongst these countries, only Belgium has formally adopted a federal solution, whereas all the others, including the UK, have opted for different types of devolution. In general, the adoption of accommodative strategies by central governments has worked in favour of internal peace and democratic legitimacy but these strategies also strengthen minority nationalist parties (Massetti & Schakel 2017) and push them to radicalise their self-government demands (Massetti & Schakel 2017). Therefore, the fact that devolution did not "kill nationalism stone dead" was not a UK exception. Aspirations for independence grew in several member states, particularly in the context of the EU, whose institutional framework provides a high reward to those with a seat in the European Council and lowers the costs of establishing a new (member) state (Cetrà & Lineira 2018).

However, together with Spain, the UK has hosted the most threatening challenge to state territorial integrity (Lineira & Cetrà 2015). In both countries we find regions where the ethno-national struggle was conducted through an armed struggle (Basque country and Northern Ireland), making the issue of secession extremely delicate and intricate; and regions where it has remained within democratic/electoral politics (Catalonia and Scotland). The latter cases have pursued independence more openly, particularly in the years following the financial/economic crisis. The so-called "Catalan process [of national self-determination]" was triggered by a "loss of autonomy" dynamic (Sirkoy and Cuffe 2015), inflicted by the 2010 sentence of the Spanish Constitutional Court. This process did not find any formal/legal means of expression, as the Spanish constitution does not allow independence referendums and Spanish governments have not been willing to concede them (Cetrà & Harvey 2019, 616–18). As a result, the controversy escalated into a full constitutional crisis in autumn 2017, when the Catalan government was temporarily suspended (and some of its ministers prosecuted) for holding an illegal referendum and declaring independence. By contrast, the flexible/political constitution of the UK provided the British government with more room for manoeuvre (ibid., 615). Cameron's perception of a low risk/high reward match pushed him to accept the challenge, providing the

Scots with an opportunity to express their view on independence (ibid., 622). Then, the referendum challenge turned out to be tougher than expected but the unionist forces managed to bring the result home, demonstrating that the unity of the UK was based on democracy and consent, not on a constitutional straitjacket.

With Brexit, the Scottish question has changed in several respects. First of all, the EU framework is no more, which entails potentially contrasting effects. On the one hand, particularly in the long term, separation from London is likely to become a more traumatic and less appealing choice for Scotland. On the other hand, in the 2012–14 referendum campaign, the UK government was able to count on the EU's assistance to undermine the Scottish bid for independence (Massetti 2022). Should there be a second chance for Scotland, it is likely that the EU will support Edinburgh, at least informally. Secondly, with Brexit, the Scottish case has become more similar to Catalonia. By not considering the result of the Brexit referendum in Scotland, and by pushing devolution back – via the EU Withdrawal Act 2018 and the Internal Market Bill 2020 – the UK government has triggered a "loss of autonomy" dynamic, similar to the one that has been experienced by Catalonia since 2010. In addition, given the high support for independence in Scotland (around 50 percent), the government is not willing to concede a second opportunity to the Scots to express their constitutional preference. The argument that a referendum on independence cannot be held more than once in a generation can probably work for some more years. Yet, this denial has already generated some temptations, in some sectors of the SNP, to follow the Catalan route of unilateral secession and open constitutional crisis. In fact, this scenario remains highly unlikely, as blatant breaches of the rule of law are rather alien to British political culture and are not generally appreciated by British public opinion. On the other hand, in the long run, keeping Scotland in the UK against the will of the Scottish people could prove to be an untenable position.

7.3 Westminster strikes back: British democracy after Brexit

The UK constitutional system has been in flux for at least 25 years and the direction of change has been at the centre of a lively debate (Hazell 2008; Bogdanor 2009; Flinders 2010; King & Crewe 2014; Judge 2014; Richards et al. 2014; King 2015). In this context, the Brexit process has represented a key litmus test, as all the major political institutions had to explicitly confront "the full range of conflicting constitutional understandings" that were present – more or less dormant or activated – in UK politics (Wincott et al. 2021, 1535). Indeed, with Brexit, that debate has recommenced and intensified (Moran 2017; Clarke et al. 2017; Bogdanor 2019; McConalogue 2020; Rose 2021a). This book contributes to the empirical part of the debate with a clear thesis, supported by the extensive evidence presented in the empirical chapters: as a result of Brexit, the UK political system has moved back towards the Westminster model.

About a decade before Brexit, authoritative scholars had proposed alternative trajectories for the UK constitutional transition (Glover & Hazell 2008). Building on two key dichotomies – concentration vs dispersal of power and political vs legal constitution – they sketched out four scenarios for the future of the UK. A return to the "Old Constitution", with the traditional mix of concentration of power and a political constitution; "Centralised constitutionalism", combining concentration of power and a legal constitution; "Westminster devolved", characterised by dispersal of power and a political constitution; and "Dispersed constitutionalism", a combination of dispersed power and a legal constitution (Glover & Hazell 2008, 16). Back then, the two scholars detected a clear movement from the "Old Constitution" towards "Dispersed constitutionalism", with the latter being identified as the most likely end point of the transition.

Our study shows that Brexit has actually represented a step back along that trajectory, moving the system in the direction of what Glover and Hazell called the "Old Constitution". In other words, after a long period of gradual distancing from the Westminster model, Brexit has led Westminster to strike back.

Indeed, at the end of the Brexit process, all the key features of the model are in place. First of all, the UK has stopped being part of the EU system of multi-level governance and has gone back to state-based democratic government. This main aspect of the reform has, in itself, deleted one level of decision-making (the EU level), thus producing a reconcentration of power. In addition, the subtraction of the UK from the jurisdiction of the European Court of Justice has removed judicial constraints on the sovereignty of Westminster, thus reasserting the political constitution. Secondly, at the end of the Brexit process, the renowned pattern of the Westminster model – SMP, two-party system, single-party majority government, and executive dominance over the legislature – has been fully re-established. Thirdly, the Brexit governments have manifested clear signs of ill-tolerance for the institutions created – and the constitutional views that emerged – during the previous (reformist) period, starting with the Supreme Court and devolution. So far, the Supreme Court has only been threatened (and it is currently under "review"), but no formal measure has been adopted to constrain, limit, or scrap it. By contrast, the unitary character of the UK has been strongly reasserted and the process of devolution has undergone a drastic halt, with some signs of reversal. This outcome cannot be considered as an automatic product of the decision to leave the EU. Indeed, key Eurosceptic actors, such as Nigel Farage, conceived Brexit as part of a wider reformist agenda to move the UK further away from the Westminster model. By contrast, the Conservative Party that "got Brexit done" clearly emanated a certain nostalgia for the traditional Westminster system and an Anglo-British hyper-unionist ideology (Aughey 2018; Kenny & Sheldon 2021; Gamble 2016; Peele 2021). Therefore, the overall Brexit outcome should be seen more as a result of a political design than of a chaotic and random process. In this respect, Brexit appears to have the potential to represent an important moment in British constitutional history (Bogdanor 2019).

However, the extent of constitutional change should not be overestimated. Brexit has not (and could not) put the clock of history back 50 years. First, as discussed above, the reacquisition of full formal sovereignty has not eliminated interdependence and the ensuing need to strike compromises with other international actors, starting with the EU. In addition, some international treaties penetrate the domestic constitution in relation to rather sensitive issues, such as the status of Northern Ireland. Secondly, the domestic reforms adopted in the previous period have not disappeared. The Supreme Court still provides a judicial review for laws and represents a supreme arbiter in controversies between institutions over the attribution of powers. Moreover, devolved administrations maintain most of their respective self-rule powers.

There is more. The reassertion of the Westminster system does not necessarily imply a full and unchallenged persistence of the BPT. Referendums have become entrenched in the UK institutional repertoire, and they are now considered as an appropriate instrument for taking decisions on the most important political issues by a considerable share of citizens (Renwick *et al.* 2022). In spite of persisting doubts on their regulation and on the quality of information in referendum campaigns, they are no longer considered as instruments of plebiscitary politics but, rather, as complementary (and corrective) tools of representative democracy. The relative ease with which both politicians and voters have become familiar with referendums might be due to their confrontational/majoritarian nature, which is perfectly in line with the type of democracy associated with the Westminster model. Yet, referendums remain clearly at odds with the elitist heritage of the BPT, as they represent a potential alternative to the "government knows best" approach and to representative democracy (Weale 2017). In addition, referendums have possibly contributed to making the constitution *de facto* more rigid (Gordon 2020). Indeed, abolishing an institution (also) created by referendum without holding another referendum could now appear as politically illegitimate, especially in the presence of an explicit legislative mandate. In this respect, devolved institutions should be more protected than the Supreme Court vis-à-vis potential nostalgia for the old Westminster system.

A further departure from the BPT manifested itself, for a substantive part of the Brexit process, in the unprecedented level of parliamentary assertiveness vis-à-vis the government. The peak of parliament's boldness was certainly reached in the rather unusual context of deep intra-party divisions and minority government (2017–19). Yet, during the discussion on the Internal Market Bill (2020), parliament clearly demonstrated that it can prevent the executive's blatant breaches of the rule of law, also in the presence of a single-party majority government. This was a particularly positive sign vis-à-vis fears that the populist genesis of Brexit would generate a "populist democracy", characterised by an even more dominant executive (Withe 2021). It showed that a healthy relationship between Government and Parliament, which provides some checks and balances, could also be found within the political constitution – rather than by adopting a legal-rigid constitution (Chalmers 2017).

As such, rather than resulting in a comprehensive constitutional overhaul, Brexit has turned out to be more of a(nother) tipping point, producing important but limited domestic reforms, which leave the UK constitution still in flux – albeit now moving in the opposite direction. If the "reformist period" (1997–2010) weakened, but did not fundamentally alter, the majoritarian features of the UK political system, Brexit has further reasserted them, but without erasing important institutional reforms and innovative practices introduced in the previous period.

In the post-Brexit scenario, a new balance between the reinvigorated Westminster system and the institutions of the "new" constitution will have to be found. Striking such a balance will depend on the preferences of the key actors – particularly the executive – and, as the political system adjusts to post-Brexit realities, it will most likely lead to further institutional strains and tensions. Persisting political polarisation – between government and oppositions as well as between the centre and peripheries – suggests that, in the medium to long term, the constitution might still be open to different potential developments (Giuliani 2021; Wincott *et al.* 2021).

Yet, for the time being, we agree with Richard Rose when he rules out the possibility of drastic constitutional transformations, both in the direction of a codified/rigid constitution and of federalism (Rose 2021a, 168). In addition, the SMP voting system was reconfirmed in a referendum in 2011. As a consequence, at least two pillars of the "Old constitution" – Westminster sovereignty and the SMP voting system – are expected to be there to stay.[9] These two pillars will have to find new equilibria of coexistence with the Supreme Court, in a way that promotes checks and balances within the political constitution; and with devolution, possibly preserving the integrity of the UK polity.

The latter objective appears to be particularly challenging, as the Brexit process has not only put Scottish independence back on the agenda, but it has also touched the delicate constitutional balance of Northern Ireland. Therefore, the post-Brexit survival of the UK polity, as we have known it since 1921, remains a moot point. However, it is important to note that the chances of secession for these two Celtic peripheries appear to be inversely distributed in the timeline. Scotland remains in the UK internal market and customs union, while Scottish nationalists (on the basis of the 2016 referendum results in Scotland) would like to bring it back within the EU. This means that the short- to medium-term perspective works in favour of independence, as the sense of injustice for having been taken out of the EU by an alien Conservative government against the Scottish will is still fresh and politically spendable. In addition, the drawbacks and policy failures experienced by the Scots in these years can easily be attributed to Brexit or, in any case, to the pro-Brexit Conservative government. By contrast, the long-term perspective works against Scottish independence, as the more the UK and the EU diverge in their internal markets, the more Scottish independence will become a traumatic move. In fact, if (as it seems) an independent Scotland would have to wait for some time before joining the EU, the independence process would entail the parallel negotiation of two separate trade agreements: one with the (rest of the) UK and one with the EU. It is therefore logical to expect that, if the UK succeeds in holding on to Scotland during the next five/ten years, in the absence of further shocks, secessionist attitudes could then gradually decline. On the contrary, Northern Ireland (*de facto*) is already in the EU's customs union and common market, and it already has a trade border with Great Britain. In addition, for Northern Ireland, secession would mean immediate unification with Ireland, with full membership of the EU. Moreover, demographic trends work in favour of the Catholic community and, therefore, of (Irish) nationalist orientations. Finally, a putative passage of Northern Ireland from the UK to the Irish Republic would constitute an extremely delicate affair, which both London and Dublin would rather manage carefully and gradually, in order to provide reassurances to the unionist community. Therefore, it is logical to expect that the short- to medium-term perspective works in favour of the status quo; while the scenario of Irish unification has more of a chance in a longer-term perspective.

In any case, within the new status quo, the central government and devolved governments need to find new systems of co-decision in areas where their respective competences intersect, rather than falling into a situation of total war, as it was often the case during the Brexit process. The newly devised three-tier system of intergovernmental relations aims to achieve that objective. Similarly, the recently established "Independent Review of Administrative Law" aims, amongst other things, to reach a satisfactory compromise between the political constitution and the role of the Supreme Court. Therefore, what we are likely to be witnessing is a gradual emergence of a reasserted but partially transformed Westminster system, whose full features are difficult to predict in detail.

More importantly, it cannot be taken for granted that the new constitutional blend, which is being created by the Conservative governments, will survive the next alternation in power. Indeed, the model of democracy reasserted by the Brexit process appears to go against some of the preferences of the British public, such as the empowerment of scientific advisers, judges, the central bank, and civil servants (Renwick et al. 2022). In addition, potential instability and tensions are not only related to the centre–periphery dimension. The Brexit referendum could be just one manifestation of a longer-term crisis of input and/ or output legitimacy in British politics. The delivery of Brexit might not provide a satisfactory answer to the deep causes of discontent, as the initially bottom-up Brexit revolt was highjacked by a Conservative Party still linked to an elitist view of politics (Hall et al. 2018). Indeed, drawing on Renwick (2010), we have conceptualised the internal dimension of Brexit as a case of constitutional reform conducted by an *elite mass interaction*. With the Brexit referendum, the masses sent a clear message of dissatisfaction to the political establishment (Marsh 2018), indirectly calling into question the basic principles of the BPT (Blick & Salter 2020). It remains to be seen if "getting Brexit done" the way that the Conservative governments did will normalise the representative–represented relationship or, rather, if anti-establishment dynamics will remain relevant in post-Brexit UK politics.

Notes

1 For very insightful perspectives on Brexit as a "policy fiasco", see Richardson and Rittberger (2020).
2 For instance, Dominic Grieve, the MP for Beaconsfield and a leading pro-remain backbencher (see Chapter 4), lost a non-binding vote of no confidence by his local constituency association in late March 2019.
3 At the same time, non-tariff barriers – such as customs checks and VAT requirements – have been introduced. In its 9 February 2022 report, the Public Accounts Committee noted "a clear increase in costs, paperwork and border delays" for UK business post-Brexit.
4 Indeed, the PM explicitly addressed this point in his reply to Frost's resignation letter: "Crucially you have helped highlight and sought to address the destabilising impact the current operation of the Northern Ireland Protocol is having on communities in Northern Ireland, which is undermining the Belfast (Good Friday) Agreement and the territorial integrity of this country" (18 December 2021).
5 It is now more than 15 years since Freedom House documented a democratic regression throughout the world (see also the last report of the Varieties of Democracy Project: "Autocratization turns viral").
6 To be sure, populist parties were not born in the last 15 years. In Italy, Silvio Berlusconi's mildly populist Forza Italia first assumed office in 1994; the FPO's participation in a government coalition in Austria dates back to 1999, while it was in 2002 that Jean-Marie Le Pen, who had founded the Front National 30 years before, got to the second round of the French Presidential elections. But if these were harbingers of the emergence of a "populist zeitgeist" (Mudde 2004), in the last decade most – if not all – Western European countries experienced the success of (especially radical-right) populist parties, with percentages similar to those obtained by UKIP in 2015 (on the peculiar rise of populism in Eastern Europe see Stanley 2017).
7 Leaving aside Northern Ireland, until 2015 the two-party competition was only challenged by parties such as the Liberal Democrats, and the SNP in Scotland (and less so by the Greens and the PC in Wales). While the SNP's success was clearly a threat to the territorial integrity of the UK polity, only UKIP was a direct threat to EU membership.
8 In different ways the electoral laws applied in these countries in recent elections are among the more disproportional inside the PR family or among the mixed-member systems currently used in Europe (see Herron et al. 2018)
9 In March 2022, with the Dissolution and Calling of Parliament Act 2022, PM Johnson even managed to restore a stronger control by the government on the date of elections, repealing the Fixed-term Parliament Act.

BIBLIOGRAPHY

Abraham, T. 2019. Most Brits Uncertain on Labour's Brexit Policy. *YouGov*. https://yougov.co.uk/topics/politics/articles-reports/2019/11/05/most-brits-uncertain-labours-brexit-policy.

Acemoglu, D. and Robinson, J. A. 2012. *Why Nations Fail: The Origins of Power, Prosperity and Poverty*. London: Profile books, Ltd.

Achen, C. and Bartels, L. M. 2016. *Democracy for Realists: Why Elections Do Not Produce Responsive Government*. Princeton, NJ: Princeton University Press.

Adam, R. G. 2020. *Brexit: Causes and Consequences*. Cham: Springer.

Albertazzi, D. and Vampa, D. (eds.) 2021. *Populism and New Patterns of Political Competition in Western Europe*. London: Routledge.

Allen, N. 2018. 'Brexit means Brexit': Theresa May and Post-referendum British Politics. *British Politics*, vol. 13, no. 1, pp. 105–120.

Allen, N. and Bartle, J. 2021. *Breaking the Deadlock: Britain at the Polls*. Manchester: Manchester University Press.

Almond, G. A. 1990. *Discipline Divided: Schools and Sects in Political Science*. London and Newbury Park, CA: Sage Publications.

Almond, G. A. and Bingham Powell, G. 1966. *Comparative Politics: A Developmental Approach*. Boston, MA: Little Brown & Co.

Almond, G. A. and Verba, S. 1963. *The Civic Culture: Political Attitudes and Democracy in Five Nations*. Princeton, NJ: Princeton University Press.

Alonso, S., Keane, J. and Merkel, W. (eds.) 2011. *The Future of Representative Democracy*. Cambridge: Cambridge University Press.

Alonso, S. 2012. *Challenging the State: Devolution and the Battle for Partisan Credibility: A Comparison of Belgium, Italy, Spain and the United Kingdom*. Oxford: Oxford University Press.

Alter, K. J. and Zurn, M. 2020. Conceptualising Backlash Politics: Introduction to a Special Issue on Backlash Politics in Comparison. *British Journal of Politics and International Relations*, vol. 22, no. 4, pp. 563–584.

American Political Science Association (APSA). 1950. Toward a More Responsible Two-Party System: A Report of the Committee on Political Parties. *The American Political Science Review*, vol. 44, no. 3, part 2 supplement.

Amery, L. 1964. *Thoughts on the Constitution*. Oxford: Oxford University Press.

Andeweg, R. and Louwerse, T. 2018. The Institutional Framework of Representative Democracy: Comparing the Populist-Majoritarian and the Liberal/Consensual Model. In R. Rohrschneider and J. Thomassen (eds.), *The Oxford Handbook of Political Representation in Liberal Democracies*. Oxford: Oxford University Press, pp. 94–112.

Andrews, L. 2021. The Forward March of Devolution Halted—And the Limits of Progressive Unionism. *The Political Quarterly*, vol. 92, no. 3, pp. 512–521.

Antoniw, M. 2018. Devolution, Brexit, and the Prospect of a New Constitutional Settlement for the Four Countries of the UK. *The Constitution Unit Blog*, 1 March. https://constitution-unit.com/2018/03/01/devolution-brexit-and-the-prospect-of -a-new-constitutional-settlement-for-the-four-countries-of-the-uk/.

Armstrong, K. A. 2017. *Brexit Time: Leaving the EU-Why, How and When?* Cambridge: Cambridge University Press.

Art, D. 2020. The Myth of Global Populism. *Perspectives on Politics*, online first.

Aughey, A. 2018. *The Conservative Party and the Nation: Union, England and Europe*. Manchester: Manchester University Press.

Awan-Scully, R. 2018. *The End of British Party Politics?* London: Biteback.

——— 2021. Unprecedented Times, a Very Precedented Result: The 2021 Senedd Election. *The Political Quarterly*, vol. 92, no. 3, pp. 469–473.

Bache, I. 2008. *Europeanization and Multilevel Governance: Cohesion Policy in the European Union and Britain*. Plymouth: Rowman & Littlefield.

Bache, I. and Jordan, A. (eds.) 2006. *The Europeanization of British Politics*. Basingstoke: Palgrave Macmillan.

Bagehot, W. 2001 [1867]. *The English Constitution*. Oxford: Oxford University Press.

Bailey, D. and Budd, L. (eds.) 2017. *The Political Economic of Brexit*. Newcastle: Agenda.

Baker, D. 2002. Britain and Europe: More Blood on the Euro-Carpet. *Parliamentary Affairs*, vol. 55, no. 2, pp. 317–330.

Baker, D., Gamble, A. and Ludlam, S. 1994. The Parliamentary Siege of Maastricht 1993: Conservative Divisions and British Ratification. *Parliamentary Affairs*, vol. 47, no. 1, pp. 37–60.

Baker, D., Gamble, A., Randall, N. and Seawright, D. 2008. 'Euroscepticism in the British Party System: 'A Source of Fascination, Perplexity, and Sometimes Frustration'. In Szczerbiak, A. and P. Taggart (eds.), *Opposing Europe? The Comparative Party Politics of Euroscepticism*. Oxford: Oxford University Press. Vol. I, pp. 93–116.

Baldini, G., Bressanelli, E. and Gianfreda, S. 2020. Taking Back Control? Brexit, Sovereignism and Populism in Westminster (2015–17). *European Politics and Society*, vol. 21, no. 2, pp. 219–234.

Baldini, G., Bressanelli, E. and Massetti, E. 2018. Who Is in Control? Brexit and the Westminster Model. *The Political Quarterly*, vol. 89, no. 4, pp. 537–544.

——— 2021. Back to the Westminster Model? The Brexit Process and the UK Political System. *International Political Science Review*, online first.

Baldini, G. and Chelotti, N. (eds.) 2022. The Brexit Effect: Special Issue. *International Political Science Review*, vol. 43, *di prossima uscita*.

Baldini, G. and Giglioli, M. 2020. Italy 2018: The Perfect Populist Storm? *Parliamentary Affairs*, 73, no. 2, pp. 363–384.

Baldini, G. and Pappalardo, A. 2009. *Elections, Electoral Systems and Volatile Voters*. Basingstoke: Palgrave.

Bale, T. 2016. *The Conservative Party from Thatcher to Cameron*. Cambridge: Polity Press.

——— 2018. Who Leads and Who Follows? The Symbiotic Relationship between UKIP and the Conservatives – And Populism and Euroscepticism. *Politics*, vol. 38, no. 3, pp. 263–277.

Bale, T. and Rovira Kaltwasser, C. 2021. *Riding the Populist Wave: Europe's Mainstream Right in Crisis*. Cambridge: Cambridge University Press.

Balsom, D. and McAllister, I. 1979. The Scottish and Welsh Devolution Referenda of 1979: Constitutional Change and Popular Choice. *Parliamentary Affairs*, vol. 32, no. 1, pp. 394–409.

Banks, A. 2016. *The Bad Boys of Brexit: Tales of Mischief, Mayhem & Guerrilla Warfare in the EU Referendum Campaign*. London: Biteback Publishing.

Bardi, L. and Mair, P. 2008. The Parameters of Party Systems. *Party Politics*, vol. 14, no. 2, pp. 147–166.

Bartolini, S. and Mair, P. 1990. *Identity, Competition and Electoral Availability*. Cambridge: Cambridge University Press.

Bartolini, S. 1999. Collusion, Competition and Democracy: Part I. *Journal of Theoretical Politics*, vol. 11, no. 4, pp. 435–470.

——— 2000. Collusion, Competition and Democracy: Part II. *Journal of Theoretical Politics*, vol. 12, no. 1, pp. 33–65.

——— 2005. *Restructuring Europe: Centre Formation, System Building and Political Structuring between the Nation State and the European Union*. Oxford: Oxford University Press.

Basta, K. and Henderson, A. 2021. Multinationalism, Constitutional Asymmetry and COVID: UK Responses to the Pandemic. *Nationalism and Ethnic Politics*, vol. 27, no. 3, pp. 293–310.

BBC News. https://www.bbc.co.uk/news/politics/eu_referendum/results, 24 June 2016.

——— *Brexit: Wales EU Continuity Bill Passes Latest Hurdle in Senedd*, 20 March 2018, Disponibile All'indirizzo. https://www.bbc.com/news/uk-wales-politics-43472526.

——— *AMs Repeal Welsh Assembly EU Continuity Law*, 22 November 2018, https://www.bbc.com/news/uk-wales-politics-46268710.

——— *Brexiteers' Letter Adds to Pressure on May*, 7 Settembre 2019, https://www.bbc.com/news/uk-politics-41190237.

——— *Nicola Sturgeon: No Shortcut Route to Indepdence*, 10 October 2019, https://www.bbc.com/news/uk-scotland-scotland-politics-50002776.

——— *NI Riots: What is behind the Violence in Northern Ireland?*, 11 April 2021 https://www.bbc.com/news/uk-northern-ireland-56664378.

Bedock, C. 2017. *Reforming Democracy: Institutional Engineering in Western Europe*. Oxford: Oxford University Press.

Beer, S. 1965. *British Politics in the Collectivist Age*. New York: Knopf.

Bellamy, R. 2019. Was the Brexit Referendum Legitimate, and Would a Second One Be So? *European Political Science*, vol. 18, no. 1, pp. 126–133.

Bennett, A. and Checkel, J. T. (eds.) 2015. *Process Tracing*. Cambridge: Cambridge University Press.

Bennett, O. 2016. *The Brexit Club: The Inside Story of the Leave Campaign's Shock Victory*. London: Biteback.

Bennie, L. G. 2002. Exploiting New Electoral Opportunities: The Small Parties in Scotland. In G. Hassan and C. Warhurst (eds.), *Tomorrow's Scotland*. London: Lawrence and Wishart, pp. 98–115.

Benton, M. and Russell, M. 2013. Assessing the Impact of Parliamentary Oversight Committees: The Select Committees in the British House of Commons. *Parliamentary Affairs*, vol. 66, no. 4, pp. 772–797.

Bernauer, J., Bühlmann, M., Vatter, A. and Germann, M. 2016. Taking the Multidimensionality of Democracy Seriously: Institutional Patterns and the Quality of Democracy. *European Political Science Review*, vol. 8, no. 3, pp. 473–494.

Bértoa, F. C. and Enyedi, Z. 2021. *Party System Closure: Party Alliances, Government Alternatives, and Democracy in Europe*. Oxford: Oxford University Press.

Berz, J. 2021. The Effect of Voters' Economic Perception, Brexit and Campaigns on the Evaluation of Party Leaders Over Time. *The British Journal of Politics and International Relations*, vol. 22, no. 2, pp. 202–219.

Best, E. and Settembri, P. 2008. Legislative Output after Enlargement: Similar Number, Shifting Nature. In E. Best, P. Settembri and T. Christiansen (eds.), *The Institutions of the Enlarged European Union: Continuity and Change*. Cheltenham: Edward Elgar Publishing, pp. 183–204.

Bevir, M. and Rhodes, R. 2001. Decentering Tradition: Interpreting British Government. *Administration and Society*, vol. 33, no. 2, pp. 107–132.

Bickerton, C. 2019. 'Parliamentary', 'Popular' and 'Pooled': Conflicts of Sovereignty in the United Kingdom's Exit from the European Union. *Journal of European Integration*, vol. 41, no. 7, pp. 887–902.

Birch, A. 1964. *Representative and Responsible Government*. London: Allen and Unwin.

Blick, A. and Salter, B. 2020. Divided Culture and Constitutional Tensions: Brexit and the Collision of Direct and Representative Democracy. *Parliamentary Affairs*, vol. 74, no. 3, pp. 617–638.

Blühdorn, I. and Butzlaff, F. 2019. Rethinking Populism: Peak Democracy, Liquid Identity and the Performance of Sovereignty. *European Journal of Social Theory*, vol. 22, no. 2, pp. 191–211.

Bochel, J. and Denver, D. 1981. The Outcome. In J. Bochel, D. Denver and A. Macartney (eds.), *The Referendum Experience: Scotland 1979*. Aberdeen: Aberdeen University Press, pp. 138–164.

Bogaards, M. 2017. Comparative Political Regimes: Consensus and Majoritarian Democracy. In *Oxford Research Encyclopedia of Politics*.

Bogdanor, V. 1981. *The People and the Party System: The Referendum and Electoral Reform in British Politics*. New York: Cambridge University Press.

––––– 2001. *Devolution in the United Kingdom*. Oxford: Oxford University Press.

––––– 2004. The Constitution and the Party System in the Twentieth Century. *Parliamentary Affairs*, vol. 57, no. 4, pp. 717–733.

––––– 2008. Referendums in British Politics. *Contemporary British History*, vol. 2, no. 4, pp. 12–14.

––––– 2009. *The New British Constitution*. Bloomsbury Publishing.

––––– 2016. Europe and the Sovereignty of the People. *The Political Quarterly*, vol. 87, no. 3, pp. 348–351.

––––– 2019. *Beyond Brexit: Towards a British Constitution*. London: I.B. Tauris.

Bolleyer, N., Swenden, W. and McEwen, N. 2014. A Theoretical Perspective on Multi-level Systems in Europe: Constitutional Power and Partisan Conflict. *Comparative European Politics*, vol. 12, no. 4/5, pp. 367–383.

Bolleyer, N. and Salat, O. 2021. Parliaments in Times of Crisis: COVID-19, Populism and Executive Dominance. *West European Politics*, vol. 44, no. 5–6, pp. 1103–1128.

Bormann, N. C. 2010. Patterns of Democracy and Its Critics. *Living Reviews in Democracy*, vol. 2, pp. 1–14.

Börzel, T. A. and Risse, T. 2000. When Europe Hits Home: Europeanization and Domestic Change. *European Integration online Papers (EIoP)*, vol. 4, no. 15. http://eiop.or.at/eiop/pdf/2000-015.pdf.

Bossetta, M. 2017. Fighting Fire with Fire: Mainstream Adoption of the Populist Political Style in the 2014 Europe Debates between Nick Clegg and Nigel Farage. *The British Journal of Politics and International Relations*, vol. 19, no. 4, pp. 715–734.

Brack, N. 2015. The Role of Eurosceptic Members of the European Parliament and Their Implications for the EU. *International Political Science Review*, vol. 36, no. 3, pp. 337–350.

Bradbury, J. and Mitchell, J. 2005. Devolution: Between Governance and Territorial Politics. *Parliamentary Affairs*, vol. 58, no. 2, pp. 287–302.

Braham, C. and Burton, J. 1975. The Referendum Reconsidered. Fabian Tract, 434, Fabian Society. https://digital.library.lse.ac.uk/objects/lse:qep733yup/read/single #page/1/mode/2up.

Brancati, D. 2008. The Origins and Strengths of Regional Parties. *British Journal of Political Science*, vol. 38, no. 1, pp. 135–159.

Brand, J. 1978. *The National Movement in Scotland*. London: Routledge & Kegan Paul.

Bressanelli, E. and Chelotti, N. 2019. Power without Influence? Explaining the Impact of the European Parliament Post-Lisbon. *Journal of European Integration*, vol. 41, no. 3, pp. 265–276.

——— 2021. Assessing What Brexit Means for Europe: Implications for EU Institutions and Actors. *Politics and Governance*, vol. 9, no. 1, pp. 1–4.

Brown, S. A. 2019. Brexit, the UK and Europe: Why, How and What Next? *Journal of European Integration*, vol. 41, no. 1, pp. 123–129.

Brusenbauch Meislova, M. 2019. Brexit Means Brexit—Or Does It? The Legacy of Theresa May's Discursive Treatment of Brexit. *The Political Quarterly*, vol. 90, no. 4, pp. 681–689.

Bulpitt, J. 1983. *Territory and Power in the United Kingdom: An Interpretation*. Manchester: Manchester University Press.

Bulmer, S. 1992. Britain and European Integration: Of Sovereignty, Slow Adaptation, and Semi-detachment. In S. George (eds.) *Britain and the European Community*. Oxford: Oxford University Press, pp. 1–29.

Butler, D. and Kitzinger, U. W. 1976. *The 1975 Referendum*. London: Macmillan.

Butler, D. and Stokes, D. 1974. *Political Change in Modern Britain*. Basingstoke: Macmillan Press.

Campbell, S. 2013. New Nationalism? The S.D.L.P. and the Creation of a Socialist and Labour Party in Northern Ireland, 1969–75. *Irish Historical Studies*, vol. XXXVIII, no. 151, pp. 422–438.

Capano, G., Howlett, M. and Ramesh, M. 2015. Bringing Governments Back in: Governance and Governing in Comparative Policy Analysis. *Journal of Comparative Policy Analysis: Research and Practice*, vol. 17, no. 4, pp. 311–321.

Carreras, M., Irepoglu Carreras, Y. and Bowler, S. 2019. Long-Term Economic Distress, Cultural Backlash, and Support for Brexit. *Comparative Political Studies*, vol. 52, no. 9, pp. 1396–1424.

Casal Bertoa, F. 2017. Political Parties or Party Systems? Assessing the 'Myth' of Institutionalisation and Democracy. *West European Politics*, vol. 40, no. 2, pp. 402–429.

Catterall, P. 2000. The British Electoral System, 1885–1970. *Historical Research*, vol. 73, no. 181, pp. 156–174.

Census. 2011a. Key Statistics for Northern Ireland (Report Published in December 2012). Available at: https://www.nisra.gov.uk/sites/nisra.gov.uk/files/publications /2011-census-results-key-statistics-northern-ireland-report-11-december-2012 .pdf.

——— 2011b. National Records of Scotland –Table KS202SC– National Identity. Available at: https://www.scotlandscensus.gov.uk/webapi/jsf/tableView/tableView .xhtml.

———— 2011c. Key Statistics for Wales –Table KS202EW– National Identity. Available at: https://www.ons.gov.uk/peoplepopulationandcommunity/populationandmigration /populationestimates/bulletins/2011censuskeystatisticsforwales/2012-12-11#ethnic -group-and-identity.

Cetrà, D. and Harvey, M. 2019. Explaining Accommodation and Resistance to Demands for Independence Referendums in the UK and Spain. *Nations and Nationalism*, vol. 25, no. 2, pp. 607–629.

Cetrà, D. and Liñera, R. 2018. Breaking-Up Within Europe: Sub-state Nationalist Strategies in Multilevel Polities. *JCMS: Journal of Common Market Studies*, vol. 56, no. 3, pp. 717–729.

Chalmers, M. 2017. *UK Foreign and Security Policy after Brexit*. RUSI Briefing Paper, Royal United Services Institute, London, January.

Chang, W. W. 2018. Brexit and Its Economic Consequences. *The World Economy*, vol. 41, no. 9, pp. 2349–2373.

Cheneval, F. and el-Wakil, A. 2018. The Institutional Design of Referendums: Bottom-up and Binding. *Swiss Political Science Review*, vol. 24, no. 3, pp. 294–304.

Chiaramonte, A. and Emanuele, V. 2017. Party System Volatility, Regeneration, and De-institutionalization in Western Europe (1945–2015). *Party Politics*, vol. 23, no. 4, pp. 376–388.

Christiansen, T. and Fromage, D. (eds.) 2019. *Brexit and Democracy: The Role of Parliaments in the UK and the European Union*. Basingstoke: Palgrave Macmillan.

Clarke, H., Goodwin, M. and Whiteley, P. 2017. *Brexit: Why Britain Voted to Leave the European Union*. Cambridge: Cambridge University Press.

Coakley, J. 2022. A Farewell to Northern Ireland? Constitutional Options for Irish Unity. *The Political Quarterly*, vol. 93, no. 2, pp. 307–315.

Colley, L. 1992. *Britons: Forging the Nation, 1707–1837*. New Haven, CT: Yale University Press.

Conti, G. 2019. *Parliament the Mirror of the Nation: Representation, Deliberation, and Democracy in Victorian Britain*. Cambridge: Cambridge University Press.

Conservative Party Manifesto. 2015. *Strong Leadership - A Clearer Economic Plan – a Brighter, More Secure Future*. London: Conservative Party.

Convery, A. 2014. Devolution and the Limits of Tory Statecraft: The Conservative Party in Coalition and Scotland and Wales. *Parliamentary Affairs*, vol. 67, no. 1, pp. 25–44.

Cooper, I. 2017. A Separate Parliament for the Eurozone? Differentiated Representation, Brexit, and the Quandary of Exclusion. *Parliamentary Affairs*, vol. 70, no. 4, pp. 655–672.

Copus, C. 2018. The Brexit Referendum: Testing the Support of Elites and Their Allies for Democracy; or, Racists, Bigots and Xenophobes, Oh My! *British Politics*, vol. 13, no. 1, pp. 90–104.

Corcoran, D. P. 2013. *Freedom to Achieve Freedom: The Irish Free State 1922–1932*. Dublin: Gill & Macmillan.

Coulter, C. and Murray, M. 2008. *Northern Ireland after the Troubles: A Society in Transition*. Manchester: Manchester University Press.

Cox, G. W. 1997. *Making Votes Count: Strategic Coordination in the World's Electoral Systems*. Cambridge: Cambridge University Press.

Cox, G. W. and McCubbins, M. D. 2005. *Setting the Agenda*. Cambridge: Cambridge University Press.

Conway, M. 2019. Brexit: 100 Years in the Making. *Contemporary European History*, vol. 28, no. 1, pp. 6–9.

Cowley, P. 2015. Parliament. In A. Seldon and M. Finn (eds.), *The Coalition Effect 2010–2015*. Cambridge: Cambridge University Press, pp. 136–158.

Cowley, P. and Stuart, M. 2014. *The Four Year Itch*. Nottingham: University of Nottingham.

Crepaz, M., Koelble, T. A. and Wilsford, D. (eds.) 2000. *Democracy and Institutions. The Life Work of Arend Lijphart*. Ann Arbor, MI: The University of Michigan Press.

Crick, B. (ed.) 1991. *National Identities: The Constitution of the United Kingdom*. Oxford: Blackwell.

Curtice, J. 2013. Politicians, Voters and Democracy: The 2011 UK Referendum on the Alternative Vote. *Electoral Studies*, vol. 32, no. 2, pp. 215–223.

———— 2016. Brexit: Behind the Referendum. *Political Insight*, vol. 7, no. 2, pp. 4–7.

———— 2020a. A Return to 'Normality' at Last? How the Electoral System Worked in 2019. *Parliamentary Affairs*, vol. 73, no. Suppl_1, pp. 29–47.

———— 2020b. Was the 2019 General Election a Success? *NatCen Social Research*. https://whatukthinks.org/eu/analysis/was-the-2019-general-election-a-success.

———— 2022. A Brexit Election? In D. Wring et al. (eds.), *Political Communication in Britain: The 2019 General Election*. Cham: Palgrave Macmillan, pp. 15–31.

Curtice, J., Clery, E., Perry, J., Phillips, M. and Rahim, N. 2019. *British Social Attitudes: The 36th Report*. London: The National Centre for Social Research.

Curtice, J., Fisher, S. and English, P. 2021. The Geography of a Brexit Election: How Constituency Context and the Electoral System Shaped the Outcome. In R. Ford, T. Bale, W. Jennings and P. Surridge (eds.), *The British General Election of 2019*. Cham: Palgrave Macmillan, pp. 461–494.

Curtice, J. and Montagu, I. 2020. Is Brexit Fuelling Support for Independence? *Scottish Social Attitudes*. Edinburgh: ScotCen, pp. 1–22.

Curtin, D. 2014. Challenging Executive Dominance in European Democracy. *Modern Law Review*, vol. 77, no. 1, pp. 1–32.

Cutts, D., Goodwin, M., Heath, O. and Surridge, P. 2020. Brexit, the 2019 General Elections and the Realignment of British Politics. *The Political Quarterly*, vol. 91, no. 1, pp. 7–23.

Cygan, A., Lynch, P. and Whitaker, R. 2020. UK Parliamentary Scrutiny of the EU Political and Legal Space after Brexit*. *Journal of Common Market Studies*, vol. 58, no. 6, pp. 1605–1620.

Dahl, R. A. 1971. *Polyarchy. Participation and Opposition*. New Haven: Yale University Press.

Daniels, L.-A. and Quo, A. 2021. Brexit and Territorial Preferences: Evidence from Scotland and Northern Ireland. *Publius: The Journal of Federalism*, vol. 51, no. 2, pp. 186–211.

Dardanelli, P. 2006. *Between Two Unions: Europeanisation and Scottish Devolution*. Manchester: Manchester University Press.

Davis, D. 2017. Parliamentary Scrutiny by Select Committees. 7 February. https://www.parliament.uk/globalassets/documents/commons-committees/european-scrutiny/letter-david-davis-070217.pdf/.

Davies, K. 2022. Sticking Together in 'Divided Britain': Talking Brexit in Everyday Family Relationships. *Sociology*, vol. 56, no. 1, pp. 97–113.

Deegan-Krause, K. and Enyedi, Z. 2010. Agency and the Structure of Party Competition: Alignment, Stability and the Role of Political Elites. *West European Politics*, vol. 33, no. 3, pp. 686–710.

De Sio, L. and Weber, T. 2014. Issue Yield: A Model of Party Strategy in Multidimensional Space. *American Political Science Review*, vol. 108, no. 4, pp. 870–885.

De Vries, C. and Hobolt, S. 2020. *Political Entrepreneurs: The Rise of Challenger Parties in Europe*. Princeton, NJ: Princeton University Press.

Denham, J. 2018. Is It the English Question or the British Question? The Three Stands of Britishness. *LSE Blog on British Politics and Policy*. https://blogs.lse.ac.uk/politicsandpolicy/is-it-the-english-or-the-british-question/.

Dennison, J. 2020. A Review of Public Issue Salience: Concepts, Determinants and Effects on Voting. *Political Studies Review*, vol. 17, no. 4, pp. 436–446.

Dennison, J. and Goodwin, M. 2015. Immigration, Issue Ownership and the Rise of UKIP. *Parliamentary Affairs*, vol. 68, no. Suppl_1, pp. 168–187.

Denver, D. 2005. 'Valence Politics': How Britain Votes Now. *British Journal of Politics and International Relations*, vol. 7, no. 2, pp. 292–299.

Denver, D. and Garnett, M. 2014. *British General Elections Since 1964: Diversity, Dealignment and Disillusion*. Oxford: Oxford University Press.

Denver, D. and Johns, R. 2022. *Elections and Voters in Britain*. Cham: Palgrave Macmillan.

Dexter, L. A. 2006. *Elite and Specialized Interviewing*. Colchester: Ecpr Press.

Diamond, P. 2014. *Governing Britain: Power, Politics and the Prime Minister*. London: I.B. Tauris.

Diamond, P., Nedergaard, P., Rosamond, B. and Lequesne, C. (eds.) 2018. *The Routledge Handbook of the Politics of Brexit*. Abingdon: Routledge.

Diamond, P. and Richards, D. 2012. The Case for Theoretical and Methodological Pluralism in British Political Studies: New Labour's Political Memoirs and the British Political Tradition. *Political Studies Review*, vol. 10, no. 2, pp. 177–194.

Dicey, A. V. 1885. *Introduction to the Study of the Law of the Constitution*. London: Macmillan.

Dorey, P. 2008. *The Labour Party and Constitutional Reform: A History of Constitutional Conservatism*. Basingstoke: Palgrave.

Dougan, M., Hayward, K., Hunt, J., McEwen, N., McHarg, A. and Wincot, D. 2020. *UK Internal Market Bill, Devolution and the Union*. Centre on Constitutional Change – Wales Governance Centre – UK in a Changing Europe.

Douglas-Scott, S. 2016. Brexit, Article 50 and the Contested British Constitution. *Modern Law Review*, vol. 79, no. 6, pp. 1019–1040.

Driver, S. 2011. *Understanding British Party Politics*. Cambridge: Polity Press.

Druckman, J. N., Martin, L. W. and Thies, M. F. 2005. Influence without Confidence: Upper Chambers and Government Formation. *Legislative Studies Quarterly*, vol. 30, no. 4, pp. 529–548.

Dunleavy, P. 1999. Elected Representatives and Accountability: The Legacy of Empire. In I. Halliday, A. Gamble and G. Parry (eds.), *Fundamentals in British Politics*. Basingstoke: Macmillan, pp. 204–230.

——— 2018. The Westminster 'Plurality Rule' Electoral System. In P. Dunleavy, A. Park and R. Taylor (eds.), *The UK's Changing Democracy: The 2018 Democratic Audit*. London: LSE Press, pp. 45–55.

Dunleavy, P. and Margetts, H. 1999. Mixed Electoral Systems in Britain and the Jenkins Commission on Electoral Reform. *British Journal of Politics and International Relations*, vol. 1, no. 1, pp. 12–38.

Duverger, M. 1951. *Les Partis Politiques*. Paris: A. Colin.

Dyson, K. and Featherstone, K. 1996. Italy and EMU as a 'Vincolo Esterno': Empowering the Technocrats, Transforming the State. *South European Society and Politics*, vol. 1, no. 2, pp. 272–299.

Dyson, S. B. 2018. Gordon Brown, Alistair Darling, and the Great Financial Crisis: Leadership Traits and Policy Responses. *British Politics*, vol. 13, no. 2, pp. 121–145.

Elazar, D. J. 1997. Contrasting Unitary and Federal Systems. *International Political Science Review*, vol. 18, no. 13, pp. 237–251.

Elias, A. 2006. From 'Full National Status' to 'Independence' in Europe – The Case of Plaid Cymru – The Party of Wales. In J. McGarry and M. Keating (eds.), *European Integration and the Nationalities Question*. London: Routledge, pp. 193–215.

Emanuele, V. and Chiaramonte, A. 2018. Explaining the Impact of New Parties in the Western European Party Systems. *Journal of Elections, Public Opinion and Parties*, vol. 29, no. 4, pp. 490–510.

EPRS. 2020. *States of Emergency in Response to the Coronavirus Crisis*. PE 659.385. Brussels, December 2020.

Eribon, G. 2013. *Retour a Reims*. Paris: Flammarion.

Ertman, T. 2010. The Great Reform Act of 1832 and British Democratization. *Comparative Political Studies*, vol. 43, no. 8–9, pp. 1000–1022.

Evans, A. 2020. A Tale as Old as (Devolved) Time? Sewel, Stormont and the Legislative Consent Convention. *Political Quarterly*, vol. 91, no. 1, pp. 166–172.

Evans, J. 2002. In Defence of Sartori. Party System Change, Voter Preference Distributions and Other Competitive Incentives. *Party Politics*, vol. 8, no. 2, pp. 155–174.

Evans, P. (ed.) 2017. *Essays on the History of Parliamentary Procedure*. Oxford and Portland: Hart Publishing.

Evans, G. 1999. Europe: A New Electoral Cleavage? In G. Evans and P. Norris (eds.), *Critical Elections: British Parties and Voters in Long-term Perspective*. London: Sage, pp. 207–222.

Evans, G. and Duffy, M. 1997. Beyond the Sectarian Divide: The Social Bases and Political Consequences of Nationalist and Unionist Party Competition in Northern Ireland. *British Journal of Political Science*, vol. 27, no. 1, pp. 47–71.

Evans, G. and Schaffner, F. 2019. Brexit Identity vs Party Identity, UK in a Changing Europe. https://ukandeu.ac.uk/wp-content/uploads/2019/01/Public-Opinion-2019 -report.pdf.

Evans, G. and Tilley, J. 2017. *The New Politics of Class: The Political Exclusion of the British Working Class*. Oxford: Oxford University Press.

Evans, G. and Menon, A. 2017. *Brexit and British Politics*. Polity Press.

Evans, G. and Mellon, J. 2019. Immigration, Euroscepticism, and the Rise and Fall of UKIP. *Party Politics*, vol. 25, no. 1, pp. 76–87.

Evans, G. and Mellon, J. 2020. The Re-shaping of Class Voting. https://www.britishelec tionstudy.com/bes-findings/the-re-shaping-of-class-voting-in-the-2019-election -by-geoffreyevans-and-jonathan-mellon.

Evans, G., De Geus, R. and Green, J. 2021. Boris Johnson to the Rescue? How the Conservatives Won the Radical-Right Vote in the 2019 General Election. *Political Studies*.

Evans, G., Noah, C. and Dennison, J. 2018. Brexit: The Causes and Consequences of the UK's Decision to Leave the EU. In M. Castells et al. (eds.), *Europe's Crises*. Cambridge: Polity, pp. 380–404.

Evans, P., Reuschmeyer, D. and Skocpol, T. 1985. *Bringing the State Back In*. New York: Cambridge University Press.

Fabbrini, S. 2010. *Compound Democracies: Why the United States and Europe Are Becoming Similar*. Oxford: Oxford University Press.

Farrell, D. M. and Scully, R. 2007. *Representing Europe's Citizens?: Electoral Institutions and the Failure of Parliamentary Representation*. Oxford: Oxford University Press.

Fasone, C. 2021. Coping with Disloyal Cooperation in the Midst of a Pandemic: The Italian Response, *VerfBlog*, 8 March 2021. https://verfassungsblog.de/coping-with-disloyal -cooperation-in-the-midst-of-a-pandemic-the-italian-response/.

Fieldhouse, E., Evans, G., Green, J., Mellon, J. and Prosser, C. 2021. *Volatility, Realignment and Electoral Shocks: Brexit and the UK General Election of 2019*, Assrn.

Fieldhouse, E., Green, J., Evans, G., Mellon, J., Prosser, C., Schmitt, H. and Van der Eijk, C. 2020. *Electoral Shocks: The Volatile Voter in a Turbulent World*. Oxford: Oxford University Press.

Fioretos, O., Falleti, T. G. and Sheingate, A. (eds.) 2016. *The Oxford Handbook of Historical Institutionalism*. Oxford: Oxford University Press.

Flinders, M. 2005. Majoritarian Democracy in Britain: New Labour and the Constitution. *West European Politics*, vol. 28, no. 1, pp. 61–93.

———— 2010. *Democratic Drift: Majoritarian Modification and Democratic Anomie in the United Kingdom*. Oxford: Oxford University Press.

———— 2018. The (Anti-)Politics of the General Election: Funnelling Frustration in a Divided Democracy. *Parliamentary Affairs*, vol. 71, no. Suppl_1, pp. 222–236.

———— 2020. Not a Brexit Election? Pessimism, Promises and Populism 'UK-Style'. *Parliamentary Affairs*, vol. 73, no. Suppl_1, pp. 225–242.

Flinders, M., Cotter, L. M., Kelso, A. and Meakin, A. 2018. The Politics of Parliamentary Restoration and Renewal: Decisions, Discretion, Democracy. *Parliamentary Affairs*, vol. 71, no. 1, pp. 144–168.

Flinders, M., Judge, D., Rhodes, R. A. W. and Vatter, A. 2022. 'Stretched But Not Snapped': A Response to Russell and Serban on Retiring the 'Westminster Model'. *Government and Opposition*, vol. 57, no. 2, pp. 353–369.

Flinders, M. and Kelso, A. 2011. Mind the Gap: Political Analysis, Public Expectations and the Parliamentary Decline Thesis. *British Journal of Politics and International Relations*, vol. 13, no. 2, pp. 249–268.

Foley, M. 1989. *The Silence of Constitutions*. London: Routledge.

Foreign & Commonwealth Office. 2014. *Review of the Balance of Competences*, 18 December. https://www.gov.uk/guidance/review-of-the-balance-of-competences.

Ford, R. and Goodwin, M. 2014. *Revolt on the Right: Understanding Support for the Radical Right in Britain*. Basingstoke: Palgrave.

Ford, R. and Jennings, W. 2020. The Changing Cleavage Politics of Western Europe. *Annual Review of Political Science*, vol. 23, no. 1, pp. 295–314.

Ford, R., Bale, T., Jennings, W. and Surridge, P. 2021. *The British General Election of 2019*. London: Palgrave Macmillan.

Foreign Policy. 2020. *A New Scottish Independence Vote Seems All But Inevitable*, 24 January. https://foreignpolicy.com/2020/01/24/a-new-scottish-independence-vote-seems-all-but-inevitable/.

Fowler, B. 2020. *Parliament's Role in Scrutinising The UK-EU Trade and Cooperation Agreement is a Farce*. Hansard Society, 29 December. https://www.hansardsociety.org.uk/blog/parliaments-role-in-scrutinising-the-uk-eu-trade-and-cooperation-agreement.

Franklin, M. N. 2010. Cleavage Research: A Critical Appraisal. *West European Politics*, vol. 33, no. 3, pp. 648–658.

Freeden, M. 2017. After the Brexit Referendum: Revisiting Populism as an Ideology. *Journal of Political Ideologies*, vol. 22, no. 1, pp. 1–11.

Fukuyama, F. 2011. *The Origins of Political Order*. New York: Farrar, Straus and Giroux.

Fukuyama, F. 2014. *Political Order and Political Decay*. New York: Farrar, Straus and Giroux.

Gaines, B. J. 2009. Does the United Kingdom Obey Duverger's Law? In B. Grofman, A. Blais and S. Bowler (eds.), *Duverger's Law of Plurality Elections: The Logic of Party Competition in Canada, India, the United Kingdom, and the United States*. New York: Springer, pp. 115–134.

Gallagher, M. and Uleri, P. V. 1996. *The Referendum Experience in Europe*. Basingstoke: Macmillan.

Gamble, A. 2003. *Between Europe and America: The Future of British Politics*. Basingstoke: Palgrave Macmillan.

—— 2006. The Constitutional Revolution in the UK. *Publius*, vol. 36, no. 1, pp. 19–35.

—— 2016. The Conservatives and the Union: The 'New English Toryism' and the Origins of Anglo-Britishness. *Political Studies Review*, vol. 14, no. 3, pp. 359–367.

—— 2018. Taking Back Control: The Political Implications of Brexit. *Journal of European Public Policy*, vol. 25, no. 8, pp. 1215–1232.

—— 2019. The Realignment of British Politics in the Wake of Brexit. *The Political Quarterly*, vol. 90, pp. 177–186.

Gänzle, S., Leruth, B. and Trondal, J. 2019. *Differentiated Integration and Disintegration in a Post-Brexit Era*. London: Routledge.

George, S. 1994. *An Awkward Partner*. Oxford: Oxford University Press.

Gee, G. and Young, A. L. 2016. Regaining Sovereignty? Brexit, The UK Parliament and the Common Law. *European Public Law*, vol. 22, no. 1, pp. 131–147.

Gidron, N. and Hall, P. 2020. Populism as a Problem of Social Integration. *Comparative Political Studies*, vol. 53, no. 7, pp. 1027–1059.

Gifford, C. 2014. The People against Europe: The Eurosceptic Challenge to the United Kingdom's Coalition Government. *JCMS: Journal of Common Market Studies*, vol. 52, no. 3, pp. 512–528.

—— 2020. Brexit and Trump: Contesting New Cleavage Formation. *Journal of Contemporary European Studies*, online first.

Ginsburg, T. and Versteeg, M. 2020. States of Emergencies: Part II. *Harvard Law Review Blog*, https://blog.harvardlawreview.org/states-of-emergencies-part-ii/.

Giovannini, A. 2016. Towards a 'New English Regionalism' in the North? The Case of Yorkshire First. *Political Quarterly*, vol. 87, no. 4, pp. 590–600.

Giovannini, A. and Mosca, L. 2021. The Year of Covid-19: Italy at a Crossroads. *Contemporary Italian Politics*, vol. 13, no. 2, pp. 130–148.

Giuliani, M. 2021a. Westminster as Usual? Three Interpretations for the UK Democracy. *Government and Opposition*, earlyview, pp. 1–17.

—— 2021b. Twelve Votes for an Exit: Compromise and Responsiveness in the Brexit Process. *Government and Opposition*, earlyview, pp. 1–20.

Glencross, A. 2016. *Why the UK Voted for Brexit: David Cameron's Great Miscalculation*. London: Palgrave Macmillan.

—— 2021. Managing Differentiated Disintegration: Insights from Comparative Federalism on Post-Brexit EU–UK Relations. *British Journal of Politics and International Relations*, vol. 23, no. 4, pp. 593–608.

Glover, M. and Hazell, R. 2008. Introduction: Forecasting Constitutional Futures. In R. Hazell (ed.), *Constitutional Futures Revisited: Britain's Constitution to 2020*. Basingstoke: Palgrave Macmillan, pp. 1–28.

Goes, E. 2015. The Liberal Democrats and the Coalition: Driven to the Edge of Europe. *The Political Quarterly*, vol. 86, no. 1, pp. 93–100.

—— 2020. Labour's 2019 Campaign: A Defeat of Epic Proportions. *Parliamentary Affairs*, vol. 73, no. Suppl_1, pp. 84–102.

Goldenberg, J. and Fisher, S. D. 2019. The Sainte-Laguë Index of Disproportionality and Dalton's Principle of Transfers. *Party Politics*, vol. 25, no. 2, pp. 203–207.

Goldsworthy, J. 2010. *Parliamentary Sovereignty: Contemporary Debates*. Cambridge: Cambridge University Press.

Goodhart, D. 2017. *The Road to Somewhere: The Populist Revolt and the Future of Politics*. London: Hurst.

Goodhart, P. 1976. *Full-Hearted Consent: The Story of the Referendum Campaign and the Campaign for the Referendum*. London: Davis-Poynter.

Goodwin, M. 2015. Ukip, the 2015 General Election and Britain's EU Referendum, Political Insight. *Political Insight*, vol. 6, no. 3, pp. 12–15.

Goodwin, M. and Heath, O. 2016. The 2016 Referendum, Brexit and the Left Behind: An Aggregate-Level Analysis of the Result. *The Political Quarterly*, vol. 87, no. 3, pp. 323–332.

Gordon, M. 2016. Brexit: A Challenge for the UK Constitution, of the UK Constitution? *European Constitutional Law Review*, vol. 12, no. 3, pp. 404–444.

——— 2019. Parliamentary Sovereignty and the Political Constitution(s): From Griffith to Brexit. *King's Law Journal*, vol. 30, no. 1, pp. 125–147.

——— 2020. Referendums in the UK Constitution: Authority, Sovereignty and Democracy after Brexit. *European Constitutional Law Review*, vol. 16, no. 2, pp. 213–248.

Gormley-Heenan, C. and Aughey, A. 2017. Northern Ireland and Brexit: Three Effects on "The Border to the Mind". *British Journal of Politics and International Relations*, vol. 19, no. 3, pp. 497–511.

Gover, D. and Kenny, M. 2016. *Finding the Good in EVEL: An Evaluation of 'English Votes for English Laws' in the House of Commons*. Edinburgh: Centre on Constitutional Change.

Gover, D. and Kenny, M. 2018. Answering the West Lothian Question? A Critical Assessment of 'English Votes for English Laws' in the UK Parliament. *Parliamentary Affairs*, vol. 71, no. 4, pp. 760–782.

Government of Wales Act. 2006. Available at: https://www.legislation.gov.uk/ukpga /2006/32/contents.

Grande, E. and Schwarzbözl, T. 2017. Politicizing Europe in the UK. Dynamics of Inter-party Competition and Intra-party Conflict. Paper prepared for the Conference 'Rejected Europe. Beloved Europe. Cleavage Europe', European University Institute, Florence, May 18–19.

Gravey, V. and Jordan, A. 2016. Does the European Union have a Reverse Gear? Policy Dismantling in a Hyperconsensual Polity. *Journal of European Public Policy*, vol. 23, no. 8, pp. 1180–1198.

Green, J. 2020. *Annual Norton Lecture, Centre for British Politics*. Online Lecture, University of Hull.

Green, J. and Hobolt, S. 2008. Owning the Issue Agenda: Party Strategies and Vote Choices in British Elections. *Electoral Studies*, vol. 27, no. 3, pp. 460–476.

Greenleaf, W. H. 1983. *The British Political Tradition Vol. 2, The Ideological Heritage*. London: Methuen.

Griffith, J. A. G. 1979. The Political Constitution. *Modern Law Review*, vol. 42, no. 1, pp. 1–21.

Griffiths, J. and Larner, J. 2021. Democratic Accountability in a Crisis: Analysing Evaluations of Government Response to COVID-19 in a Multi-nation State. Public Opinion and Voting Behavior Working Paper, 14 June 2021, APSA Preprint: 10.33774/apsa-2021-p1dpl.

Grogan, J. 2020. Parliament Still Does Not Have the Power to Scrutinise the Coronavirus 2020 Act Properly. *LSE Blog*, 30 October. https://blogs.lse.ac.uk/covid19/2020/10 /30/parliament-still-does-not-have-the-power-to-scrutinise-the-coronavirus-act -2020-properly/.

Grube, D. and Howard, C. 2016. Is the Westminster System Broken Beyond Repair? *Governance*, vol. 29, no. 4, pp. 467–481.

Guerrera, A. 2019. Philip Hammond: Why Boris Johnson Will Let down Brexiteers in a British "Parliamentary Dictatorship". *La Repubblica*, 18 December. https://www.repubblica.it/esteri/2019/12/18/news/philip_hammond_why_boris_johnson_will_let_down_the_brexiteers_in_a_british_parliamentary_dictatorship_-243744640/.

Guerrina, R. and Masselot, A. 2018. Walking into the Footprint of EU Law: Unpacking the Gendered Consequences of Brexit. *Social Policy and Society*, vol. 17, no. 2, pp. 319–330.

Gurr, T. R. and Moore, W. H. 1997. Ethnopolitical Rebellion: A Cross-sectional Analysis of the 1980s with Risk Assessments for the 1990s. *American Journal of Political Science*, vol. 41, no. 4, pp. 1079–1103.

Hall, M. 2011. *Political Traditions and UK Politics*. Basingstoke: Palgrave.

Hall, M., Marsh, D. and Vines, E. 2018. A Changing Democracy: Contemporary Challenges to the British Political Tradition. *Policy Studies*, vol. 39, no. 4, pp. 365–382.

Hansard Society. 2019. *Private Members' Bills*. https://www.hansardsociety.org.uk/publications/guides/private-members-bills.

Harvey, D. 2021. Brexit and Covid-19. *King's Law Journal*, vol. 32, no. 1, pp. 26–36.

Hay, C. 2020. Brexistential Angst and the Paradoxes of Populism: On the Contingency, Predictability and Intelligibility of Seismic Shifts. *Political Studies*, vol. 68, no. 1, pp. 187–206.

Hayton, R. 2022. Brexit and Party Change: The Conservatives and Labour at Westminster. *International Political Science Review*, online first.

Hazareesingh, S. 1994. *Political Traditions in Modern France*. Oxford: Oxford University Press.

Hazell, R. 2006. The English Question. *Publius: the Journal of Federalism*, vol. 36, no. 1, pp. 37–56.

——— 2007. The Continuing Dynamism of Constitutional Reform. *Parliamentary Affairs*, vol. 60, no. 1, pp. 3–25.

——— (ed.) 2008. *Constitutional Futures Revisited: Britain's Constitution to 2020*. London: Palgrave Macmillan.

Henderson, A., Jeffery, C., Linera, R., Scully, R., Wincott, D. and Wyn Jones, R. 2016. England, Englishness and Brexit. *The Political Quarterly*, vol. 87, no. 2, pp. 187–199.

Henderson, A. and Wyn Jones, R. 2021. *Englishness: The Political Force Transforming Britain*. Oxford: Oxford University Press.

Hennessy, P. 1995. *The Hidden Wiring: Unearthing the British Constitution*. London: Gollancz.

Héritier, A. 2007. *Explaining Institutional Change in Europe*. Oxford: Oxford University Press.

Herron, E. S., Pekkanen, R. J. and Shugart, M. S. (eds.) 2018. *The Oxford Handbook of Electoral Systems*. Oxford: Oxford University Press.

Hertner, I. 2016. "Seven, or Seven and a Half Out of 10": Jeremy Corbyn's Conspicuous Absence from the Referendum Campaign. *LSE Brexit*, 13 June. https://blogs.lse.ac.uk/brexit/2016/06/13/seven-or-seven-and-a-half-out-of-10-jeremy-corbyns-conspicuous-absence-from-the-referendum-campaign/.

Hix, S. 2017. Decentralised Federalism: A New Model for the EU. In B. Martill and U. Staiger (eds.), *Brexit and Beyond: Rethinking the Futures of Europe*. London: UCL Press, pp. 72–80.

——— 2018. Brexit: Where is the EU–UK Relationship Heading? *Journal of Common Market Studies*, vol. 56, no. 4, pp. 11–27.

HM Government. 2021. *Global Britain in a Competitive World*. 16 March. https://www.gov.uk/government/publications/global-britain-in-a-competitive-age-the-integrated-review-of-security-defence-development-and-foreign-policy/global-britain-in-a-competitive-age-the-integrated-review-of-security-defence-development-and-foreign-policy.

Hobolt, S., Leeper, T. J. and Tilley, J. 2020. Divided by the Vote: Affective Polarization in the Wake of the Brexit Referendum. *British Journal of Political Science*, vol. online first.

Hobolt, S. and Tilley, J. 2021. British Public Opinion towards EU Membership. *Public Opinion Quarterly*, vol. 85, no. 4, pp. 1128–1152.

——— 2022. Do 'Remainers' and 'Leavers' Still Exist? In *British Politics after Brexit, UK in a Chaning Europe Report*. London, pp. 39–42.

Hobolt, S. B. 2016. The Brexit Vote: A Divided Nation, a Divided Continent. *Journal of European Public Policy*, vol. 23, no. 9, pp. 1259–1277.

Hochshild, A. R. 2016. *Strangers in Their Own Land*. New York: The Free Press.

Hoff, S. 2015. Locke and the Nature of Political Authority. *The Review of Politics*, vol. 77, no. 1, pp. 1–22.

Holmes, M. 2014. Britain and the Politics of European Integration. In B. Jones and P. Norton (eds.), *Politics UK*, 8th edition. New York: Routledge, pp. 556–575.

Holyrood. 2018. *EU Continuity Bill was within Competence of the Scottish Parliament When it was Passed*, by Jenny Davidson, 13 December 2018. https://www.holyrood.com/news/view,eu-continuity-bill-was-within-competence-of-scottish-parliament-when-it-was-passed_9642.htm.

Hooghe, L. and Marks, G. 2009. A Postfunctionalist Theory of European Integration: From Permissive Consensus to Constraining Dissensus. *British Journal of Political Science*, vol. 39, no. 1, pp. 1–23.

——— 2018. Cleavage Theory Meets Europe's Crises: Lipset, Rokkan, and the Transnational Cleavage. *Journal of European Public Policy*, vol. 25, no. 1, pp. 109–135.

Hooghe, L., Marks, G. and Schakel, A. H. 2010. *The Rise of Regional Authority: A Comparative Study of 42 Countries*. London: Routledge.

Hooghe, L., Marks, G., Schakel, A. H., Chapman-Osterkatz, S., Niedzwiecki, S. and Shair-Rosenfield, S. 2016. *Measuring Regional Authority. Volume I: A Postfunctionalist Theory of Governance*. Oxford: Oxford University Press.

Hooghe, L., Marks, G., Schakel, A. H., Niedzwiecki, S., Chapman-Osterkatz, S. and Shair-Rosenfield, S. 2021. Regional Authority Index (RAI) v. 3. *EUI Research Data 2021*. Robert Schuman Centre. http://diana-n.iue.it:8080/handle/1814/70298.

Hooghe, L., Marks, G. and Wilson, C. J. 2002. Does Left/Right Structure Party Positions on European Integration? *Comparative Political Studies*, vol. 35, no. 8, pp. 965–989.

Hopkin, J. 2017. When Polanyi Met Farage: Market Fundamentalism, Economic Nationalism, and Britain's Exit from the European Union. *British Journal of Politics and International Relations*, vol. 19, no. 3, pp. 465–478.

Hopkins, S. 2002. Election Report – UK General Election 2001: Northern Ireland. *Regional and Federal Studies*, vol. 12, no. 19, pp. 207–217.

Horgan, G. and Gray, A. M. 2012. Devolution in Northern Ireland: A Lost Opportunity? *Critical Social Policy*, vol. 32, no. 3, pp. 467–478.

Hough, D. and Jeffery, C. 2006. *Devolution and Electoral Politics*. Manchester: Manchester University Press.

House of Lords. 2017. *Salisbury Convention in a Hung Parliament*. Library Briefing, 20 June. https://researchbriefings.files.parliament.uk/documents/LLN-2017-0030/LLN-2017-0030.pdf.

———— 2018. Library Briefing: Referendums and Parliamentary Democracy Debate on 19 July 2018. Available at: https://researchbriefings.files.parliament.uk/documents/LLN-2018-0080/LLN-2018-0080.pdf.

———— 2021. *Government Defeats in the House of Lords*, 28 April. https://www.parliament.uk/about/faqs/house-of-lords-faqs/lords-govtdefeats/.

———— 2022. *Government Defeats in the House of Lords*. https://www.parliament.uk/about/faqs/house-of-lords-faqs/lords-govtdefeats/.

House of Lords – Constitution Committee. 2010. *Twelfth Report "Referendums in the United Kingdom"*. https://publications.parliament.uk/pa/ld200910/ldselect/ldconst/99/9902.htm.

House of Lords – Select Committee on the Constitution. 2020. *Brexit Legislation: Constitutional Issues*, 6° Report of Session 2019–21, 9 June. https://publications.parliament.uk/pa/ld5801/ldselect/ldconst/71/71.pdf.

Huhe, N., Naurin, D. and Thomson, R. 2020. Don't Cry for Me Britannia: The Resilience of the European Union to Brexit. *European Union Politics*, vol. 21, no. 1, pp. 152–172.

Inglehart, R. 1977. *The Silent Revolution, Changing Values and Political Styles among Western Publics*. Princeton, NJ: Princeton University Press.

Inglehart, R. and Norris, P. 2017. Trump and the Populist Authoritarian Parties: The Silent Revolution in Reverse. *Perspectives on Politics*, vol. 15, no. 2, pp. 443–454.

Inglis, D. 2021. Brexit Barbarization? The UK Leaving the EU as De-civilizing Trend. *Journal of Sociology*, vol. 57, no. 1, pp. 59–76.

Institute for Government. 2017. *Devolution: Common Frameworks and Brexit*. https://www.instituteforgovernment.org.uk/explainers/brexit-devolution-and-common-frameworks.

———— 2018. *EU Withdrawal Bill: Amendments and Debates*, 21 June. https://www.instituteforgovernment.org.uk/explainers/eu-withdrawal-bill-amendments-and-debates.

———— 2020a. *Parliamentary Monitor 2020*, 20 May. https://www.instituteforgovernment.org.uk/publications/parliamentary-monitor-2020.

———— 2020b. *UK Internal Market Bill: Key Amendments*, 22 December. https://www.instituteforgovernment.org.uk/explainers/internal-market-bill-amendments.

Ipsos Mori. 2019. *How Britain Voted in the 2019 Election*. https://www.ipsos.com/ipsos-mori/en-uk/how-britain-voted-2019-election.

Jennings, I. W. 1933. *The Law and the Constitution*. London: University of London Press.

Jennings, W. 2009. The Public Thermostat, Political Responsiveness and Error-Correction: Border Control and Asylum in Britain, 1994–2007. *British Journal of Political Science*, vol. 39, no. 4, pp. 847–870.

Jennings, W. and Lodge, M. 2019. Brexit, the Tides and Canute: The Fracturing Politics of the British State. *Journal of European Public Policy*, vol. 26, no. 5, pp. 772–789.

Jennings, W., McKay, L. and Stoker, G. 2021. The Politics of Levelling Up. *The Political Quarterly*, vol. 92, no. 2, pp. 302–311.

Jennings, W. and Stoker, D. 2017. Tilting Towards the Cosmopolitan Axis? Political Change in England and the 2017 General Election. *The Political Quarterly*, vol. 88, no. 3, pp. 359–369.

Jensen, M. D. and Snaith, H. 2018. Brexit and the European Union: Hanging in the Balance? In P. Diamond, P. Nedergaard and B. Rosamond (eds.), *Routledge Handbook of the Politics of Brexit*. London: Routledge, pp. 254–265.

Jensen, M. J. and Kelstrup, J. D. 2019. House United, House Divided: Explaining the EU's Unity in the Brexit Negotiations. *JCMS: Journal of Common Market Studies*, vol. 57, no. S1, pp. 28–39.

Jessop, B. 2017. The Organic Crisis of the British State: Putting Brexit in its Place. *Globalizations*, vol. 14, no. 1, pp. 133–141.

John, P. 2018. *The Political Science of British Politics: Institutions Are Back Again*. Available on SSRN 2846736.

Johnes, M. 2007. Eighty Minute Patriots? National Identity and Sport in Modern Wales. *International Journal of the History of Sport*, vol. 17, no. 4, pp. 93–110.

Johns, R. 2021. As You Were: The Scottish Parliament Election of 2021. *The Political Quarterly*, vol. 92, no. 3, pp. 493–499.

Johns, R., Mitchell, J. and Carman, C. J. 2013. Constitution or Competence? The SNP's Re-Election in 2011. *Political Studies*, vol. 61, no. S1, pp. 158–178.

Johnson, B. 2016. 'Please Vote Leave on Thursday, Because We'll Never Get This Chance Again'. *The Telegraph*, 19 June.

Johnston, R. 2006. What Is and Isn't to Be Defended as British Politics: Whose Past, Whose Present, and Whose Future? A Comment on Kerr and Kettell. *British Politics*, vol. 1, no. 1, pp. 413–418.

Johnston, R., Pattie, C., and Hartman, T. 2020. Who Follows the Leader? Leadership Heuristics and Valence Voting at the UK's 2016 Brexit Referendum. *Innovation: the European Journal of Social Science Research*, online first.

Johnston, R., Pattie, C. and Rossiter, D. 2021. *Representative Democracy? Geography and the British Electoral System*. Manchester: Manchester University Press.

Jones, B., Norton, P. and Hertner, I. (eds.) 2022. *Politics UK*, 10th edition. London: Routledge.

Jones, T. 2019. *The Uneven Path of British Liberalism*. Manchester: Manchester University Press.

Jordan, G. and Cairney, P. 2013. What is the 'Dominant Model' of British Policymaking? Comparing Majoritarian and Policy Community Ideas. *British Politics*, vol. 8, no. 3, pp. 233–259.

Jordan, G. and Richardson, J. 1979. *Governing under Pressure: The Policy Process in a Post-parliamentary Democracy*. Oxford: Martin Robertson.

Judge, D. 2005. *Political Institutions in the United Kingdom*. Oxford: Oxford University Press.

Judge, D. 2014. *Democratic Incongruities*. Palgrave Macmillan UK.

Jupille, J. 2004. *Procedural Politics: Issues, Influence and Institutional Choice in the European Union*. Cambridge: Cambridge University Press.

Kanagasooriam, J. and Simon, E. 2021. Red Wall: The Definitive Description. *Political Insight*, vol. 12, no. 3, pp. 8–11.

Katz, R. and Mair, P. 1995. Changing Models of Party Organization and Party Democracy: The Emergence of the Cartel Party. *Party Politics*, vol. 1, no. 1, pp. 5–28.

Kavanagh, D. 2012. Referendums in British Politics. In A. Torre and J. O. Frosini (eds.), *Democrazia rappresentativa e referendum nel Regno Unito*. Ravenna: Maggioli Editore, pp. 113–124.

Kaufmann, E. 2018. *Whiteshift*. London: Allen Lane.

Keating, M. 2001. *Plurinational Democracy: Stateless Nations in a Post-sovereignty Era*. Oxford: Oxford University Press.

——— 2018. Brexit and the Territorial Constitution of the United Kingdom. *Droit et Société*, vol. 98, no. 1, pp. 53–69.

———— 2019. *The Repatriation of Competences in Agriculture after Brexit, Centre on Constitutional Change – UK in a Changing Europe* (Revised Version February 2019).

———— 2021a. *State and Nation in the United Kingdom: The Fractured Union*. Oxford: Oxford University Press.

———— 2021b. Taking Back Control? Brexit and the Territorial Constitution of the United Kingdom. *Journal of European Public Policy*, online first.

Keegan, W., Marsh, D. and Roberts, R. 2017. *Six Days in September: Black Wednesday, Brexit and the Making of Europe*. London: OMFIF.

Kellner, P. 2020. How M&S Closures Illuminate Brexit Britain and Last Month's Election. https://kellnerpolitics.com/2020/01/02/how-ms-closures-illuminate-brexit-britain -and-last-months-election/.

———— 2022. Can a Progressive Alliance Ever Win in the UK? *Prospect Magazine*. https://www.prospectmagazine.co.uk/politics/can-a-progressive-alliance-ever-win -in-the-uk.

Kelso, A. 2016. Political Leadership in Parliament: The Role of Select Committee Chairs in the UK House of Commons. *Politics and Governance*, vol. 4, no. 2, pp. 115–126.

———— 2017. The Politics of Parliamentary Procedure: An Analysis of Queen's Speech Debates in the House of Commons. *British Politics*, vol. 12, no. 2, pp. 267–288.

Keman, H. and Pennings, P. 1995. Managing Political and Societal Conflict in Democracies: Do Consensus and Corporatism Matter? *British Journal of Political Science*, vol. 25, no. 2, pp. 271–281.

Kenny, M. and Sheldon, J. 2021. When Planets Collide: The British Conservative Party and the Discordant Goals of Delivering Brexit and Preserving the Domestic Union, 2016–2019. *Political Studies*, vol. 69, no. 4, pp. 965–984.

Kerr, P. and Kettell, S. 2006. In Defence of British Politics: The Past, Present and Future of the Discipline. *British Politics*, vol. 1, no. 1, pp. 3–25.

Key, V. O. 1955. A Theory of Critical Elections. *The Journal of Politics*, vol. 17, no. 1, pp. 3–18.

King, A. 1966. *British Politics: People, Parties and Parliament*. Boston, MA: D. C. Heath and Company.

———— 2009. *The British Constitution*. Oxford: Oxford University Press.

———— 2015. *Who Governs Britain?* New York: Penguin Books.

King, A. and Crewe, I. 2014. *The Blunders of Our Governments*. Simon and Schuster.

Kirkup, J. 2016. *The Lib–Lab Pact: A Parliamentary Agreement, 1977–78*. Basingstoke: Palgrave Macmillan.

Knapp, A. 2018. Structure versus Accident in the Defeat of France's Mainstream Right, April–June 2017. *Parliamentary Affairs*, vol. 71, no. 3, pp. 558–577.

Knight, J. 1992. *Institutions and Social Conflict*. Cambridge: Cambridge University Press.

Kriesi, H. P., Grande, E., Dolezal, M., Helbling, M., Höglinger, D., Hutter, S. and Wüest, B. 2012. *Political Conflict in Western Europe*. Cambridge: Cambridge University Press.

Kriesi, H., Grande, E., Lachat, R., Dolezal, M., Bornschier, S. and Frey, T. 2006. Globalization and the Transformation of the National Political Space: Six European Countries Compared. *European Journal of Political Research*, vol. 45, no. 6, pp. 921–956.

Labour Party Manifesto. 2019. *It's Time for Real Change*. London: Labour Party.

Ladrech, R. 2002. Europeanization and Political Parties: Towards a Framework for Analysis. *Party Politics*, vol. 8, no. 4, pp. 389–403.

Laffan, B. 2018. Brexit: Re-opening Ireland's 'English Question'. *Political Quarterly*, vol. 89, no. 4, pp. 568–575.

192 Bibliography

————— 2021. Sovereignty: Driving British Divergence. In F. Fabbrini (ed.), *The Law & Politics of Brexit: Volume III: The Framework of New EU-UK Relations*. Oxford: Oxford University Press, pp. 240–259.

Liable, J. 2008. *Separatism and Sovereignty in the New Europe*. New York: Palgrave Macmillan.

Lang, A., McGuinness, T. and Miller, V. 2017. *European Union (Notification of Withdrawal) Bill: Analysis of Lords' Amendments*. House of Commons Library, briefing paper 7922, 10 March.

Langlands, R. 1999. Britishness or Englishness? The Historical Problem of National Identity in Britain. *Nations and Nationalism*, vol. 5, no. 1, pp. 53–69.

Lavery, S., McDaniel, S. and Schmid, D. 2019. Finance Fragmented? Frankfurt and Paris as European Financial Centres after Brexit. *Journal of European Public Policy*, vol. 26, no. 10, pp. 1502–1520.

Lees, C. 2021. Brexit, the Failure of the British Political Class, and the Case for Greater Diversity in UK Political Recruitment. *British Politics*, vol. 16, no. 1, pp. 36–57.

Levi, M. and Hechter, M. 1985. A Rational Choice Approach to the Rise and Decline of Ethnoregional Political Parties. In A. Tiryakian and R. Rogowski (eds.), *New Nationalism of the Developed West*. Boston, MA: Allen & Unwin, pp. 128–146.

Lijphart, A. 1968. Typologies of Democratic Systems. *Comparative Political Studies*, vol. 1, no. 1, pp. 3–44.

————— 1977. *Democracy in Plural Societies: A Comparative Exploration*. New Heaven CT: Yale University Press.

————— 1984. *Democracies: Patterns of Majoritarian and Consensus Government in Twenty-One Countries*. New Haven, CT and London: Yale University Press.

————— 1999. *Patterns of Democracy: Government Forms and Performance in Thirty-Six Countries*. New Haven, CT and London: Yale University Press.

————— 2012. *Patterns of Democracy: Government Forms and Performance in Thirty-Six Countries*, 2nd edition. New Haven, CT and London: Yale University Press.

Liñera, R. and Cetrà, D. 2015. The Independence Case in Comparative Perspective. *The Political Quarterly*, vol. 86, no. 2, pp. 257–264.

Lipset, S. M. and Rokkan, S. 1967. Cleavage Structures, Party Systems and Voter Alignments: An Introduction. In S. M. Lipset and S. Rokkan (eds.), *Party Systems and Voter Alignments: Cross-National Perspectives*. New York: Free Press, pp. 1–64.

Lodge, M. and Wegrich, K. 2012. Introduction: Executive Politics, Crises and Governance. In M. Lodge and K. Wegrich (eds.), *Executive Government in Times of Crises*. Basingstoke: Palgrave, pp. 1–15.

Lustik, I. S., Miodonwnik, D. and Eidelson, R. J. 2004. Secessionism in Multicultural States: Does Sharing Power Prevent or Encourage It? *American Political Science Review*, vol. 98, no. 2, pp. 209–229.

Lynch, P. 1996. *Minority Nationalism and European Integration*. Cardiff: University of Wales Press.

————— 2007. Party System Change in Britain: Multi-party Politics in a Multi-level Polity. *British Politics*, vol. 2, no. 3, pp. 323–346.

————— 2015. Conservative Modernisation and European Integration: From Silence to Salience and Schism. *British Politics*, vol. 10, no. 2, pp. 185–203.

Lynch, P. and Whitaker, R. 2008. A Loveless Marriage: The Conservatives and the European People's Party. *Parliamentary Affairs*, vol. 61, no. 1, pp. 31–51.

Lynch, P. and Whitaker, R. 2013. Where There is Discord, Can They Bring Harmony? Managing Intra-party Dissent on European Integration in the Conservative Party. *The British Journal of Politics and International Relations*, vol. 15, no. 3, pp. 317–339.

Lynch, P., Whitaker, R. and Cygan, A. 2019. Brexit and the UK Parliament: Challenges and Opportunities. In T. Christiansen and D. Fromage (eds.), *Brexit and Democracy*. London: Palgrave Macmillan, pp. 51–80.

Lynggard, K., Jensen, M. D. and Kluth, M. F. 2022. *Governments' Responses to the COVID-19 Pandemic in Europe: Navigating the Perfect Storm*. Cham: Palgrave Macmillan.

Loughlin, M. 2013. *The British Constitution: A Very Short Introduction*. Oxford: Oxford University Press.

Low, S. 1904. *The Governance of England*. London: T. Fisher Unwin.

MacCormick, N. 1998. The English Constitution, the British State and the Scottish Anomaly. *Scottish Affairs*, vol. 25, no. 2, pp. 129–145.

Macinnes, A. I. 2007. *Union and Empire: The Making of the United Kingdom in 1707*. Cambridge: Cambridge University Press.

MacLeod, G. and Jones, M. 2018. Explaining 'Brexit Capital': Uneven Development and the Austerity State. *Space and Polity*, vol. 22, no. 2, pp. 111–136.

Magistro, B. and Wittstock, N. 2021. Changing Preferences versus Issue Salience: The Political Success of Anti-immigration Parties in Italy. *South European Society and Politics*. https://doi.org/10.1080/13608746.2021.2009107.

Mair, P. 2000. The Limited Impact of Europe on National Party Systems. *West European Politics*, vol. 23, no. 4, pp. 27–51.

—— 2006a. Cleavage. In R. Katz and W. Crotty (eds.), *Sage Handbook of Party Politics*. London: Sage, pp. 371–376.

—— 2006b. Party System Change. In R. Katz and W. Crotty (eds.), *Sage Handbook of Party Politics*. London: Sage, pp. 63–73.

—— 2009. The Party System. In M. Flinders, C. Hay, A. Gamble and M. Kenny (eds.), *Oxford Handbook of British Politics*. Oxford: Oxford University Press, pp. 283–302.

Manin, B. 1997. *The Principles of Representative Government*. Cambridge: Cambridge University Press.

March, J. G. and Olsen, J. P. 1984. The New Institutionalism: Organizational Factors in Political Life. *American Political Science Review*, vol. 78, no. 3, pp. 734–749.

Marinetto, M. 2003. Governing beyond the Centre: A Critique of the Anglo-Governance School. *Political Studies*, vol. 5, no. 3, pp. 592–608.

Marquand, D. 2008. *Britain Since 1918, the Strange Career of British Democracy*. London: Phoenix.

Marshall, H. and Drieschova, A. 2018. Post-truth Politics in the UK's Brexit Referendum. *New Perspectives*, vol. 26, no. 3, pp. 89–105.

Marks, G., Attewell, D., Rovny, J. and Hooghe, L. 2021. Cleavage Theory. In M. Riddervold et al. (eds.), *The Palgrave Handbook of EU Crises*. Palgrave Studies in European Union Politics, pp. 173–187.

Marsh, D. 2018. Brexit and the Politics of Truth. *British Politics*, vol. 13, no. 3, pp. 79–89.

Marshal, H. and Drieshova, A. 2018. Post-truth Politics in the UK's Brexit Referendum. *New Perspectives*, vol. 26, no. 3, pp. 89–105.

Martill, B. 2020. The 2019 European Parliament Election in the UK. *Italian Political Science Review/Rivista Italiana di Scienza Politica*, vol. 50, no. 3, pp. 368–381.

—— 2021a. Deal or no Deal: Theresa May's Withdrawal Agreement and the Politics of (Non-) Ratification. *Journal of Common Market Studies*, vol. 59, pp. 1607–1622.

—— 2021b. Prisoners of Their Own Device: Brexit as a Failed Negotiating Strategy. *British Journal of Politics and International Relations*, early view.

Massetti, E. 2009. Explaining Regionalist Party Positioning in a Multi-dimensional Ideological Space: A Framework for Analysis. *Regional and Federal Studies*, vol. 19, no. 4–5, pp. 501–531.

—––– 2010. *Political Strategy and Ideological Adaptation in Regionalist Parties in Western Europe: A Comparative Study of the Northern League, Plaid Cymru, the South Tyrolese People's Party and the Scottish National Party.* PhD Thesis, University of Sussex.

—––– 2022. The European Union and the Challenge of 'Independence in Europe': Straddling between (Formal) Neutrality and (Actual) Support for Member-States' Territorial Integrity. *Regional and Federal Studies*, vol. 32, no. 3, pp. 307–330.

Massetti, E. and Schakel, A. H. 2016. Between Autonomy and Secession: Decentralization and Regionalist Party Ideological Radicalism. *Party Politics*, vol. 22, no. 1, pp. 59–79.

—––– 2017. Decentralization Reforms and Regionalist Parties Strength: Accommodation, Empowerment or Both? *Political Studies*, vol. 65, no. 2, pp. 432–451.

Massey, C. 2020. A New Era? Keir Starmer's Labour Leadership. *Political Insight*, vol. 11, no. 3, pp. 4–7.

Matthews, F. 2017. Whose Mandate Is It Anyway? Brexit, the Constitution and the Contestation of Authority. *Political Quarterly*, vol. 88, no. 4, pp. 603–611.

Matthews, F. and Flinders, M. 2017. Patterns of Democracy: Coalition Governance and Majoritarian Modification in the United Kingdom, 2010–2015. *British Politics*, vol. 12, no. 2, pp. 157–182.

Mattinson, D. 2020. *Beyond the Red Wall.* London: Biteback.

Mcconalogue, J. 2019. The British Constitution Resettled? Parliamentary Sovereignty after the EU Referendum. *The British Journal of Politics and International Relations*, vol. 21, no. 2, pp. 439–458.

—––– 2020. *The British Constitution Resettled – Parliamentary Sovereignty Before and After Brexit.* Cham: Palgrave Macmillan.

McCurdy, C., Gardiner, L., Gustafsson, M. and Handscomb, K. 2020. *Painting the Towns Blue, Demography, Economy and Living Standards in the Political Geographies Emerging from the 2019 General Election.* Resolution Foundation. https://www.resolutionfoundation .org/publications/painting-the-towns-blue/.

McEwen, N. 2017. Brexit and Scotland: Between Two Unions. *British Politics*, vol. 13, no. 1, pp. 65–78.

—––– 2018. Still Better Together? Purpose and Power in Intergovernmental Councils in the UK. *Regional and Federal Studies*, vol. 27, no. 5, pp. 667–690.

—––– 2019. Legislating for EU Withdrawal: Do the Devolved Institutions Really Have 'No Role'? *Blogpost Del Centre on Constitutional Change.* https://www.centreoncon stitutionalchange.ac.uk/news-and-opinion/legislating-eu-withdrawal-do-devolved -institutions-really-have-no-role.

—––– 2022. Worth the Wait? Reforming Intergovernmental Relations. Centre on Constitutional Change. Available at: https://www.centreonconstitutionalchange.ac .uk/news-and-opinion/worth-wait-reforming-intergovernmental-relations.

McEwen, N. and Remond, A. 2019. *The Repatriation of Competences in Climate and Energy Policy after Brexit: Implications for Devolution and Multi-level Government, Centre on Constitutional Change – UK in Changing Europe.*

McEwen, N., Kenny, M., Sheldon, J. and Brown-Swan, C. 2020. Intergovernmental Relations in the UK: Time for a Radical Overhaul? *The Political Quarterly*, vol. 9, no. 3, pp. 632–640.

McGarry, J. and O'Leary, B. 2016. Power-Sharing Executives: Consociational and Centripetal Formulae and the Case of Northern Ireland. *Ethnopolitics*, vol. 15, no. 5, pp. 497–519.

McGowan, L. 2018. *Preparing for Brexit: Actors, Negotiations and Consequences*. London: Palgrave Macmillan.

McHarg, A. and Mitchell, J. 2017. Brexit and Scotland. *British Journal of Politics and International Relations*, vol. 19, no. 3, pp. 512–526.

McLean, I. and McMillan, A. 2005. *State of the Union: Unionism and the Alternatives in the United Kingdom Since 1707*. Oxford: Oxford University Press.

McLoughlin, P. J. 2009. The SDLP and the Europeanization of the Northern Ireland Problem. *Irish Political Studies*, vol. 24, no. 4, pp. 603–619.

Mellon, J. 2021. Tactical Voting and Electoral Pacts in the 2019 UK General Election. *Political Studies Review*, earlyview.

Mendelson, M. and Parkin, A. (eds.) 2001. *Referendum Democracy: Citizens, Elites and Deliberation in Referendum Campaigns*. Basingstoke: Palgrave.

Menon, A. and Scazzieri, L. 2020. The United Kingdom: Towards a Parting of the Ways. In S. Bulmer and C. Lequesne (eds.), *The Member States of the European Union*. Oxford: Oxford University Press, pp. 257–279.

Menon, A. 2022. Covid Has Been an Easy Scapegoat for Economic Disruption, but Brexit Is Biting. *The Guardian*, 31 January.

Mezey, M. L. 1979. *Comparing Legislatures*. Durham, NC: Duke University Press.

Middleton, A. 2021. *Communicating and Strategising Leadership in British Elections*. Basingstoke: Palgrave Macmillan.

Minto, R., Hunt, J., Keating, M. and McGowan, L. 2016. A Changing UK in a Changing Europe: The UK State between European Union and Devolution. *Political Quarterly*, vol. 87, no. 2, pp. 179–186.

Mitchell, D. 2018. Non-nationalist Politics in a Bi-national Consociation: The Case of the Alliance Party of Northern Ireland. *Nationalism and Ehtnic Politics*, vol. 24, no. 3, pp. 336–347.

Mitchell, J. 1998. The Evolution of Devolution: Labour's Home Rule Strategy in Opposition. *Government and Opposition*, vol. 33, no. 4, pp. 479–496.

——— 2000. New Parliament, New Politics in Scotland. *Parliamentary Affairs*, vol. 53, no. 3, pp. 605–621.

——— 2006. Evolution and Devolution: Citizenship, Institutions, and Public Policy. *Publius: The Journal of Federalism*, vol. 36, no. 1, pp. 153–168.

——— 2010a. Introduction: The Westminster Model and the State of Unions. *Parliamentary Affairs*, vol. 63, no. 1, pp. 85–88.

——— 2010b. The Narcissism of Small Differences: Scotland and Westminster. *Parliamentary Affairs*, vol. 63, no. 1, pp. 98–116.

——— 2015. Sea Change in Scotland. *Parliamentary Affairs*, vol. 68, no. 1, pp. 88–100.

——— 2016. Seachange in Scotland. *Parliamentary Affairs*, vol. 68, no. S1, pp. 88–100.

Moran, M. 2011. *Politics and Governance in the UK*, 2nd edition. Basingstoke: Palgrave Macmillan.

——— 2017. *The End of British Politics?* Basingstoke: Palgrave.

Mitchell, P. 2005. The United Kingdom: Plurality Rule under Siege. In M. Gallagher and P. Mitchell (eds.), *The Politics of Electoral Systems*. Oxford University Press, pp. 157–184.

Mitchell, P., Evans, G. and O'Leary, B. 2009. Extremist Outbidding in Ethnic Party Systems is not Inevitable: Tribune Parties in Northern Ireland. *Political Studies*, vol. 57, no. 2, pp. 391–421.

Mitchell, P., O'Leary, B. and Evans, G. 2001. Northern Ireland: Flanking Extremists Bite the Moderates and Emerge in their Clothes. *Parliamentary Affairs*, vol. 54, no. 4, pp. 725–742.

Moravcsik, A. 2016. Brexit: Welcome, Britain, to the Hotel California. https://paw .princeton.edu/article/brexit-welcome-britain-hotel-california.

Morel, L. 2001. The Rise of Government-initiated Referendums in Consolidated Democracies. In M. Mendelson and A. Parkin (eds.), *Referendum Democracy: Citizens, Elites and Deliberation in Referendum Campaigns*. Basingstoke: Palgrave, pp. 47–64.

Morgan, K. O. 2017. Britain in the Seventies – Our Unfinest Hour? *Revue Française de Civilisation Britannique*. [online], XXII, Hors Série.

Morphet, J. 2021. *The Impact of COVID-19 on Devolution: Recentralising the British State Beyond Brexit?* Bristol: Policy Press.

Mudde, C. 2004. The Populist Zeitgeist. *Government and Opposition*, 39, no. 4, pp. 541–563.

——— 2021. Populism in Europe: An Illiberal Democratic Response to Undemocratic Liberalism (The Government and Opposition/Leonard Schapiro Lecture 2019). *Government and Opposition*, vol. 56, no. 4, pp. 577–597.

Munck, R. 1992. The Making of the Troubles in Northern Ireland. *Journal of Contemporary History*, vol. 27, no. 1, pp. 211–229.

Murphy, M. C. 2018. *Europe and Northern Ireland's Future: Negotiating Brexit's Unique Case*. Newcastle: Agenda Publishing.

Murphy, M. C. 2022. The Rise of the Middle Ground in Northern Ireland: What Does It Mean? *The Political Quarterly*. Early View. https://doi.org/10.1111/1467-923X.13175.

Murtagh, B. and Shirlow, P. 2012. Devolution and the Politics of Development in Northern Ireland. *Environment and Planning. Part C: Government and Policy*, vol. 30, no. 1, pp. 46–61.

National Records of Scotland – Census 2011. https://www.scotlandscensus.gov.uk/ webapi/jsf/tableView/tableView.xhtml.

Nice, A. 2021. European Structural Funds: The UK Shared Prosperity Fund. *Institute of Government*. 21/07/2021. Available at: https://www.instituteforgovernment.org.uk/ explainers/structural-funds.

Norris, P. 1995. The Politics of Electoral Reform in Britain. *International Political Science Review*, vol. 16, no. 1, pp. 65–78.

——— 2019. Was Farage the Midwife Delivering Johnson's Victory? The Brexit Party and the Size of the Conservative Majority. *LSE Blog*, 19 December https://blogs.lse .ac.uk/politicsandpolicy/ge2019-brexit-party-impact/.

North, D. C., Wallis, J. J. and Weingast, B. R. 2009. *Violence and Social Orders: A Conceptual Framework for Interpreting Recorded Human History*. Cambridge: Cambridge University Press.

Norton, P. 1975. *Dissension in the House of Commons: Intra-party Dissent in the House of Commons' Division Lobbies 1945–1974*. London and Basingstoke: Macmillan.

——— 1997. The Case for First-Past-the-Post. *Representation*, vol. 34, no. 2, pp. 84–88.

——— 2001. Playing by the Rules: The Constraining Hand of Parliamentary Procedure. *Journal of Legislative Studies*, vol. 7, no. 3, pp. 13–33.

——— 2011. *The British Polity*, 5a edition. London and New York: Pearson, I.B. Tauris.

——— 2020. *Governing Britain*. Manchester: Manchester University Press.

Nwokora, Z. and Pelizzo, R. 2014. Sartori Reconsidered: Toward a New Predominant Party System. *Political Studies*, vol. 62, no. 4, pp. 824–842.

O'Brien, B. 1999. *The Long War: The IRA and Sinn Féin*. New York: Syracuse University Press.

Offe, C. 2017. Referendum vs. Institutionalized Deliberation: What Democratic Theorists Can Learn from the 2016 Brexit Decision. *Dædalus*, vol. 146, no. 3, pp. 14–27.

Olivas Osuna, J. J., Kiefel, M. and Katsouyanni, K. G. 2021. Place Matters: Analyzing the Roots of Political Distrust and Brexit Narratives at a Local Level. *Governance*, vol. 34, no. 4, pp. 1019–1038.

Oliver, T. 2018. *Understanding Brexit. A Concise Introduction*. Bristol: Bristol University Press.

——— 2019. Brexitology: Delving into the Books on Brexit. *International Politics Reviews*, vol. 7, no. 1–2, pp. 1–24.

Oppermann, K. 2008. The Blair Government and Europe: The Policy of Containing the Salience of European Integration. *British Politics*, vol. 3, no. 2, pp. 156–182.

Outhwaite, W. 2017. *Brexit Sociological Response*. London: Anthem Press.

Panelbase. 2020. *Online Survey, 28–31 January 2020*. Available at: https://www.drg.global /wp-content/uploads/W14874-ScotGoesPop-tables-for-publication-v3-310220.pdf

Patberg, M. 2019. After the Brexit Vote: What's Left of 'Split' Popular Sovereignty? *Journal of European Integration*, vol. 40, no. 7, pp. 923–937.

Patel, O. and Reh, C. 2016. *Brexit: The Consequences for the EU's Political System*. UCL Constitution Unit Briefing Paper.

Pattie, C., Hartman, T. and Johnston, R. 2018. A Close-Run Thing? Accounting for Changing Overall Turnout in UK General Elections. *Representation*, vol. 55, no. 1, pp. 101–116.

Paun, A., Sargeant, J. and Klemperer, D. 2020. Devolution: Common Frameworks and Brexit. Institute for Government. 05/10/2020. https://www.instituteforgovernment .org.uk/explainers/devolution-common-frameworks-brexit.

Peele, G. 2021. Post Brexit and Post-Covid: Reflections on the Contemporary Conservative Party. *The Political Quarterly*, vol. 92, no. 3, pp. 404–411.

Pérez-Díaz, V. M., Dâiaz, V. P. and Díaz, V. P. 1999. *Spain at the Crossroads: Civil Society, Politics, and the Rule of Law*. Harvard University Press.

Pickard, J. 2019. Ken Clarke: The Tory Grandee Who Wants a Soft Brexit. *Financial Times*, 1 April. https://www.ft.com/content/42c75142-548c-11e9-a3db-1fe89bedc16e.

Pierson, P. 2000. Increasing Returns, Path Dependence, and the Study of Politics. *American Political Science Review*, vol. 94, no. 2, pp. 251–267.

Pierson, P. and Skocpol, T. 2002. Historical Institutionalism in Contemporary Political Science. In *Political Science: The State of the Discipline*. New York: W.W. Norton, pp. 693–721.

Politico. 2020. *How Boris Johnson's Internal Market Bill Went down Close to Home*, 9 September. https://www.politico.eu/article/boris-johnson-internal-market-bill -went-down-close-to-home/.

Posner, E. A. and Vermeule, A. 2011. *The Executive Unbound: after the Madisonian Republic*. Oxford: Oxford University Press.

Power, S., Bale, T. and Webb, P. 2020. Mistake Overturned, so I Call It a Lesson Learned: The Conservatives. *Parliamentary Affairs*, vol. 73, no. Suppl_1, pp. 65–83.

Powell, G. B. 2000. *Elections as Instruments of Democracy*. New Haven, CT: Yale University Press.

Prosser, C., Fieldhouse, E., Green, J., Mellon, J. and Evans, G. 2020. Tremors but no Youthquake: Measuring changes in the age and turnout gradients at the 2015 and 2017 British general elections. *Electoral Studies*, vol. 60, no. 4, pp. 1021–1029.

Prosser, C. 2021. The End of the EU Affair: The UK General Election of 2019. *West European Politics*, vol. 44, no. 2, pp. 450–461.

Pulzer, P. 1967. *Political Representation and Elections; Parties and Voting in Great Britain*. London: Praeger.

Quinn, T. 2013. From Two-Partism to Alternating Predominance: The Changing UK Party System, 1950–2010. *Political Studies*, vol. 61, no. 2, pp. 378–400.

Quinn, T., Allen, N. and Bartle, J. 2022. Why Was There a Hard Brexit? The British Legislative Party System, Divided Majorities and the Incentives for Factionalism. *Political Studies*, pp. 1–22. https://doi.org/10.1177/00323217221076353

Raunio, T. 2009. National Parliaments and European Integration: What We Know and Agenda for Future Research. *The Journal of Legislative Studies*, vol. 15, no. 4, pp. 317–334.

Reif, K. and Schmitt, H. 1980. Nine Second-Order National Elections– A Conceptual Framework for the Analysis of European Election Results. *European Journal of Political Research*, vol. 8, no. 1, pp. 3–44.

Renwick, A. 2010. *The Politics of Electoral Reform*. Cambridge: Cambridge University Press.

——— 2017. Referendums. In K. Arzheimer, J. Evans and M. S. Lewis-Beck (eds.), *The Sage Handbook of Electoral Behaviour*. London: Sage, pp. 433–458.

Renwick, A., Lauderdale, B., Russell, M. and Cleaver, J. 2022. *What Kind of Democracy Do People Want*. London: Constitution Unit.

Renwick, A., Palese, M. and Sargeant, J. 2018. Discussing Brexit—Could We Do Better? *The Political Quarterly*, vol. 89, no. 4, pp. 545–552.

Rhodes, R. A. 1988. *Beyond Westminster and Whitehall*. London: Routledge.

——— 1997. *Understanding Governance: Policy Networks, Governance, Reflexivity and Accountability*. Buckingham and Philadelphia: Open University Press.

Richards, D., Diamond, P. and Wager, A. 2019. Westminster's Brexit Paradox: The Contingency of the 'Old' versus 'New' Politics. *British Journal of Politics and International Relations*, vol. 21, no. 2, pp. 330–348.

Richards, D. and Smith, M. 2017. Things Were Better in the Past' Brexit and the Westminster Fallacy of Democratic Nostalgia. *LSE Politicsandpolicy Blog*, 20 May. https://blogs.lse.ac.uk/politicsandpolicy/brexit-and-the-westminster-fallacy-of -democratic-nostalgia/.

Richards, D. and Smith, M. J. 2015. In Defence of British Politics against the British Political Tradition. *The Political Quarterly*, vol. 86, no. 1, pp. 41–51.

Richards, D., Smith, M. and Hay, C. 2014. Conclusion: Apres Le Deluge? Crisis, Continuity and Change in UK Institutions. In *Institutional Crisis in 21st-Century Britain*. London: Palgrave Macmillan, pp. 256–272.

Richardson, J. 2018. The Changing British Policy Style: From Governance to Government? *British Politics*, vol. 12, no. 2, pp. 1–19.

Roberts, B. 1995. Welsh Identity in a Former Mining Valley: Social Images and Imagined Communities. *Contemporary Wales*, vol. 7, no. 1, pp. 77–95.

Robinson, J. S. R. 2008. Tackling the Anxieties of the English: Searching for the Nation through Football. *Soccer and Society*, vol. 9, no. 2, pp. 215–230.

Rodríguez-Pose, A. 2018. Commentary: The Revenge of the Places that Don't Matter (and What to Do about It). *Cambridge Journal of Regions, Economy and Society*, vol. 11, no. 1, pp. 189–209.

Roe-Crines, A. 2021. A Problem of Communication: Keir Starmer's Labour Leadership. *Political Insight*, vol. 12, no. 4, pp. 22–24.

Rokkan, S. and Urwin, D. 1982. Introduction: Centres and Peripheries in Western Europe. In S. Rokkan and D. Urwin (eds.), *The Politics of Territorial Identity: Studies in European Regionalism*. London: Sage, pp. 1–17.

Rosamond, B. 2016. Brexit and the Problem of European Disintegration. *Journal of Contemporary European Research*, vol. 12, no. 4, pp. 864–871.

———— 2020. European Integration and the Politics of Economic Ideas: Economists and Market Contestation in the Brexit Debate. *Economics*, vol. 58, no. 5, pp. 1085–1106.

Rose, R. 2001. *The Prime Minister in a Shrinking World*. Cambridge: Polity Press.

———— 2020. *How Referendums. Challenge European Democracy: Brexit and Beyond*. Cham: Palgrave.

———— 2021a. *How Sick is British Democracy?: A Clinical Analysis*. Cham: Springer Nature.

———— 2021b. How Sick is British Democracy? A Clinical Diagnosis. *Political Insight*, vol. 12, no. 3, pp. 28–30.

Rose, R. and McAllister, I. 1986. *Voters Begin to Choose: From Closed Class to Open Elections in Britain*. London: Sage.

Rose, R. and Urwin, D. W. 1970. Persistence and Change in Western Party Systems Since 1945. *Political Studies*, vol. 18, no. 3, pp. 287–319.

Rudolph, L. 2020. Turning Out to Turn Down the EU: The Mobilisation of Occasional Voters and Brexit. *Journal of European Public Policy*, vol. 27, no. 12, pp. 1858–1878.

Rudolph, J. R. and Thompson, R. J. (eds.) 1989. *Ethnoterritorial Politics, Policy, and the Western World*. London: Lynne Rienner.

Russack, S. (ed.) 2021. *The Effect of COVID on EU Democracies*. EPIN, European Policy Institutes Network, Report, 30 April.

Russell, M. 2013. *The Contemporary House of Lords: Westminster Bicameralism Revived*. Oxford: Oxford University Press.

Russell, M. and Cowley, P. 2016. The Policy Power of the Westminster Parliament: The "Parliamentary State" and the Empirical Evidence. *Governance*, vol. 29, no. 1, pp. 121–137.

Russell, M. and Cowley, P. 2018. Modes of UK Executive-Legislative Relations Revisited. *The Political Quarterly*, vol. 89, no. 1, pp. 18–28.

Russell, M. and Gover, D. 2017. *Legislation at Westminster: Parliamentary Actors and Influence in the Making of British Law*. Oxford: Oxford University Press.

Russell, M. and Paun, A. 2007. *The House Rules? International Lessons for Enhancing the Autonomy of the House of Commons*. London: UCL, The Constitution Unit.

Russell, M. and Serban, R. 2021. The Muddle of the 'Westminster Model': A Concept Stretched Beyond Repair. *Government and Opposition*, vol. 56, no. 4, pp. 744–756.

———— 2022. Why it is indeed time for the Westminster model to be retired from comparative politics. *Government and Opposition*, vol. 57, no. 2, pp. 370–384.

Russell, M., Gover, D. and Wollter, K. 2016. Does the Executive Dominate the Westminster Legislative Process?: Six Reasons for Doubt. *Parliamentary Affairs*, vol. 69, no. 2, pp. 286–308.

Russell, M., Gover, D., Wollter, K. and Benton, M. 2017. Actors, Motivations and Outcomes in the Legislative Process: Policy Influence at Westminster. *Government and Opposition*, vol. 52, no. 1, pp. 1–27.

Russell, M. and Serban, R. 2022. Why it is indeed time for the Westminster model to be retired from comparative politics. *Government and Opposition*, vol. 57, no. 2, pp. 370–384.

Saalfeld, T. 2003. The United Kingdom: Still a Single 'Chain of Command'? The Hollowing Out of the 'Westminster Model. In K. Strom, W. Muller and T. Bergman (eds.), *Delegation and Accountability in Parliamentary Democracies*. Oxford: Oxford University Press, pp. 620–646.

Sampson, T. 2017. Brexit: The Economics of International Disintegration. *Journal of Economic Perspectives*, vol. 31, no. 4, pp. 163–184.

Sandbrook, D. 2012. *Seasons in the Sun: The Battle for Britain, 1974–1979*. London: Allen Lane.

Sanders, D. 2017. The UK's Changing Party System: The Prospects for a Party Realignment at Westminster. *Journal of the British Academy*, vol. 5, pp. 91–124.

Sartori, G. 1969. From the Sociology of Politics to Political Sociology. In S. M. Lipset (ed.), *Politics and the Social Sciences*. New York: Oxford University Press, pp. 65–100.

Sartori, G. 1976. *Parties and Party Systems: A Framework for Analysis*. Cambridge: Cambridge University Press.

———— 1986. The Influence of Electoral Systems: Faulty Laws or Faulty Method? In B. Grofman and A. Lijphart (eds.), *Electoral Laws and Their Political Consequences*. New York: Agathon Press, pp. 43–68.

———— 1990. From the Sociology of Politics to Political Sociology. In P. Mair (ed.), *The West European Party System*. New York: Oxford University Press, pp. 150–182.

———— 1994. *Comparative Constitutional Engineering*. London: Macmillan.

Saunders, R. 2016. A Tale of Two Referendums: 1975 and 2016. *The Political Quarterly*, vol. 87, no. 3, pp. 318–322.

———— 2018. *Yes to Europe!: The 1975 Referendum and Seventies Britain*. Cambridge: Cambridge University Press.

Savanta ComRes. 2020. *Scottish Political Tracker – 17 December 2020*, Online Survey, 11–15 December 2020.

———— 2021. *State of the Union Poll (Scotland) – 4 March 2021*, Online Survey, 18–22 February 2021.

Schakel, A. and Massetti, E. 2020. Regional Institutions and the European Union. In F. Laursen (ed.), *The Encyclopedia of European Union Politics*. New York: Oxford University Press.

Schimmelfennig, F. 2018. Brexit: Differentiated Disintegration in the European Union. *Journal of European Public Policy*, vol. 25, no. 8, pp. 1154–1173.

Schmidt, S. K. 2020. No Match Made in Heaven: Parliamentary Sovereignty, EU Over-Constitutionalization and Brexit. *Journal of European Public Policy*, vol. 27, no. 5, pp. 779–794.

Schmidt, V. A. 2006. Adapting to Europe: Is It Harder for Britain? *The British Journal of Politics and International Relations*, vol. 8, no. 1, pp. 15–33.

Schmitt, K. 2005. *Political Theology: Four Chapters on the Concept of Sovereignty*. Chicago: University of Chicago Press.

Schrimsley, R. 2020. 'Maoist' Downing Street Faces Its Own Revolution. *Financial Times*, 5 October. https://www.ft.com/content/1588da49-0cd5-414a-a745-07532d2d99bb.

Schuette, L. A. 2021. Forging Unity: European Commission Leadership in the Brexit Negotiations. *JCMS: Journal of Common Market Studies*, vol. 59, no. 5, pp. 1142–1159.

Scotland Act 2016. Available at: https://www.legislation.gov.uk/ukpga/2016/11/contents/enacted.

Scottish Government. 2019. 19 December. https://www.gov.scot/publications/scotlands-right-choose-putting-scotlands-future-scotlands-hands/pages/1/.

Scottish National Party. 2016. *Re-Elect*. Election Manifesto.

Seldon, A. 2020. *May at 10: The Verdict*. London: Biteback Publisher.

Setala, M. 2006. On the Problems of Responsibility and Accountability in Referendums. *European Journal of Political Research*, vol. 45, no. 4, pp. 701–723.

Setala, M. and Schiller, T. 2009. *Referendums and Representative Democracy: Responsiveness, Accountability and Deliberation*. London: Routledge.

Seyd, B. 2016. Exploring Political Disappointment. *Parliamentary Affairs*, vol. 69, no. 2, pp. 327–347.

Sherrington, P. 2006. Confronting Europe: UK Political Parties and the EU 2000–2005. *British Journal of Politics and International Relations*, vol. 8, no. 1, pp. 69–78.

Shipman, T. 2016. *All Out War: The Full Story of How Brexit Sank Britain's Political Class*. London: William Collins Publisher.

Shugart, M. S. 2008. Inherent and Contingent Factors in Reform Initiation in Plurality Systems. In A. Blais (ed.), *To Keep or to Change First Past the Post?: The Politics of Electoral Reform*. Oxford: Oxford University Press, pp. 7–60.

Simson Caird, J. 2018. *Grieve 2: An Amendable Motion?* House of Commons Library, 19 June. https://commonslibrary.parliament.uk/brexit/legislation/grieve-2-an -amendable-motion.

——— 2019. Why the New Speaker May Not Always Be Able to Play a Straight Bat. UCL: The Constitution Unit. 16 November 2019. https://constitution-unit.com /2019/11/16/why-the-new-speaker-may-not-always-be-able-to-play-a-straight -bat/#more-8734.

Siroky, D. S. and Cuffe, J. 2015. Lost Autonomy, Nationalism and Separatism. *Comparative Political Studies*, vol. 48, no. 1, pp. 3–34.

Slapin, J. B., Kirkland, J. H., Lazzaro, J. A., Leslie, P. A. and O'Grady, T. 2018. Ideology, Grandstanding, and Strategic Party Disloyalty in the British Parliament. *American Political Science Review*, vol. 112, no. 1, pp. 15–30.

Smith, G. 1976. The Functional Properties of the Referendum. *European Journal of Political Research*, vol. 4, no. 1, pp. 1–23.

Smith, J. E. 2012. The European Dividing Line in Party Politics. *International Affairs*, vol. 88, no. 6, pp. 1277–1295.

——— 2019. Fighting to 'Take Back Control': The House of Lords and Brexit. In T. Christiansen and D. Fromage (eds.), *Brexit and Democracy*. London: Palgrave Macmillan, pp. 81–103.

Smith, M. J. 1999. *The Core Executive in Britain*. London: Macmillan.

Sobolewska, M. and Ford, R. 2020. *Brexitland: Identity, Diversity and the Reshaping of British Politics*. Cambridge: Cambridge University Press.

Sorens, J. 2009. The Partisan Logic of Decentralisation Reforms. *Regional and Federal Studies*, vol. 19, no. 2, pp. 255–272.

Sounders, R. 2018. *Yes to Europe! The 1975 Referendum and the Seventies Britain*. Cambridge: Cambridge University Press.

Stanley. 2017. Populism in Central and Eastern Europe. In C. R. Kaltwasser, P. Taggart, P. Ochoa Espejo and P. Ostiguy (eds.), *The Oxford Handbook on Populism*. Oxford: Oxford University Press, pp. 140–160.

Stephens, J. D. 1979. Class Formation and Class Consciousness: A Theoretical and Empirical Analysis with Reference to Britain and Sweden. *The British Journal of Sociology*, vol. 30, no. 4, pp. 389–414.

Stolz, K. 2019. Should Unionists Support PR? Electoral Systems, Party Systems and Territorial Integration in the United Kingdom. *British Politics*, vol. 14, no. 3, pp. 269–289.

Surridge, P. 2021. Post-Brexit British Politics: A Reunited Kingdom? *Political Insight*, vol. 1, no. 1, pp. 8–11.

Sumption, J. 2020. Brexit and the British Constitution: Reflections on the Last Three Years and the Next Fifty. *Political Quarterly*, vol. 91, no. 1, pp. 107–115.

Taagepera, R. 2003. Arend Lijphart's Dimensions of Democracy: Logical Connections and Institutional Design. *Political Studies*, vol. 51, no. 1, pp. 1–19.

Taggart, P. and Pirro, A. 2021. European Populism before the Pandemic: Ideology, Euroscepticism, Electoral Performance, and Government Participation of 63 Parties in 30 Countries. *Italian Political Science Review/Rivista Italiana Di Scienza Politica*, vol. 51, no. 3, pp. 281–304.

Taylor, A. 2007. The Strategic Impact of the Electoral System and the Definition of 'Good' Governance. *British Politics*, vol. 2, no. 1, pp. 20–44.

Taylor, M. 2019. Brexit and the British Constitution: A Long View. *The Political Quarterly*, vol. 90, no. 4, pp. 719–726.

The Financial Times. 2017. *Sturgeon Sends Official Letter to May Seeking Scottish Referendum*, 31 March. https://www.ft.com/content/9d8e574e-1611-11e7-80f4-13e067d5072c.

The Guardian. 2017a. *Brexit Bill to Cause Constitutional Clash with Scotland and Wales*, 14 July. https://www.theguardian.com/politics/2017/jul/13/scotland-wales-brexit -great-repeal-bill-naked-power-grab-nicola-sturgeon-carwyn-jones.

——— 2017b. *Theresa May Rejects Nicola Sturgeon's Referendum Demand*, 16 March. https://www.theguardian.com/politics/2017/mar/16/theresa-may-rejects-nicola -sturgeons-scottish-referendum-demand.

——— 2018. *Scottish Parliament Decisively Rejects EU Withdrawal Bill*, 15 May. https:// www.theguardian.com/politics/2018/may/15/scottish-parliament-decisively-reject -eu-withdrawal-bill-brexit.

——— 2020. *Devolution 'A Disaster North of the Border', Says Boris Johnson*, 16 November. https://www.theguardian.com/uk-news/2020/nov/16/scotland-devolution-a -disaster-north-of-the-border-says-boris-johnson.

The Independent. 2016. 8 November https://www.independent.co.uk/news/uk/politics /brexit-nicola-sturgeon-scotland-theresa-may-legal-challenge-supreme-court -appeal-case-a7404591.html.

The New European. 2020. *Boris Johnson a 'Great Recruiting Agent' for Scottish and Welsh Independence, Says Plaid Leader*, 29 November. https://www.theneweuropean.co.uk/ brexit-news/plaid-cymru-adam-price-on-boris-johnson-6568890.

The Scotsman. 2021. 8 April https://www.scotsman.com/news/politics/nicola-sturgeon -to-fall-short-of-majority-as-alex-salmonds-alba-party-deprives-snp-of-key-list -seats-poll-shows-3192641.

The Supreme Court. 2016. Written Case by the Lord Advocate (UKSP, 2016/0196). file:///F:/Westminster%20alla%20prova%20della%20Brexit/Sources/Judicial%20c ases/Miller%20vs%20Secretary%20of%20State/UKSC_2016_0196_Written%20cas e%20of%20the%20Lord%20Advocate%20for%20Scotland.pdf.

The Supreme Court. 2017. Judgement 24 January. https://www.supremecourt.uk/cases/ docs/uksc-2016-0196-judgment.pdf.

——— 2018. Judgement 13 December. https://www.supremecourt.uk/cases/uksc-2018-0.

——— 2019. Judgement 24 September. https://www.supremecourt.uk/cases/uksc-2019 -0192.html.

Thelen, K. 1999. Historical Institutionalism in Comparative Politics. *Annual Review of Political Science*, vol. 2, no. 1, pp. 369–404.

Thimont Jack, M. 2020. *EU Withdrawal Bill: Amendments and Debates*. London: Institute for Government, 25 February.

Thompson, H. 2017. Inevitability and Contingency: The Political Economy of Brexit. *British Journal of Politics and International Studies*, vol. 19, no. 3, pp. 434–449.

——— 2021. The European Geopolitical Space and the Long Path to Brexit. *Government and Opposition*, vol. 56, no. 3, pp. 385–404.

Thompson, L. 2020a. From Minority Government to Parliamentary Stalemate: Why Election 2019 Was Needed to Break the Brexit Logjam. *Parliamentary Affairs*, vol. 73, no. Suppl_1, pp. 48–64.

———— 2020b. *The End of the Small Party? Change UK and the Challenges of Parliamentary Politics*. Manchester: Manchester University Press.

Thompson, L. and Pearson, M. 2022. "Enter Parliament but Never Become Part of It" How Have the Greens in the United Kingdom Approached Opposition? *The British Journal of Politics and International Relations*, online first.

Tierney, S. 2004. *Constitutional Law and National Pluralism*. Oxford: Oxford University Press.

———— 2005. Reframing Sovereignty: Sub-state National Societies and Contemporary Challenges to the Nation-State. *International and Comparative Law Quarterly*, vol. 54, no. 1, pp. 161–183.

———— 2009. Constitutional Referendums: A Theoretical Enquiry. *Modern Law Review*, vol. 72, no. 3, pp. 360–383.

Tilley, J., Evans, G. and Mitchell, C. 2008. Consociationalism and the Evolution of Political Cleavages in Northern Ireland, 1989–2004. *British Journal of Political Science*, vol. 38, no. 4, pp. 699–717.

Tomkins, A. 2010. The Role of the Courts in the Political Constitution. *University of Toronto Law Journal*, vol. 60, no. 1, pp. 1–22.

Tonge, J. 2017. Supplying Confidence or Trouble? The Deal between the Democratic Unionist Party and the Conservative Party. *The Political Quarterly*, vol. 88, no. 3, pp. 412–416.

———— 2022. Voting into a Void? The 2022 Northern Ireland Assembly Election. *The Political Quarterly*, vol. 93, no. 3, pp. 524–529.

Tonge, J., Wilks-Heeg, S. and Thompson, L. 2020. Introduction: A Conservative Victory Like No Other? In J. Tonge, S. Wilks Heeg and L. Thompson (eds.), *Britain Votes: The 2019 General Election*. Oxford: Oxford University Press, pp. 1–6.

Toubeau, S. and Massetti, E. 2013. The Party Politics of Territorial Reforms in Europe. *West European Politics*, vol. 36, no. 2, pp. 297–316.

Treib, O. 2021. Euroscepticism is Here to Stay: What Cleavage Theory Can Teach Us about the 2019 European Parliament Elections. *Journal of European Public Policy*, vol. 28, no. 2, pp. 174–189.

Trystan, D., Scully, R. and Wyn Jones, R. 2003. Explaining the 'Quiet Earthquake': Voting Behaviour in the First Election to the National Assembly for Wales. *Electoral Studies*, vol. 22, no. 4, pp. 635–650.

UK Government – Cabinet Office. 2019. *Revised Frameworks Analysis*, April 2019.

Vachudova, M. A. 2021. Populism, Democracy, and Party System Change in Europe. *Annual Review of Political Science*, vol. 24, no. 1, pp. 471–498.

van Bergeijk, P. 2019. *Deglobalization 2.0: Trade and Openness During the Great Depression and the Great Recession*. Cheltenham: Edward Elgar.

Van Kessel, S., Chelotti, N., Drake, H., Roch, J. and Rodi, P. 2020. Eager to Leave? Populist Radical Right Parties' Responses to the UK's Brexit Vote. *The British Journal of Politics and International Relations*, vol. 22, no. 1, pp. 65–84.

Vasilopoulou, S. 2020. Brexit and the 2019 EP Election in the UK. *Journal of Common Market Studies*, vol. 58, no. S1, pp. 80–90.

Vatter, A. 2009. Lijphart Expanded: Three Dimensions of Democracy in Advanced OECD Countries? *European Political Science Review*, vol. 1, no. 1, pp. 125–154.

Vittori, D. 2021. Threat or Corrective? Assessing the Impact of Populist Parties in Government on the Qualities of Democracy: A 19-Country Comparison. *Government and Opposition*, pp. 1–21. https://doi.org/10.1017/gov.2021.21.

Von Schoultz, Å. 2017. Party Systems and Voter Alignments. In K. Arzheimer, J. Evans and M. S. Lewis-Beck (eds.), *The Sage Handbook of Electoral Behaviour 1*. London: Sage, pp. 30–55.

Wager, A., Bale, T., Cowley, P. and Menon, A. 2021. The Death of May's Law: Intra-And Inter-Party Value Differences in Britain's Labour and Conservative Parties. *Political Studies*. doi: 0032321721995632.

Wall, S. 2008. *A Stranger in Europe: Britain and the EU from Thatcher to Blair*. Oxford: Oxford University Press.

Walter, S. 2021. Brexit Domino? The Political Contagion Effects of Voter-Endorsed Withdrawals from International Institutions. *Comparative Political Studies*, vol. 54, no. 13, pp. 2382–2415.

Ward, J. and Ward, B. 2021. From Brexit to COVID-19: The Johnson Government, Executive Centralisation and Authoritarian Populism. *Political Studies*, online first.

Weale, A. 2017. The Democratic Duty to Oppose Brexit. *The Political Quarterly*, vol. 88, no. 2, pp. 170–181.

Webb, P. 2000. *The Modern British Party System*. London: Sage.

——— 2002. Political Parties in Britain: Secular Decline or Adaptive Resilience? In P. Webb, D. Farrell and I. Holliday (eds.), *Political Parties in Advanced Industrial Democracies*. Oxford: Oxford University Press, pp. 16–45.

Webb, P. and Fisher, J. 1999. The Changing British Party System: Two-Party Equilibrium or the Emergence of Moderate Pluralism? In D. Broughton and M. Donovan (eds.), *Changing Party Systems in Western Europe*. London and New York: Macmilland and St.Martin's Press, pp. 8–29.

Webb, P. and Bale, T. 2021. *The Modern British Party System*. Oxford: Oxford University Press.

Wellings, B. and Vines, E. 2016. Populism and Sovereignty: The EU Act and the In-Out Referendum, 2010–2015. *Parliamentary Affairs*, vol. 69, no. 2, pp. 309–326.

Welsh Government – Census 2011, Statistical Bulletin 126/2012.

Wheatley, J. 2019. *The Changing Shape of Politics*. Cham: Palgrave.

Whigham, S. 2014. 'Anyone but England'? Exploring Anti-English Sentiment as Part of Scottish National Identity in Sport. *International Review for the Sociology of Sport*, vol. 49, no. 2, pp. 152–174.

Whitaker, R. 2020. *Whoever Leads Labour Next Will Struggle to Influence EU-UK Relations*. Labourlist, 23 March 2020.

White, J. 2019. *Politics of Last Resort: Governing by Emergency in the European Union*. Oxford: Oxford University Press.

White, S. 2021. Brexit and the Future of the UK Constitution. *International Political Science Review*, vol. 43, no. 3, pp. 359–373.

White, S. G. 2022a. Brexit and the Future of the UK Constitution. *International Political Science Review*, vol. 43, no. 3, pp. 359–373.

——— 2022b. The Referendum in the UK's Constitution: From Parliamentary to Popular Sovereignty? *Parliamentary Affairs*, vol. 75, no. 2, pp. 263–280.

Whiteley, P., Seyd, P. and Clarke, H. D. 2021. The Conservative Party: The Victory of the Eurosceptic. In *Breaking the Deadlock*. Manchester: Manchester University Press, pp. 64–88.

Whiteley, P. F., Goodwin, M. and Clarke, H. D. 2018. The Rise and Fall of UKIP 2007–2017. In A. Nicholas and J. Bartle (eds.), *None Past the Post: Britain at the Polls 2017*. Manchester: Manchester University Press, pp. 78–99.

Whitehead, L. 2013. The Westminster System "Model" or "Muddle"? *Taiwan Journal of Democracy*, Special Issue, May, pp. 9–38.

Whyman, B. and Petrescu, A. I. 2020. *The Economics of Brexit*. Revisited. Cham: Palgrave.

Wilford, R. 2010. Northern Ireland: The Politics of Constraint. *Parliamentary Affairs*, vol. 63, no. 1, pp. 134–155.

Willet, J. and Giovannini, A. 2014. The Uneven Path of UK Devolution: Top-Down vs. Bottom-Up Regionalism in England – Cornwall and the North-East Compared. *Political Studies*, vol. 62, no. 2, pp. 343–360.

Williams, G. 1979. *Religion, Language and Nationality in Wales*. Cardiff: University of Wales Press.

Wilson, W. 1885. *Congressional Government: A Study in American Politics*. Boston, MA: Houghton Mifflin.

Wincott, D. 2017. Brexit Dilemmas: New Opportunities and Tough Choices in Unsettled Times. *The British Journal of Politics and International Relations*, vol. 19, no. 4, pp. 680–695.

——— 2020. Symposium Introduction: The Paradox of Structure: The UK State, Society and 'Brexit'. *JCMS: Journal of Common Market Studies*, vol. 58, no. 6, pp. 1578–1586.

Wincott, D., Davies, G. and Wager, A. 2021. Crisis, What Crisis? Conceptualizing Crisis, UK Pluri-Constitutionalism and Brexit Politics. *Regional Studies*, vol. 55, no. 9, pp. 1528–1537.

Wood, J. R. 1981. Secession: A Comparative Analytical Framework. *Canadian Journal of Political Science*, vol. 14, no. 1, pp. 107–134.

Wright, A. 2020. *British Politics: A Very Short Introduction*. Oxford: Oxford University Press.

Wring, D., Mortimore, R. and Atkinson, S. (eds.) 2019. *Political Communication in Britain: Campaigning, Media and Polling in the 2017 General Election*. Cham: Palgrave Macmillan.

Wyn Jones, R. and Scully, R. 2006. Devolution and Electoral Politics in Scotland and Wales. *Publius: The Journal of Federalism*, vol. 36, no. 1, pp. 115–134.

Young, H. 1998. *This Blessed Plot, Britain and Europe from Churchill to Blair*. London: Macmillan.

Zulianello, M. 2020. Varieties of Populist Parties and Party Systems in Europe: From State-of-the-Art to the Application of a Novel Classification Scheme to 66 Parties in 33 Countries. *Government and Opposition*, vol. 55, no. 2, pp. 327–347.

APPENDIX

A. List of interviews

Interviewee	Date	Time	Place	No. (*cited)
Scholar	10.12.2018	10.00 am	London	1*
Scholar	10.12.2018	12.00 am	London	2
Scholar	10.12.2018	4.30 pm	London	3*
Scholar	10.12.2018	2.30 pm	London	4*
Plaid Cymru MP	12.12.2018	4.00 pm	House of Commons, London	5*
Scholar	14.12.2018	10.00 am	London	6*
Scholar	14.12.2018	3.00 pm	London	7
Labour MP	17.12.2018	12.00 am	House of Commons, London	8
Scholar	17.12.2018	2.15 pm	London	9
Politician	17.12.2018	4.15 pm	London	10
Conservative Peer	18.12.2018	10.30 am	House of Lords, London	11*
Scholar	18.12.2018	3.30 pm	London	12
SNP MP	19.12.2018	4.00 pm	House of Commons, London	13*
Clerk	11.02.2019	11:30 am	Portcullis House, London	14*
Scholar	11.02.2019	5:00 pm	London	15*
Lib-Dem MP	12.02.2019	11:15 am	Portcullis House, London	16
Plaid Cymru MP	12.02.2019	1:00 pm	Portcullis House, London	17
Scholar	12.02.2019	2:45 am	London	18

(Continued)

(*Continued*)

Interviewee	Date	Time	Place	No. (*cited)
SNP MP	13.02.2019	10:00 am	Portcullis House, London	19
Conservative MP	13.02.2019	11:00 am	Portcullis House, London	20
Scholar	13.02.2019	2:00 pm	London	21*
SNP MP	13.02.2019	3:30 pm	Portcullis House, London	22
Scholar	13.02.2019	5:00 am	London	23*
Scholar	14.02.2019	10:00 am	London	24*
Civil servant	14.02.2019	10:30 am	London	25*
Scholar	15.02.2019	10:00 am	London	26*
Scholars (joint interview)	15.02.2019	12:30 am	London	27*
Scholar	18.02.2019	9:30 am	Edinburgh	28*
Civil servant	18.02.2019	10:00 am	Scottish Government, St Andrew's House, Edinburgh	29
Civil servant	18.02.2019	5:30 am	Edinburgh	30
Scholar	19.02.2019	9:00 am	Edinburgh	31
Conservative MSP	19.02.2019	11:00 am	Scottish Parliament, Edinburgh	32
Green MSP	19.02.2019	3:00 pm	Scottish Parliament, Edinburgh	33
Scholar	19.02.2019	4:15 pm	Edinburgh	34*
Labour MSP	20.02.2019	2:00 pm	Scottish Parliament, Edinburgh	35
SNP MSP	20.02.2019	3:15 pm	Scottish Parliament, Edinburgh	36
Labour MSP	21.02.2019	9:00 am	Scottish Parliament, Edinburgh	37
Lib-Dem MSP	21.02.2019	4:15 pm	Scottish Parliament, Edinburgh	38
SNP MSP	21.02.2019	5:30 pm	Scottish Parliament, Edinburgh	39
Scholar	04.03.2019	2:00 pm	Online – Skype	40*
Scholar	07.03.2019	2:00 pm	Online – Skype	41*
Scholar	18.09.2019	4.30 pm	London	42*
Scholar	20.09.2019	9.00 am	London	43
Scholar	20.09.2019	11.00 am	London	44*
Scholar	23.09.2019	1.00 pm	London	45
(Former) Conservative MEP	23.09.2019	2.30 pm	London	46
UKIP MS	25.09.2019	10.00 am	National Assembly for Wales, Cardiff	47

(*Continued*)

(*Continued*)

Interviewee	Date	Time	Place	No. (*cited)
Brexit Party MS	25.09.2019	11.30 am	National Assembly for Wales, Cardiff	48
Labour MS	25.09.2019	13.30 am	National Assembly for Wales, Cardiff	49
Labour MS	25.09.2019	3.00 pm	National Assembly for Wales, Cardiff	50
Civil servant	26.09.2019	11.00 am	Cardiff	51
Conservative MS	26.09.2019	2.00 pm	National Assembly for Wales, Cardiff	52
Labour MS	26.09.2019	4.00 pm	National Assembly for Wales, Cardiff	53
Labour MS	28.09.2019	4.45 pm	Cardiff	54
Labour MSP	30.09.2019	9.30 am	Edinburgh	55
Conservative MSP	30.09.2019	11.30 am	Scottish Parliament, Edinburgh	56
SNP MSP	30.09.2019	4.00 pm	Scottish Parliament, Edinburgh	57
SNP MSP	01.10.2019	10.00 am	Scottish Parliament, Edinburgh	58
Labour MSP	01.10.2019	11.00 am	Scottish Parliament, Edinburgh	59
Conservative MSP	01.10.2019	2.00 pm	Scottish Parliament, Edinburgh	60
SNP MSP	01.10.2019	3.00 pm	Scottish Parliament, Edinburgh	61
SNP MSP	01.10.2019	4.00 pm	Scottish Parliament, Edinburgh	62
SNP MSP	02.10.2019	10.00 am	Scottish Parliament, Edinburgh	63
SNP MSP	02.10.2019	11.00 am	Scottish Parliament, Edinburgh	64
SNP MSP	02.10.2019	12.00 am	Scottish Parliament, Edinburgh	65
SNP MSP	02.10.2019	2.00 pm	Scottish Parliament, Edinburgh	66
SF MLA	03.10.2019	10.00 am	Stormont, Belfast	67
UUP MLA	03.10.2019	11.00 am	Stormont, Belfast	68
Alliance MLA	03.10.2019	12.00 am	Stormont, Belfast	69
UUP MLA	04.10.2019	10.30 am	Stormont, Belfast	70
Scholar	04.10.2019	4.00 pm	Belfast	71
Labour MS	08.10.2019	3.45 pm	Online – Skype	72

APPENDIX

B. Timeline of events

Key moments in the EU-UK relations ahead of Brexit

1961: the UK applies to EEC membership under conservative PM Harold MacMillan.

1963: the French president, Charles De Gaulle, vetoes UK membership.

1973: the third membership application, with Edward Heath as PM, is successful.

1975: referendum on UK membership in the EEC, approving it.

1988: the "Bruges Speech" by PM Margaret Thatcher is very critical of political integration and moves the Conservative Party firmly into the Eurosceptic camp.

2005: David Cameron, leader of the Conservative Party, moves his party out of the Group of the European People's Party in the European Parliament.

2011: the *European Union Act* introduces a "referendum lock": any further reform of the EU treaties would need to be approved by a referendum.

The road to the Brexit referendum

23 January 2013: "Bloomberg Speech" by PM Cameron endorses a referendum on EU membership.

22 May 2014: UKIP wins the EP elections gaining 24 seats.

18 September 2014: referendum on Scottish independence. 55.3 percent of the votes are against it.

14 April 2015: a referendum on membership is indicated in the election manifesto of the Conservative Party.

7 May 2015: general elections in the UK. Cameron heads a single-party Conservative government. UKIP wins only one seat, but it obtains almost 3,900,000 votes (12.6 percent of the total).

17 December 2015: the *European Union Referendum Act* receives royal assent.

22 February 2016: "new settlement" between the UK and the EU. Cameron announces the date of the referendum and communicates his intention to campaign to remain in a reformed EU.

From the referendum to the 2017 general election

23 June 2016: referendum. Leave (51.9 percent) wins over Remain (48.1 percent).

24 June 2016: following defeat of the option endorsed by the Government, PM Cameron resigns.

14 July 2016: Theresa May is the new PM.

24 January 2017: ruling of the Supreme Court (*Miller case*). In order to trigger Art. 50 and start the withdrawal process, an Act of Parliament is necessary.

16 March 2017: the *European Union (Notification of Withdrawal) Act* receives royal consent: the Brexit process – formally lasting two years – starts.

29 March 2017: the process of withdrawal from the EU starts.

30 March 2017: the Scottish First Minister Nicola Sturgeon sends a letter to PM Theresa May asking for a new referendum on Scottish independence.

8 June 2017: general election. PM May leads a Conservative minority government.

Theresa May's minority government

26 June 2018: the *European Union (Withdrawal) Bill* receives royal assent.

14 November 2018: withdrawal agreement between the EU and the UK.

13 December 2018: ruling of the Supreme Court on the *Scotland Continuity Bill case*. The supremacy of the Westminster Parliament vis-á-vis the national parliaments, also in devolved policy areas, is restated.

15 January 2019: the House of Commons rejects the withdrawal agreement with a very large majority (432 vs 202).

5 February 2019: the Brexit Party is registered with the Electoral Commission.

12 March 2019: the House of Commons rejects the withdrawal agreement for a second time.

27 March 2019: the House of Commons organises a series of "indicative votes" on Brexit. No option is backed by a majority of MPs.

29 March 2019: the House of Commons rejects, for the third time, the withdrawal agreement (without the "political declaration"). Exit date is postponed for the first time.

1 April 2019: further "indicative votes" in the Commons. No vote is backed by a majority of MPs.

23 May 2019: European Parliament elections in the UK. The Brexit Party is the most-voted party.

24 May 2019: Theresa May resigns, but she remains in office until her successor is chosen by the Tory party.

Boris Johnson's governments until "Brexit Day"

23 July 2019: Boris Johnson is the new leader of the Tory Party.

24 July 2019: Johnson becomes PM.

28 August 2019: prorogation of Parliament (from 9 September to 14 October).

9 September 2019: the *European Union (Withdrawal) (No. 2) Act* – also known as Benn Act – is approved.

24 September 2019: the Supreme Court – unanimously – rules that the prorogation of Parliament is unlawful.

19 October 2019: Johnson presents the new withdrawal agreement with the EU to Parliament.

22 October 2019: the House of Commons votes against the business motion on the *EU (Withdrawal Agreement) Bill*. Johnson withdraws the bill.

31 October 2019: for the second time, the Brexit date is postponed.

12 December 2019: general election in the UK. Johnson wins a clear majority in the House of Commons.

19 December 2019: the Scottish First Minister Nicola Sturgeon sends a letter – together with the document *Scotland's Right to Choose* – to PM Johnson, demanding a second referendum on Scottish independence.

23 January 2020: the *European Union (Withdrawal Agreement) Act* receives royal assent.

31 January 2020: the withdrawal of the UK from the EU takes place – *Brexit Day*.

1 February 2020: the transition period starts.

After Brexit Day: the transition period

30 June 2020: the deadline to ask for an extension of the transition period expires.

9 September 2020: the government introduces the *UK Internal Market Bill* to Parliament. The bill is officially criticised by the EU not to respect the terms of the withdrawal agreement.

17 December 2020: the *UK Internal Market Bill* is approved.

24 December 2020: the Trade and Cooperation Agreement for the new post-Brexit relationship between the EU and the UK is signed.

30 December 2020: Parliament approves the *European Union (Future Relationship) Bill*.

31 December 2020: at midnight (or 11 pm GMT), the transition period ends, and the UK abandons the common market and the customs union.

INDEX

Page numbers in **bold** denote tables, those in *italic* denote figures.